THE PILGRIMAGE TO COMPOSTELA
IN THE MIDDLE AGES

Council of Europe Sign Marking the Road to Santiago

The Pilgrimage to Compostela in the Middle Ages

Edited By
Maryjane Dunn
Linda Kay Davidson

Routledge
New York and London

First paperback edition published in 2000 by
Routledge
29 West 35th Street
New York, NY 10001

Published in Great Britain by
Routledge
11 New Fetter Lane
London EC4P 4EE

Routledge is an imprint of the Taylor & Francis Group

Copyright © 1996 by Maryjane Dunn and Linda Kay Davidson
Previously published in hardback as vol. 1829 in the Garland Reference Library of the Humanities.

Library of Congress Cataloging-in-Publication Data

The pilgrimage to Compostela in the Middle Ages / edited by Maryjane
Dunn and Linda Kay Davidson.
      p. cm.
      Includes bibliographic references and indexes.
      ISBN 0-8153-1638-0 (alk. paper)
      ISBN 0-415-92895-8 (pbk.)
      1. Christian pilgrims and pilgrimages–Spain–Santiago de
Compostela–History. 2. Europe–Church history–600-1500. 3. Christians
pilgrims and pilgrimages in literature. 4. Santiago de Compostela
(Spain)–Church history. I. Dunn, Maryjane. II. Davidson, Linda Kay.
  BX2321.S3P55 1996
  263'.0424611–dc20   97-24453
                                       CIP

Printed on acid-free, 250-year-life paper
Manufactured in the United States of America

10 9 8 7 6 5 4 3 2 1

Contents

List of Contributors

VICENTE ALMAZÁN
Professor of Spanish
Emeritus
University of Wisconsin
Oshkosh, WI 54901

VINCENT CORRIGAN
Associate Professor of Music
Bowling Green State University
Bowling Green, OH 43403
vcorrig@bgnet.bgsu.edu

JOHN DAGENAIS
Professor of Spanish
University of California
Los Angeles, CA 90095
dagenais@humnet.ucla.edu

LINDA KAY DAVIDSON
Instructor of Spanish
University of Rhode Island
Kingston, RI 02881
davidson@uriacc.uri.edu

MARYJANE DUNN
Instructor of Spanish
Metropolitan Community College
Omaha, NE 68103
mdunn@metro.mccneb.edu

ALBERTO FERREIRO
Professor of History
Seattle Pacific University
Seattle, WA 98119
beto@spu.edu

DAVID M. GITLITZ
Professor of Hispanic Studies
University of Rhode Island
Kingston, RI 02881
dgitlitz@uriacc.uri.edu

JEANNE E. KROCHALIS
Associate Professor of English
Pennsylvania State University
New Kensington, PA 16802
jek4@psu.edu

CONNIE L. SCARBOROUGH
Associate Professor of Spanish
University of Cincinnati
Cincinnati, OH 45221
connie.scarborough@uc.edu

COLIN SMITH
Professor of Spanish
Emeritus
Cambridge, U.K. CB3 OLL

Illustrations

Madrid Youth Pilgrimage Group Arriving in Sobrado de Monjes, July 1993

The Pilgrimage to Compostela: Time and Place

Maryjane Dunn and Linda Kay Davidson

> We stopped in Santa Catalina to buy food. . . . A youth at the village bar told us we would have to wait until his grandmother returned from a shopping expedition to a nearby farm. Forty minutes later we were still waiting. . . . . I caught myself becoming impatient. The young man offered us beer. Suddenly I was ashamed of myself for expecting the working of this hamlet to run according to the dictates of my inner timetable. Where was I trying to get to so fast, anyway? Among other destinations, a state of being in which I would have the confidence to stop being dominated by the clock! (Dennett 179)

Americans, caught up in the minutiae of their daily lives, acting according to the items listed in their agendas, or syllabi, or daily-planners, wearing watches with at least one alarm clock function, often have lost track of the larger "circle of life"[1] as we move to meet timeclocks and deadlines. We live in secular society, a technological, state-of-the-art, digitized existence. Calendars also tie us to time. Whether based on lunar or solar calculations, they mark our passage through days, months, seasons, and years. Through their measurements, cultures and individuals coordinate and celebrate religious ceremonies, political and social events, and organize personal time.

We are likewise part of a broader continuum of time and, in many ways, the calendars and rhythms and saints and cyclical processes generated in a culture a millennium and sometimes two millennia ago continue to have an impact on our world. In many predominantly Catholic cultures, for example, dates within the year are identified with a saint or special religious occurrence of that day. The most obvious instance of this is December 25, the date identified with the birth of Jesus Christ. "See you on Christmas" is a time reference that all Christians, and probably all people living in a Christian-dominated society, understand immediately. St. Valentine's Day and St. Patrick's

Day function in the same manner. In Europe, this style of reference is a more accepted pattern. One can speak of leaving on the Assumption or on returning on St. Cecilia's Day. More than just the farmers in Spain know what the phrase "Cada puerco su San Martín" connotes.[2]

When dates, saints, and places become commingled, then we have situations similar to what Ernest Hemingway probably recognized:

Uno de enero, dos de febrero
tres de marzo, cuatro de abril,
cinco de mayo, seis de junio
siete de julio, San Fermín.[3]

This poem and its references to dates beckoned the American author and still calls to his would-be imitators to the running of the bulls down the streets of Pamplona (Navarra, Spain). Many Americans can associate March 28 with a little place called Capistrano, or better yet, the swallows returning to San Juan Capistrano. In this instance the saint's feast day has peremptorily set the important date for the small town in southern California, and it really doesn't matter that the swallows don't always return then, just about that time of the early spring.[4]

As San Juan Capistrano, California has become intertwined with a saint's life and a natural phenomenon, and San Fermín has become a part of the cultural life of Pamplona, other saints over time became identified with a specific geographical locale, as well, perhaps because it's the saint's birthplace, or the site of a miracle attributed to the saint, or perhaps because of the name of the most important church in the town: St. Anne of Beaupré (Canada), St. Francis with Assisi, St. Peter with Rome, and St. Mary with Fatima, Lourdes, and Medjugorje. Towns are named for a variety of reasons. Choosing the urban name generally involves some thought for a proper, meaningful word that emotes or signifies something special to the residents. All sorts of considerations enter in—personal, political, religious, economic, even the mere date may be an important factor. Captain James Cook "named St. Augustine AK [Alaska] for Augustine of Canterbury on May 26, 1778, the day of the Saint" (Stewart 418). We see the cultural footprints of the European immigrants to the New World who marked time by the calendar of saints and left signs of their presence in the hundreds of saints' names in toponyms. In these names we have the relics of the religious past. A farmer in the hills of San Martín Cuautlalpan in Mexico may not have a clue where Tours, France is, or of its nominal relationship with his Mexican *pueblo*. Later, post-colonial, immigrant cultures, on the other hand, may preserve the Saint's days' processions and feasts as a touchstone of their ethnic identity, celebrations that have their origins, or roots, in an age-old religious rite, but displaced by an ethnic, culturally-based need. The

Saint protects their move, their settling into a new place, and it continues their identity, for good or bad, as one of belonging to their original homeland. So important does this saint become to the group that the descendants carry on the traditions, celebrating the feast day and making the saint part of the new locale's activities.

The year 1992 reminded residents in the "New World" of the 500th anniversary of Columbus' journey to the Americas; and every year the "Columbus Day Parade" in October ostensibly proffers the same reminder. Approximately 18 cities in the United States carry the name Columbus, an obvious reference to the long-accepted, if not totally accurate, denomination of Columbus as the "Discoverer of the New World."[5] Over the last few years, however, attendance at the Providence, Rhode Island Columbus Day / Día de la Raza celebration had been waning. Three years ago, its participants walked the parade route twice, "because the parade was so short," the festival spokesperson Rick Simone commented.[6] On 8 October 1995 the Knights of Columbus parade included a new participant: St. Gennaro, the patron saint of the city's Neapolitan community. Mr. Simone calculated that about 16,000 spectators observed the two-and-a-half hour parade; this time the participants did not have to walk the route twice.[7]

In Spain, St. James[8] has had the fame of being the Patron Saint of the entire country since the early Middle Ages. His reported exploits aided in the wresting of most of the Iberian Peninsula from the Moorish civilization and in the conquest of the Hispanic New World. His supposed burial site in the northwest corner of Spain, in Compostela, yielded a new name for the site, Santiago de Compostela, which became the locus of a huge cathedral and an entire corpus of activities meant to pay homage to the Saint while simultaneously visiting the city. That the Saint imbued not only the area around his tomb with his presence, but all of the Iberian Peninsula, is evident with a glance at a map of Spain, which indicates more than fifty towns named Santiago. Many more towns have a church dedicated to him.

Similarly, along the several routes throughout Europe that wend toward the southwest, towns and chapels and fountains contain the Saint's name. There are so many along the routes of the pilgrimage to Compostela, that virtually every *patria chica* or region in France and the Iberian Peninsula has had an author who has enumerated and discussed the villages and their churches. In France, not only are there fourteen towns, but also 485 parishes dedicated to St. Jacques. Other towns along the Routes to Compostela carry names like *Montjoie* or *Camin romieu*, adding to the total references to Santiago, Compostela, and the pilgrimage, a final number which is probably not accurately calculable.[9]

The same is true throughout Hispanic America. Most persons, even those who are aware of St. James' biography, do not realize that there are records of more than a dozen apparitions of Santiago in the New World, that at least 581 towns and geographical features, including one volcano, bear his name and even more churches are dedicated to him.[10] But even though the Saint is the patronymic for towns and churches, his attributes as pilgrim and Saint-come-from-the-sea, whose symbol is the scallop shell, are all but lost on this side of the Atlantic. Modern representations in the Americas tend to present a generic Apostle; while older representations focus on the Saint in his second role as "Matamoros," or, in some places in Hispanic America, "Mataindios."

The influence and presence of Spain's Patron Saint in the conquest and settlement of the Americas is little appreciated here in the United States.[11] Secular, time-conscious America is not consciously cognizant of the imprints of our religious pasts, either the one our ancestors brought with them when they landed, or the one they sought to escape. The same is true for the surrounding saintly paraphernalia: roads are not named for saints, but for Presidents; feast days surround Thanksgiving and the Super Bowl; indulgence is a term most likely understood in context of grandparents; and the scallop shell is tourist ware in Florida and Newport, RI and other beach resorts.

Not only is the practice of making a pilgrimage to a holy spot foreign to the inhabitants of the U.S., but American understanding of pilgrimage has little place in American religious practice. Thus, while the year 1993 passed largely unnoticed in the United States as an important year and July 25 is a red-letter date in few U.S. citizens' calendars, in Spain and some parts of Hispanic America, the case should be, and was, different. In 1993 tens of thousands of pilgrims journeyed to Santiago de Compostela, Spain, in order to pay homage to St. James during a Holy Year, the first time in eleven years that Santiago's feast day had fallen on a Sunday. Both the Spanish government and the Catholic Church made great press about the anniversary, holding grand celebrations, aiding in providing lodging and, as did also the Council of Europe, helping mark the routes leading to Compostela throughout the Iberian Peninsula, and from as far away as the Scandinavian countries. Popular singer Julio Iglesias was the celebrity representative, in an effort to reach out to a wide audience.

The meaningful year's journey received slight press in North America, with its primarily Protestant background. We do not know exactly how many (although calculations indicate that more than two hundred fifty) people from North America joined with more than 99,000 persons who took the opportunity and the time to make the pilgrimage on the Road to Santiago, recreating, in essence, a religious activity which has seen a resurgence in interest and devotion after having been nearly abandoned since the Reformation by all but a handful of faithful devotees.[12] The guides, maps, and devotionals published in great number, the signposts, the newly-worked trails and hospices—all helped lead pilgrims from the Pyrenees across the north of Spain to the goal in the northwest corner of Spain.[13] Some walked more than 1000 kilometers, others only the mandated 200. Others biked or rode horses or led pack animals. People traveled alone or in groups of 10, 20, or even up to 1700.[14]

By walking, hiking, or galloping along the ancient Road, pilgrims went to celebrate the Holy Year and for personal motives that they may not even have recognized. By becoming part of the mass of people who surged toward the *autonomía* of Galicia, whether we may have identified ourselves as such or not, we became *pilgrims* replicating an ancient ritual. Ironically, the term *pilgrim* in the United States has taken several idiosyncratic twists. We have already commented in another place on its specialized use to refer to the first English colonizers on the East Coast.[15] Even within the religious meaning, the term's intention is often skewed: the weekly *Times* devoted a page to the portrayal of "Pilgrim of the Week," nominating Pope John Paul II because of his then-impending visit to the United States' East Coast, to hold services in places such as a baseball stadium.[16] Shortly before, the *Providence Journal-Bulletin* had published a large color picture of many people awaiting the Pope's visit, commenting, "R.I. Pilgrims drawn to Pope."[17] How baroque that pilgrims can visit another pilgrim in a secular site, and that the mode of transportation for one is the now-famous "Pope-mobile."

The Holy Year 1993 has passed, but the general impetus and interest still remain. The numbers fell from more than 99,000 to nearly 17,000 in 1994. We go to press waiting the data for 1995 and more of the continuing series of sociological reports about the pilgrims to Compostela. It is clear that the pilgrimage is not disappearing, that whatever cause or causes sparked the renewal of an essentially medieval activity, it will be with us for a long time. The caretakers of the various *refugios* [hospices] are struggling with the pros and cons of this activity which for some is religious; for others, personal; and for others, hedonistic, and most likely a combination of the three possibilities. Hardly was the ink dried on the last *Compostela* signed in 1993[18] when planners in the Compostela Cathedral and the Galician *Xunta* turned to the next Holy Year, 1999, the eve of a new century, the end of the millennium, and Rome's holy jubilee celebration: an occasion when time and the measurement of it takes on multiple meanings.

Although we live in a multi-national, multi-cultural, multi-religious world, there is something about the pilgrimage to Santiago de Compostela that has a lasting impact on more people and in more ways and in more countries than those Galician peasants who directed Bishop Theodomir's eyes to a pile of bones could ever have envisioned. While Fatima, Lourdes, Medjugorje are primarily and essentially Catholic shrines, Compostela is much more and serves as a goal for a far broader public. Along this longest hiking trail through Europe lie a thousand years of art and culture, music and literature. We enter a church to rest and pray, and we look at the art, we touch the thousand-year old ⟨illegible⟩ every beautiful glen and mountain has been photographed by the hikers. From wild thyme along the Road to T-shirts festooned with pilgrimage motifs for sale in the villages, pilgrims partake of the natural and commercial as they hike their kilometers. In 1993 pilgrim groups were followed by TV camera-persons and interviewed along the way; children beckoned hungry pilgrims to enter their parents' bar, "Good prices for you, pilgrim!" Parish priests sermonized to us about the correct motives and attitudes as we performed this ancient and rugged ritual. We all carried our scallop shell and our pilgrim's passport. The forward-looking pilgrim looks not only to the goal of reaching Compostela, but to the ecological and environmental impact that the thousands of pilgrims are having along the narrow corridor. This Road and all of its physical trappings are to modern medievalists what the Gothic cathedrals were to Henry Adams and his generation. For the generation of the 1970s in Spain, walking this Road, alone or in the company of others in a Church group or the Scouts or just friends, is a rite of passage and a renewal of national spirit and pride.

The millennium is almost upon us. One cycle of time is drawing to a close and another will begin. Once again a large group of people are coming together, engaging with their passions and diverse perspectives a pilgrimage whose origins lie in another, earlier, millennium, a half a world away.

OUR THANKS

As we prepared this volume, we were pleased to be able to work with professionals who showed great dedication and energy in producing their essays. It was wonderful to be involved with them, and we appreciate their patience in working with two editors who were tyrannical in the technicalities of format, style, and bibliography. We thank one and all for bending to our editorial marks and for meeting our deadlines.

Once again, Garland Publishing has been enthusiastic about our project and has helped in many of the details. To Series Editor Joyce

Salisbury and vice-president Gary Kuris, our thanks for their patient attention to details, and advice on our multitude of questions.

We hope that these essays answer questions and pique interest, but that they do not sate the appetite to know more. We dedicate these musings to novices and scholars alike who share an interest in the Camino de Santiago.

NOTES

[1] "The Circle of Life"
From the day we arrive on the planet
And blinking, step into the sun
There's more to see than can ever be seen,
More to do than can ever be done.
There's far too much to take in here
More to find than can ever be found
But the sun rolling high
Through the sapphire sky
Keeps great and small on the endless round.
It's the circle of life
And it moves us all
Through despair and hope
Through faith and love
Till we find our place
On the path unwinding
In the circle,
The circle of life.
Lyrics, Tim Rice; music, Elton John; performed by Carmen Twillie. ©1994
Walt Disney Music Co./ Wonderland Music Co. (BMI). 60858-2.

[2] Literally, "for every pig, his Saint Martin's Day." This Saint's feast
day is 11 November, when the weather is generally cold enough to slaughter
the pigs for winter.

[3]

The first of January, and second of February,
Third of March, fourth of April,
Fifth of May, Sixth of June,
Seventh of July, San Fermín.

[4] St. John Capistrano (San Giovanni Capestrano; 1358?-1456) was a
Franciscan mission preacher throughout Italy. He led Hungarian troops to
victory against the Turks in Belgrade in 1456.

[5] The first town to be named Columbus may have been in Ohio, ca.
1812. Prior to that the name Columbia was preferred to refer to the explorer
and discovery.
    Celebrating another favorite saint, there are, at last count, three towns
named Santa Claus: the oldest one is in Indiana; the other two in Alaska and
Arizona (Stewart 107; 424).

[6] From an article in the *Providence Journal-Bulletin* (9 Oct. 1995): C3.
See Turgeon.

[7] St. Januarius (d. ca. 305?) was the bishop of Benevento and was martyred near Naples. He appears in fifth-century writings and pictures. His relics were and are held in Naples. Most important is a vial of his blood. St. Januarius has three feast days, and on all three days his blood liquefies. His primary feast day is 19 September; the translation of his relics is celebrated on the first Saturday in May; his third feast day on 16 December also commemorates the threatened eruption of Mt. Vesuvius in 1631.

Simone attributes the growth in size and "stature" of the parade to the Society of San Gennaro's joining the efforts. Thus the secular in the United States benefits by the inclusion of the Old World style of identity with the Saint (Turgeon C1).

[8] In this book we shall refer to the Saint as St. James or Santiago, the Spanish name. Compostela refers to the town, generally called Santiago de Compostela, where the tomb of the Apostle is revered.

[9] Jacomet (55). The map is well worth a look. His statistics are outweighed by the multitude of studies by various authors over the last century about individual regions, for example, Aymard. Baudot cites at least 193 different forms for *Jacques* found throughout France. La-Orden has nice appendices with topographical information about England. Scudieri discusses Italy. Portugal's towns are listed in Badía and "Santiago" offers a total of 156 places dedicated to St. James. Hüffer offers some information about Germany. Henggeler has an astonishing list for Switzerland, Krötzl for Sweden, and Almazán for the entire area of Denmark, Sweden, Alsace.

[10] Mexico accounts for more than three hundred towns, villages, and rivers. The list we consulted for this total (*Santiago e América* 100-15) is probably not complete.

A nice summary of the importance of this Saint in the Americas can be found in the 437-page book *Santiago e América,* which accompanied the 1993 Exhibit in the Compostela Monasterio de San Martín Pinario, jointly published by the Xunta of Galicia and the Compostela Archbishopry.

[11] There are towns named St. James in Arkansas, Illinois, Michigan, Minnesota, Missouri, New York. In California there is a San Diego not related to this St. James and several uses of *Santiago* in toponymy. In the eastern portion of the U.S. most of these towns pay only bare homage to St. James the Apostle, their names chosen for other reasons. For instance, the town in Minnesota bearing the name St. James is simply because the railroad president couldn't remember the long Indian name that had been chosen for the site some three years earlier. So in 1872, the place was named St. James because he could remember that name. (Information thanks to Librarian Shirley Coleman, narrating from the *Minnesota Geographic Names*.) Or, in another instance, St. James, Missouri was founded by the James family. Since there was already a "Jamestown" in Missouri, they happened on the name St. James. (Information according to Ms. Jenkins in the St. James Public Library.)

[12] Data from *Compostela: Revista de la Archicofradía del Glorioso* indicates that between 1989 and 1993 approximately 375 Americans have made the pilgrimage. In 1993, 262 Americans, or 0.26 % of the total number for that year, registered in the Confraternity Office (25-35).

[13] Author Davidson was one of eight in an academic program connected with the University of Rhode Island who walked from southern France to Compostela during 1993. See Note 24 in the Introduction.

[14] Returning from Compostela, at the end of our pilgrimage, we encountered a group of approximately 1700 youth pilgrims from Madrid, led in groups of about fifty, along the back roads of Galicia. Their goal for that evening was the monastery of Sobrado de Monjes. We watched as the few monks in residence took pictures of the arriving pilgrims. Food was boxed and numbered much as rations in for a large army troupe.

[15] See opening pages of *Pilgrimage in the Middle Ages: A Research Guide*. The earliest Hispanic settlers tend to be referred to as the *conquistadores*.

[16] 9 Oct. 1995: 17. See "Pilgrim."

[17] 4 Oct. 1995: B1, B4. See Dujardin.

[18] This is the church document which testifies that the bearer has completed the pilgrimage in the necessary way and that, if the pilgrim makes a religious confession and attends mass, he will receive the promised indulgences.

[19] See, for example, Herb McGrew's serialized narrative of his pilgrimage and commentary on the food in France and Spain in the *Newsletter* of the Friends of the Road to Santiago, and, more generally, in *Gourmet* (May 1991).

Acknowledgments

The frontispiece photograph and others accompanying the Introduction were taken by David M. Gitlitz during several pilgrimages, and in Cuzco, Peru.

The map of the Centers of Ecclesiastical and Lay Culture *circa* 533 is reproduced with permission from Pierre Riché, *Education and Culture in the Barbarian West*. Trans. John J. Contreni. Columbia: U of South Carolina P, 1976.

The reproductions of the various scenes of the fifteenth-century altarpiece are made with permission from the Indianapolis Museum of Art. Copyright, Indianapolis Museum of Art, James E. Roberts Fund.

Statue of Santiago Matamoros in Cuzco, Peru Procession

Bibliography of the Pilgrimage: The State of the Art

Maryjane Dunn and Linda Kay Davidson

> The whole story is so exceedingly unlikely and so clearly concocted to provide a suitable focus for Christian unity in Spain against Islam, that it would be easy to dismiss it all as mere legend. But none of that matters; it is the pilgrimage itself which, from the very moment that the Saint's grave was discovered . . . has created its own momentum, rationale and legacy. The myth is what matters, inspiring unnumbered men and women to lead—if only for a time—lives of hardship and self-sacrifice, buoyed up by the spiritual ecstasy which their journey created. . . . Going on a pilgrimage helped me to see some things much more clearly. Perhaps that has always been the purpose, whether pilgrims sought expiation of their sins or eternal salvation (Hanbury-Tenison 154-5).

Santiago de Compostela, in the northwest corner of Spain, is the supposed resting place of the bones of St. James the Greater, one of the twelve apostles. Purportedly, after Jesus' death he preached in Spain, but had little success. He returned to Jerusalem, was beheaded (the first of the apostles to suffer martyrdom), and his body was left outside the city walls. His friends gathered his head and body and placed them in a boat which miraculously carried them to the Galician coast. Only after a series of trials placed on the Jamesian disciples by a pagan, perhaps queen, named Lupa, and involving miraculous escapes from fire, human treachery, and wild animals could his body be interred on a hill called Libredón, approximately eight kilometers inland. His burial place was then forgotten for nearly eight centuries.

This summary of the martyrdom and *Translatio* of St. James is the information traditionally cited by scholars and authors, based on evidence in early church documents, medieval chronicles and, of most importance, the *Liber Sancti Jacobi*. It is the "bare bones" of the story, assembled from bits and pieces, not divinely imparted to a single scribe in one sitting. During the early centuries in Christendom, little is known and practically nothing is written about the Saint and his burial place. Then, beginning in the seventh century, the Church's "Saint's Lives" and other religious writings began insinuating allusions to the Iberian Peninsula into their references to this St. James. After the Muslim invasions, when James began to be viewed as an aid to the beleaguered Spanish Christians, he received increasing attention. When the Christian groups found that the tomb of this apostle could indeed prove a focal point for their political and warring struggles, other formal writings, political poems for example, began exclaiming the truths of the Saint's importance to the Iberian Peninsula Christians.[1]

This legend of Santiago has overshadowed much of the earlier history of the Christianization of the Galician region of the Iberian Peninsula. There is, however, a growing interest in that epoch and a desire to understand the state of the pre-Santiago religious environment since it forms the basis for the later cult of St. James. In 1976 Henry Chadwick, in *Priscillian of Avila: The Occult and the Charismatic in the Early Church*, suggested that perhaps the heretical Priscillian was the real body buried at Compostela. Since that time, others (although not primarily English-language scholars) have continued to investigate this possibility and others about the true beginnings of the Spanish fascination with Compostela. We are fortunate to be able to open our *Book of Essays* devoted to St. James with Alberto Ferreiro's seminal article, "The Cult of Saints and Divine Patronage in *Gallaecia* before Santiago," about cults in Galicia before the advent of Santiago's. By understanding the bases upon which the Santiago structure was imposed and erected we can better comprehend how the process was effected. Ferreiro shows us that the taint of Priscillianism, the efforts of Martin of Braga, and the political battles of the Sueves and their relationship with the Catholic church paved the way for the development of a cult of French Saint Martin of Tours, a cult which was eclipsed in the seventh and eighth centuries by the cult of St. James.

Exactly when pilgrimages began to the shrine of St. James is unknown. Certainly local visits must have occurred fairly early after the announcement of the discovery. Taliani avers to have found indication of Italian pilgrims as early as the seventh century.[2] By the ninth century we do have notice of some few pilgrims.[3] There is evidence that the first pilgrim to Santiago de Compostela, whose name we know and about whom we have some, very modest, detail, was a French bishop from LePuy, Gotescalc, who traveled to the shrine in 950 "to beg mercy and help from God and Santiago."[4] For these few early pilgrims—perhaps two dozen in all—we find a reference, a name in a list, a will, a comment in an ecclesiastical record. As with the development of the written history of the Saint, the written history of the Saint's followers, his pilgrims, begins with a name here, a piece of data there: not so much as to fill an entire ledger sheet.

Questions about whether the body of St. James the Apostle actually lies in the tomb in the Compostela Cathedral, while important for many, have not slowed the traffic of pilgrims to the site. The pilgrims returned home, the fame of the Saint's shrine grew, and other pilgrims began to replicate the journey. By the twelfth century several well-established routes to Compostela had developed. The westward route across Spain narrowed to primarily one main road, termed the "French Road," the "Road of Stars," or the "Path of the Milky Way." This route actually arises at four principal French starting places: Paris, Vézelay, LePuy, and Arles. Current research stresses how these cities served as gathering points, but in no way indicate the actual distance from which pilgrims came. Investigation into microtoponymy, monastery records, internment records, and heraldry show that pilgrims came from as far away as Scandinavia, eastern Germany, England, and southern Italy. In his article for our volume, "The Pilgrim-Shell in Denmark," Vicente Almazán provides graphic details of Santiago's popularity in Denmark. The Saint's emblem, the scallop shell, is evident on escutcheons, fountains, seals, and calendars. Most importantly, a number of real pilgrims' shells have been found in graves throughout the area. The reach of the Saint and his pilgrimage obviously extended beyond the countries bordering on the Iberian Peninsula.

The four French routes, however, became the most renowned roads perhaps largely because of how they were described in the first European guidebook, the "Liber peregrinationis." This guidebook was either written or copied, or both, or neither, by one Aimeric Picaud, a French cleric. The book is marvelously organized and consists of a listing of the four principal routes; the towns along them; basic brief biographies of several famous people or saints connected to the route; detailed descriptions of the rivers, regions, and peoples to be encountered; a reliquary guide to famous saints buried along the route; and, finally, a detailed description of the town of Compostela and its basilica.[5]

The Guide was not the most copied or adapted portion of the *Liber Sancti Jacobi* (LSJ), the twelfth-century manuscript in which it is found.[6] There is little information of a spiritual or emotive nature in the guide. It is highly practical in its information, even to the point of offering helpful phrases to be used in the Basque region. The author has little good to say about the Navarrese or the Basques, their food or their customs.[7] Whether Picaud actually traveled the route himself is still open to question. Yet the information that the "Liber peregrinationis" author offers indicates that he was very opinionated. He states his views as if he had experienced the incidents himself. His, then, is not only the first guidebook of the Route; it is simultaneously the oldest account in first-person narrative of apparently personal experiences:

While we were proceeding towards Santiago, we found two
Navarrese seated on [the] banks [of the Río Salado] and
sharpening their knives. . . . To our questions they answered
with a lie saying that the water was indeed healthy. . . .
Accordingly, we watered our horses in the stream, and had no
sooner done so, than two of them died. . . (chapter VI; Melczer
88-90).

I myself have verified what I am saying. I have once seen
somebody in the town of the saint [St. Gilen] who, the day he
had invoked him, escaped, under the protection of the blessed
confessor, from the house of a certain shoemaker Peyrot; this
house, old and decrepit, soon after collapsed (chapter VIII;
Melczer 98).

This "Guide" is the fifth of the five books of the LSJ, a
compendium of the Saint's liturgy; his biography, stories of his
martyrdom and *Translatio* (in two versions), and narrations of his
various miracles; it also contains a book of adventures featuring
Charlemagne and Roland (called the *Pseudo-Turpin*); it closes with the
Pilgrim's Guide. The LSJ is the bibliophile's dream book: it is all-
encompassing; it has music; it has adventure; it has clear instructions
about travel; it tells what dangers to avoid; occasionally it even gives
currency exchange rates. It tells how the Saint lived and died, why we
should revere him, how we should do so, and how we get to the Saint's
relics. For the previous five centuries references to the Saint and the
pilgrimage had been sparse, but suddenly, in the mid-twelfth century, a
book was created which codified the pilgrimage to Compostela. What
we as scholars and pilgrims must face is that practically everything
since that creation is imitation, commentary, or exegesis of the original
work. For many years, what was written in the LSJ was regarded as The
Source, The Bible of the pilgrimage. It is not until the late nineteenth
century that readers and scholars begin to question the information it
contains. In the century since over a thousand published studies have
delved into the true essence of the LSJ and the pilgrimage.

It is obvious that the author-compiler of the LSJ was very
concerned that the proper liturgies be established and performed for the
Saint's various feast days. The musical annotations and completeness of
the prayers made the LSJ an important tome for the Cathedral. Vincent
Corrigan's very clear explanation of the abundant music in Book I for
us in this volume, in "Music and the Pilgrimage," is perhaps the first
comprehensive overview of this music's structure and its incorporation
into the liturgical year. Book IV's story of Roland and Charlemagne[8] is
the most copied and adapted of all the five LSJ books. Colin Smith's

paper in this volume, "The Geography and History of Iberia in the *Liber Sancti Jacobi*," presents an excellent view of the medieval perspective of the historical reality as it is divulged in the LSJ, primarily through this book with its references to Charlemagne and others important to the politico-geographical control of the Peninsula, the dangers along the journey's route, and what opinions the pilgrims might have held about the place and people that they were setting out to visit.

There is a paucity of writing about the pilgrimage to Santiago during the thirteenth century. Scholars of the phenomenon once again resort to ecclesiastical records and legal documents to find pilgrims' names and glean information about them. It is in the fourteenth century that other works similar to the *Pilgrim's Guide* begin to appear. Itineraries, now in the romance languages of French and Italian, list distances and occasionally a snippet of information about a town or a river along the Road to Santiago. From the fourteenth century on, more records survive, and we are fortunate to be able to gather specific data and to gain an occasional glimpse of a personal reaction to a particular aspect of the pilgrimage. From records of this sort, Constance Storrs and F.R. Cordero Carrete estimate that approximately 3600 pilgrims traveled from the British Isles to Compostela during the fourteenth century ("Peregrinos ingleses"). Storrs is also responsible for an important study of English pilgrims' land and sea travel, their licensing and preparations, based on ships' records, charters, and licenses.[9]

It was in the fifteenth century that the full panoply of eye-witness materials emerged: itineraries and journals written by pilgrims and travelers—Italian, French, English, German, a Polish man, an Armenian bishop. Some left records of their experiences in the form of diaries, or in simple expense reports and itineraries. Still others reported not only what they themselves had heard and seen, but also copied down what they found interesting that others before them had written.[10] The pilgrims who visited the Saint's tomb came from many places. The Appendices to this Introduction will show that the majority of pilgrims' names that have been culled from the various records and ledgers are those of non-residents of the Iberian Peninsula. The same is true for the written logs, the guides, and narratives. No Spanish journal or guide is known from before the eighteenth century. William Wey, an English pilgrim, left an account of his impressions of his three pilgrimages, including one to Compostela in 1456.[11] Among his comments is the narration of a miracle that he witnessed. Another loquacious pilgrim-traveler was Hieronymus Münzer, who visited Compostela in 1493. He seems to combine medieval religious concerns with an early Renaissance spirit. He copied many sections from the LSJ to take back with him to his personal library. He chose certain portions of the Book I Sermons, especially of the famous "Veneranda dies" diatribe against unscrupulous people (both pilgrims and merchants serving pilgrims) along the Route, and selections from the *Pseudo-Turpin,* Book IV of the LSJ. Yet he does not appear to have noticed the pilgrim rituals that he himself must have followed when he arrived at the Cathedral. For our volume, Jeanne Krochalis' comments and translation of Hieronymus Münzer's excerpts from the *Codex Calixtinus*, in her article "1494: Hieronymus Münzer, Compostela, and the *Codex Calixtinus,*" place into perspective the attitude toward pilgrimage in the late Middle Ages, and confirm the importance of the journey to Compostela for adventure seekers and the curious, not just for those wishing for a miracle from the Saint.

Although it is commonly believed that the Reformation served as the death knell for pilgrimages of all sorts, this was not really the case for Compostela. Even Erasmus[12] wrote of his travels to Santiago's shrine. Vázquez de Parga asserts that the character and quality of pilgrims did change: more were poor, many were vagrants begging along the route, and still others traveled for non-religious reasons.[13] There was also a general change in attitude from devout, spiritual pilgrimage to more secular, general travel, but there does not appear to ever have been a complete abandonment of the spiritual *Camino.* We learn about these pilgrims either from legal or ecclesiastical records or by the narratives that they themselves penned, many of which sound more like travelogues rather than devotionals, although there is an occasional spiritual nature to their end result. Some of the travelers were clearly Catholic pilgrims, completing a devotional exercise, such as Jacques Lemesre, who, in 1685, left on pilgrimage to Compostela. He was captured by pirates and imprisoned in Constantinople for 3 years. He never reached Compostela. There were others whose comments about the customs and conditions along the route show their predisposition toward travel adventure, such as Guillaume Manier, who wrote a diary of his four-month pilgrimage from Picardy during 1726, and Paolo Bacci whose diary of his pilgrimage from Arezzo (1763-4) contains several commentaries on Galician lodging and clothing. None of the routes was deserted: Frenchman François de Tours traveled along the Portuguese route during the period from 1698 to 1700, and Spanish author Diego de Torres Villarroel described his experiences along the *via de la plata* in the mid-1720s. For later periods for which we have access to official records, we find names of pilgrims from France, Belgium, Germany, Italy, and Spain fairly easily: for example, a German couple had a baby in Estella in 1759 on their way to Compostela. There were dangers along the route then as in all times. The diary of his pilgrimage from Naples to Compostela by Nicola Albani (ca. 1743-5) contains watercolors and engravings of scenes of his pilgrimage, including a robbery and attempted murder of the pilgrim.[14] In all of these examples, we have been able to give pertinent information about specific pilgrims because some data has been left behind. Not everyone could leave a personal diary, and it is fortuitous that any records still exist, and are still being discovered, that shed light on the nature of the pilgrimage.[15] Records from the Hospital Real de Santiago are especially important for they document over a long time span the numbers of people who used the facilities as a resting place at the end of their pilgrimage. The record-keepers may not have been infallible, but they did manage to maintain some statistics of their patients, such as origin, profession, and gender.[16]

The nineteenth century opened the door to Spain even wider for the traveler. It is apparent that visits and pilgrimages to Compostela were still popular, for we have records of some narrations, such as Edmond Jaspar's *Relation d'un pèlerinage,* published in Douai in 1883 and J.M. Gil's short "Recuerdos de viaje por Galicia" (1850).[17] What was different (but not new, of course) was the publication of guides for the tourist-pilgrim that beckoned not just to those who might walk the route. Neira de Mosquera's volume, *Manual del viajero en la Catedral de Santiago,* was published in 1847 in Madrid; Moreno Astray's work, *El viajero en la ciudad de Santiago. Reseña histórica, descriptiva, monumental, artística y literaria de la antigua capital del Reino de Galicia,* was published in Santiago in 1865. Fernández Sánchez and Freire Barreiro's *Guía de Santiago y sus alrededores* was published in Santiago in 1885. It contained train schedules, a list of clothes to pack, and detailed information on the July 25th festivities, all in a whopping 576-page book, whose main portion is a detailed study of the cult of St. James. These efforts were quite in line with what was happening in the Cathedral itself in the late 1870s as the ecclesiastical authorities sought, through scientific excavations, to find the tomb of the Apostle. This enterprise's successful result, in January 1879, paved the way for Pope Leo XIII to proclaim, in 1884, the veracity of St. James' *Translatio.*[18] Other Cathedral personnel, especially Antonio López Ferreiro and José Villaamil y Castro, worked from the 1860s through the first decade of the twentieth century publishing records and old documents, writing on various aspects of the history of the Compostela Cathedral and the Saint enshrined there.[19] In all of these publications and activities we discern a concerted effort to promote the pilgrimage to Compostela with its venerable history and sites meriting both visit and study.

Continental Europeans were (and are) not the only ones engrossed with, and calling attention to, the Santiago pilgrimage. The attitudes of the English and American writers and travelers come to the forefront in the nineteenth century.[20] Victorian travelers composed their reports to describe the unusual sights and customs they experienced. This pre-tourist era spawned curiosity-seekers looking for adventure, excitement, and new frontiers. Their stories were often published by smaller presses or in serials.[21] While the more intrepid may have gone to the Holy Land and Africa, the more timid found that Spain offered an exotic ambiance with fewer dangers and less hardship: Africa in a sense really did begin at the Pyrenees. Lured by sunny skies and cheap prices, they found Spain fascinating, but often by-passed Compostela as being gloomily Celtic and far from their stereotype expectations of wine, olives, bullfights, and flamenco so often depicted. Yet it was Richard Ford's *Hand-Book for Travellers in Spain,* published in 1845, which may have been the first guidebook since the LSJ to mention the Compostela Cathedral in any detail, focusing on the Pórtico de la Gloria in his description.[22]

Almost all these travel reports were written by men. However, an example of one woman who did travel to Compostela was Katherine Lee Bates, who wrote of her experiences in *Spanish Highways and Byways* (1905). She offered the basic legend of Santiago and considered herself a "pilgrim" for putting up with the hardships she encountered as she traveled to Compostela for Holy Day (July 25). Her descriptions hardly reflect the Christian spirit in their smug and condescending language:

> Our indoor hours in Compostela, an incessant battle against dirt, bad smells, and a most instructive variety of vermin, were a penance that must have met all pilgrim requirements. And yet these people spared no pains to make us comfortable, so far as they understood comfort. . . . But we had come to the festival of Santiago, and it was worth its price (406-7).

Bates' writings are proof of the continued pilgrimage to Compostela, and of the medieval trappings with which it was still celebrated:

> Peasants in gala dress, bright as tropic birds, stood in deferential groups about the pilgrims on the scene, men and women whose broad hats and round capes were sewn over with scallop-shells, and whose long staffs showed little gourds fastened to the upper end. They wore rosaries and crucifixes in profusion, and their habit was spangled with all manner of charms and amulets, especially the tinsel medals with their favorite device of St. James riding down the Moors. . ." (424).

The pilgrims whom she observed were more than just characters playing a part, or travelers dressed to fulfill a role, but seem to have been truly devout Christians making their journey to Santiago's shrine as thousands before had done:

> Even now, at the end of the 19th century, our first glance, as we entered the lofty, dim, and incense-perfumed nave, fell on a woman-pilgrim dragging herself painfully on her knees up the

aisle toward the High Altar, and often falling prostrate to kiss the pavement with groans and tears (425).

Pilgrims were still then available for observation in the late nineteenth and early twentieth centuries, but those travelers who called themselves pilgrims did not actually profess to any sort of emotional attachment to the Shrine itself.

The two most important travel narratives of the first seventy-five years of the twentieth century changed drastically the way of describing the Route. In 1920 an American professor of art, Georgiana Goddard King, published *The Way of St. James*, and 1957 saw the publication of Irishman Walter Starkie's *The Road to Santiago*.

King spent three years in Spain, and seven more studying in order to produce her three-volume work, which began as an iconographic, architectural study, but soon became much more, as she identified with the Spanish character and began offering more detailed history, literary quotations, musical themes, and her own, most kind, generous, lyrical descriptions of the countryside and peoples, in addition to the monuments she had originally planned to describe. Although she was not a religious pilgrim, she was open to the spiritual, emotional transformation which she experienced in her studies. In her closing she offers her own personal feelings toward the Saint:

> Who goes in pilgrimage to a god must await his work: or soon or long, he cannot leave till he has his answer. It is well to abide in expectation, and make not haste in time of trouble. I have waited, sometimes, on the great St. James, but I never went away without the word (3: 3-4).

Her work is often punctuated by verbatim transcriptions of dialogues in which she partook, and she often includes her own personal musings:

> One night, I remember, as I travelled, the Camino de Santiago hung straight across the sky, frothy white as the surf on a night in August, and I knew that under it lay the grand church . . . stars that I did not know were there, stars that I had never seen, swarming like bees, various not in three or seven or ten but in fifty magnitudes, every one differing from another in glory. A shooting-star struck down for token that another soul was released upon its far journey. . . (3: 3-4).

King also saw true pilgrims on her travels, spoke with them, and described them:

> Through all these days I saw gravity, but on the whole little devotion, except sometimes in the case of women. . . . At the shrine you see men kneeling a little awe-struck, at the gold, or at the age? You find a group of women saying litanies. But St. James means nothing to them, he is only the means of making magic (3: 23-4).

With these words, she perhaps captures more of the essence of medieval pilgrimage than what we would expect. St. James and Compostela become separate, inward reflections to King; she is able to understand and face her own emotions, flaunting them at others less sincere in their devotion. Catholic or not, pilgrim or not, the pilgrimage process changed her, and so the goal of a "true" pilgrimage has been attained.

While this work opened the doors to many about the architecture, literature, history, cult of St. James, and the beauty of Spain through its lyrical descriptions, it is truly Starkie's book which ushered in a new age of pilgrimage and reinvented the Route of the Milky Way, as many travelers now know it. The format of his work, an opening history offering background on both the cult and legend, and on his own background, set the mold for the typical opening in contemporary pilgrimage writings. The majority of Starkie's work, however, is a first person narration of his experiences along the route from Arles in 1954 in fulfillment of a vow. If Starkie had lived in the twelfth century, this would not have been unusual, but in the twentieth century it strikes us as "medieval." In fact, his final words call others to return to a new, higher plane of pilgrimage, based on the medieval model, a return to a more devout, inward, spiritual journey:

> Today in the age of easy and rapid globe-trotting we are apt to forget that pilgrimage in the religious sense sprang from a primitive instinct of mankind, which expressed itself in journeys to the shrine of an Egyptian god or a Greek or Roman goddess, or in an annual excursion to the Temple at Jerusalem. . . . My own experiences in pilgrimages. . . have convinced me that modern enterprise, by facilitating rapid mass travel and eliminating dangers, discomforts and delays on the way to the shrines of the saints, has created the cult of 'pilgrimages without tears' for the millions, which is in complete antithesis to the original idea of pilgrimage transmitted by the saints to the Middle Ages. . . . Pilgrims today are even more gregarious in spirit and more robot-like than they were in my younger days, thirty years ago. . . . Nevertheless, even today, there are still in every country a number of lonely pilgrims who forsake the rapid-moving supervised pilgrimages and make the long journey guided

solely by the myriads of wandering souls in the star-dust of the Milky Way (323-4).

The pilgrimage did not ever die out completely, although few records or statistics document the pilgrimages on foot in the early twentieth century. We have occasional reports of individuals and some groups making their trek to Compostela, the latter especially during Holy Years during the Franco reign.[23] The Falange often organized a pilgrimage, with Francisco Franco appearing with them in front of the Cathedral doors to make the *ofrenda nacional*. In the 1950s and 1960s the Delegación Nacional de Juventudes organized pilgrimages as well. Although during the 1940s and 1950s the Holy Years were not especially touted, the 1965 Holy Year was a different case. It was the first Holy Year in eleven years, just as was 1993, and there was a concerted effort, both political and religious, to celebrate gloriously with expositions, laudatory articles, special advertisements, and reproductions of documents from the sixteenth and seventeenth centuries. The Archicofradía's periodical journal, *Compostela*, (in existence since 1948) counted 109,000 pilgrims to Compostela in the first four months of 1965. The recent nadir for pilgrimage, especially pilgrimage on foot, seems to have been the early to mid-1970s, when only a handful of persons traveled the Route: approximately 70 in 1979.[24] Steadily, from the 1980s until today, there have been growing spiritual, cultural, and research interests in the route, witnessed by the extensive number of publications in a wide variety of languages that have appeared in the last 25 years. The journal *Compostela*, which had ceased publication in 1974, began a second series in October, 1993.[25] One very important champion of the rebirth of the pilgrimage was Elías Valiña Sampedro, priest in the small village of Cebreiro. He had already published a short guide of the pilgrimage route in 1971. His final version of the guide, *El Camino de Santiago. Guía del Peregrino*, was published in 1985. It has become the model for many later guides, both in information and style.[26]

Until the eighteenth century, Iberian Peninsula pilgrims apparently did not feel the need to explain themselves or detail their activities. Diego de Villarroel's narrative is the first printed account of a personal pilgrimage by a Spaniard. Yet the 1965 and 1993 Holy Years' results are different. In 1965, narratives appeared early and continuously through the Holy Year. A similar phenomenon is apparently happening for the 1993 Holy Year: published by big companies and small enterprises, a substantial number of personal narratives that have appeared are from the pens (and computers) of Spanish pilgrims to Compostela.[27]

There are many people who have heard Starkie's calling in the English-speaking world as well as in other countries of Western

Europe, and even Japan.[28] More than a dozen personal pilgrimage narratives have been published in English between 1985-1995, by American, Canadian, and British authors.[29] Their narratives share several themes, based on both King and Starkie. They show a curiosity and interest in the past—in physical structures, art, culture, and history—and review their ideas about the same in the beginning of their books to set the scene for the later pilgrimage description. Most admit to a spirituality or emotive force, but this is not necessarily Catholic or religious in nature. At the end of their journeys each author describes an unexpected change in belief, a sort of liminal experience, in which they enter over into a new, different realm of the spirit. There is generally an emphasis on the journey, rather than on the goal, but the narrations typically end in either Compostela or Finisterre, rather than examining the return home and how it affects the traveler. Ellen Feinberg's account evokes the medieval ambiance as she recounts her own experiences:

> A month before, I had been afraid . . . now I was happy to sleep out in the fresh, sweet country air. Away from city lights and city pollution, we saw the Milky Way, spreading its starry trail like a protective blanket over us. It had pointed out the way to Charlemagne, it pointed out the way to us. I saw a star lift out of the sky and drop. It seemed to fall into the field below us. A thousand years ago, would I have thought that was a message from God. . . ? (206)

Stanton offers a typical summary of a pilgrim's feelings upon completing the Route, confirming Starkie's affirmation about the value of pilgrimage:

> This much I know: most of my companions and I have been uprooted from our former lives. To make the pilgrimage has been a way of proving that we could free ourselves from our daily existence, from all those small routines and obligations that mean nothing by themselves but together can prevent us from being ourselves. . . . The world we saw was so rotten that we knew it must be ripe for a transformation. Now we know the change must begin inside ourselves because the Camino has calmed the war in our own hearts (187).

Not all contemporary pilgrims are so overwhelmed with positive thoughts, however, and Hitt stands in stark contrast to Stanton's sense of wonder:

> Trying to romance the road to Santiago is a lost cause, and all efforts to attempt any such thing ended provinces ago. A pilgrimage resembles nothing so much as a forced march. We have resigned ourselves to it and are relieved only by the

comedy of our burden and the relaxation that comes with each evening (240).

Two men, of approximately the same age and background, walking the same Route, but with decidedly different outlooks. As more pilgrims publish their experiences, it will be interesting to examine whether there will be a general change in perspective from the earlier "Starkie" reflective model to a more cynical "Bates" style travelogue.

The obvious popularity of the cult in the Peninsula and throughout all parts of Europe, and, later and in different ways, in the New World Hispanic colonies, occasioned the development of local cults of the Saint, the creation of buildings and artistic works representing St. James as Pilgrim or Moor-slayer, the formation of confraternities, and preparation of local celebrations. While the aforementioned authors lived the medievalness of a pilgrimage on foot or horseback, replicating the activities of their counterparts during the previous eight centuries, others, primarily scholars, have chosen to continue to delve into the background of the pilgrimage and how it appears in medieval art, architecture, literature, chronicles, religion, music, or daily life. Scholars have relied on manuscripts, archaeological digs, the same ecclesiastical and secular ledgers that have offered up names of earlier pilgrims, confraternity rules and membership lists, and their own eyes while attempting to discern what made the medieval pilgrimage to Compostela so special and different from the other two major medieval pilgrimages to Rome and Jerusalem. The Dunn and Davidson bibliography contains 2941 entries; 2493 of the works annotated in the bibliography were published in the twentieth century, 1358 of this number since the 1965 Holy Year.[30] The boom of publications in this last century of the millennium is not due mainly to personal narratives or guides: they comprise only approximately 10 % of the publications. Most of the other 90 % are studies about the various aspects of the pilgrimage, both modern and medieval. This flood of publications is truly international. While authors such as Vázquez de Parga, Huidobro y Serna, and Vera and Helmut Hell were composing some of the fundamental studies of the pilgrimage and its routes, others such as Robert Plötz and Klaus Herbers were studying the development of the cult of the Saint in its early manifestations and often with relationship to Germany; Suzanne Martinet, Fernando Romero, Flóris Holik, Lucia Gai, and René de La Coste-Messèliere were delving into the archives throughout Europe and making long-hidden and needed data available to all scholars.[31] Awakening interest in the pilgrimage also brought forth the founding of numerous small groups, confraternities or centers, to study the pilgrimage and to aid those going on it: in 1950, the Société des Amis in Paris; in 1956, the Centro de estudios jacobeos which began publication of the journal *Compostellanum*; in 1963, the Amigos del Camino in Estella; in 1985, the small newsletter

Peregrino, published by Elías Valiña Sampedro from Cebreiro, expanded into a glossy format journal in 1987. It is now published under the auspices of the Federación de Asociaciones Españolas de Amigos del Camino de Santiago in Santo Domingo de la Calzada and is one of the most important tools for staying current with the pilgrimage. Similar groups appeared in Belgium and Italy in the 1980s.[32]

It is not widely acknowledged that English-language publications have proven to be important ground-breakers, although in several subject areas this is the case. Walter Muir Whitehill, for example, was an American graduate student when he began the transcription of the *Liber Sancti Jacobi* in the late 1930s, the only edition of the complete work until 1993 saw the publication of the facsimile by Kaydeda. Early editions of the fourth book of the LSJ (the *Pseudo-Turpin*) and the only edition of the *Mass* of St. James were done by English-speaking authors.[33] American and British researchers have also added to the knowledge of and the theories about the pilgrimage. To name just a few—again, these as examples of a much larger corpus: Brian Kemp, who worked on the materials surrounding the Hand of St. James and Reading Abbey, John Freed who wrote on the Thurn family of Salzburg, Horton and Marie Hélène Davies who studied the entire pilgrimage phenomenon, Jerome O'Malley who studied the hymns of St. James as literature, Irene Silverblatt who has found a relationship between Santiago and pre-Columbian colonial area gods in the Peruvian Andes. Some of the early twentieth-century studies are now considered to be seminal works, like those by Kingsley Porter (*Romanesque Sculpture of the Pilgrimage Roads*, 1923), Kenneth Conant (*The Early Architectural History of the Cathedral of Santiago de Compostela*, 1926), Anselm Biggs (*Diego Gelmirez, First Archbishop of Compostela*, 1949). The first English-speaking confraternity, based in England, began in 1983. It currently has a membership of over 1000 members and sponsors a pilgrim refuge ("Gaucelmo") in Rabanal del Camino, Spain. The American counterpart, the Friends of the Road to Santiago, is a more modest organization, but continues to publish a newsletter twice a year.

Santiago scholarship has intensified into the 1990s: The papers presented at the 1988 Colloquium "The *Codex Calixtinus* and the Shrine of St. James" held at Pittsburgh were published by Gunter Narr Verlag in Germany. In Kalamazoo, Michigan, at the 28th Annual International Congress of Medieval Studies in 1993, there were several sessions on pilgrimage in general, and on the pilgrimage to Compostela in particular. The exhibit "Celebrating the Holy Year: Santiago, a Saint of Two Worlds/Spanish Sketches—Marking the Millennium," sponsored by the Friends of the Road to Santiago, displayed photographs by Joan Myers[34] and made clear the connection between the medieval pilgrimage to Compostela and Spain's Patron Saint's presence during the conquest and colonization of the New World. Ceramics by Marcia Selsor (U. Montana) replicated medieval, monastic architecture in modern form. As part of this American contingent of Santiago studies, we are pleased to be able to offer in this *Book of Essays* new papers all written in the English language. Two of them deal with the artistic output of the pilgrimage. In Connie Scarborough's study, "The Pilgrimage to Santiago de Compostela in the *Cantigas de Santa Maria*," we see the pilgrims as they passed through dangerous places, hopeful of divine help. Scarborough reminds us how other saints vied for attention along the Route to Compostela and that themes inherent in the cult of St. James occasionally detoured to other shrines and appeared in literature not always closely connected to the pilgrimage. David Gitlitz's study, "The Iconography of St. James in the Indianapolis Museum's Fifteenth-Century Altarpiece," takes us to many places—to the site of the cult in Compostela, to the Road which the pilgrims traversed, to Flemish lands, and to Indianapolis, Indiana—as he discusses the iconography of a triptych created in an artist's atelier in a Flemish city that ended up in the mid-section of the United States. He details the eight stories of the Saint's life and legend as they are depicted in the triptych, signaling the changes that have occurred in the several centuries between the codification of that legend in the LSJ and its portrayal by the fifteenth-century artist.

In Europe and the United States hundreds of books have been published celebrating the 1993 Holy Year and the act of making a pilgrimage, and by extension they commemorate the medieval pilgrimage to Compostela. As a whole, we estimate that nearly 500 new titles have appeared since the final preparation of our bibliography in 1993. The Archicofradía and the Xunta de Galicia have embarked on a course of editing and publishing materials dealing with the pilgrimage to Compostela, from reports on the statistics gleaned in surveys in Compostela to republications of seminal works, such as the Spanish translation of the *Liber Sancti Jacobi* done in the 1950s by Moralejo, et al., and C. Storrs' unpublished thesis on medieval British Isles' boat travelers to Compostela. We applaud these efforts gratefully. The expositions and exhibitions occasioned by the 1993 Holy Year, especially those in Spain, were done with great care, fanfare, and exquisite accompanying volumes, some very costly. Almost every major town along the Road to Compostela—and that Road extends far throughout all of Europe—now has an association and an accompanying bulletin.[35] What is imperative is that the data not be lost, that all scholars and pilgrims be able to maintain contact with each other, and that the bulletins and journals and exposition pamphlets and publications not be discarded in the deluge of paper. Those of us in the United States seemingly have to work harder at this: we are outside of the mainstream, off the Road, and European publishers do not always publicize here; mailings to the US addresses are sometimes confusing; and because the population of the United States is most often interpreted as the flitting tourist, here today, gone tomorrow, the European groups seem unable to interpret our interest as a serious one.

We must ask ourselves where the medieval pilgrimage to Compostela will take us in the twenty-first century. Far from dying, it is taking on new life, promising even greater numbers of pilgrims and more planning, commercialism, and excitement for the next Holy Year, 1999, the year that also marks the end of the millennium, and the Roman Jubilee Year. The "Virgin Mary has [a] home page in Cyberspace" says the Cox News Service.[36] A World Wide Web page exists that offers answers to the FAQ's ("frequently asked questions," in modern computerese) and illustrations about her. The Vatican has another page devoted to the apparitions of the Virgin Mary. The pilgrimage to Compostela has been on the WWW for more than a year. Until the time when we can join the throngs ourselves, we can participate vicariously, as John Dagenais' study in this *Book of Essays,* "A Medieval Pilgrimage to Santiago de Compostela on the Information Highway," points out. The medieval pilgrimage has come full circle and its art, literature, and music can now be experienced while surfing the Internet. Instead of needing permission from one's bishop, now one only need permission to hook-up via modem with a graphics platform. Each pilgrim can travel alone, listening in on the discussion of others, or may participate fully, joining the merry band as they travel along the cyberspace Camino.[37] What do we envision for the future of the Camino? As in the Middle Ages, the end of the millennium brings the possibility of frightening change. The Road may become a secular excursion, or it may be the needed item to revitalize the spirituality of the Catholic Church. Social change in the villages may occur through economic rebirth due to the numbers of pilgrims traveling through them. Whatever the physical, spiritual, or emotional changes that occur, the boom in bibliography is almost certain to continue.

APPENDIX I: EARLY MEDIEVAL PILGRIMS TO COMPOSTELA[38]

DATE	NAME and NATIONALITY

7th century:
?	Italians

9th century:
ca. 850	St. Evermaro of Frisia
?	Algazel, Arab poet
?	Reynalda and Zanelo, Papal legates

10th century:
950	Gotescalc (France)
959	Caesar, Abbot of Catalan monastery Santa Cecilia
961	Raymond II, Marquis of Gothia, assassinated on the Route
961	Hugo of Vermandois
968-71	Nordic pilgrim
983	Simeon of Armenia, Hermit

11th century:
?	San Theobald (Teobaldo), barefoot
?	S. Guillermo de Vercilli, founder of hermitage of Monte Virgen, at the age of 14
1023	Geribert and Bofill, clerics from Cataluña
1056	Group of many people from Liège, led by Robert
1064	Galtier Giffart
1070s	Count Eberhard V von Nellenburg and his wife Ita
1072	Siegried of Mainz, Archbishop
1072	Grafin Richardis von Sponheim
1072 (1084)	Baudowin [VII] of Guines, Count of Flanders
1072 (1084)	Chatelain of Lillers
1080	Siegfried, Bishop of Maine
1095	Archbishop Hugh of Lyon (France)
1097	Alfonso VI
1097	don Enrique, King of Braga
1097 (?)	Fernando el Magno with Queen doña Sancha
1097 (?)	Empress Matilde [daughter of Henry I of England]

12th century:
ca. 1100	Ansgot of Burwell/de la Haye (Lincolnshire, England)

ca. 1102	St. Godric of Finchale
1105	Richard Mauleverer
1108-9	Sigurd Jorsalafar (Nordic) [also went to the Holy Land]
1117 (?)	Jean (de Bonnevaux?)
1129	Hugues II, Duke of "Bourgogne"
1130s	Oliver of Merlimond
1137	Luis VI of France
1137	Duke Guillaume X de Aquitaine
1139-59	Robert II, Earl of Derby
1141-1161	William de Roumare, Earl of Lincoln
1145	Waleran de Beaumont
1146-7	Frederick III of Haunsberg
1153	Nicholas, Bishop of Cambray
1154	Louis VII, King of France [returning from Palestine]
1160	Geoffroi IV, Viscount of Thouars
1162	Graf Eberhard von Altena
1164	Archbishop Konrad von Wittelsbach
1165-6	Raymond II, Viscount of Turenne
1169	Guillaume IV of Parthenay
1172	Phillip, Duke of Flanders
1173-84	Emery, son of Audin de Hunmanby
1175	Countess Sophia of Holland
1180	Anon. cleric from Sweden
1182	Fernando II
1190	Egidia (Italy)
1195	Frederick I of Austria
1198	Guillaume, Archbishp of Reims
?	Saint Paulina of Italy
?	Ponce de Leras [brigand in the French central mountains who abandoned his life, made restitution, went on pilgrimage to Compostela, returned to a Cistercian monastery he had founded]

13th century:

1204	Alfonso IX of León [penitential pilgrimage]
1209	"Rheingraf" Wolfran and wife Gilda
1212	William II, Archbishop of Burdeos
1212	Godefried, Bishop of Nantaes
1212	Leopold VI of Austria
1214	St. Francis of Asissi
1217	William of Holland
1220	Hugo, Bishop of Liège
ca. 1220	Santo Domingo de la Calzada

1224	Jean of Jerusalem
1230	Sordello di Goito, trovador of Mantua
1232	San Fernando
<1237	Stalberg (Frankfort, Germany)
ca. 1237	Violante, wife of Alfonso X
1244	Sancho II of Portugal
1245	St. Isabel of Portugal
1245	Berlion, knight of Oullins
ca. 1250	St. Buenaventura of Italy
1254	John Mansfeld, chaplain of Henry III of England
1267	Raimund Llull
1270	Ingrid and Melchtild, of Sweden
ca. 1275	Goberto, later Abbot of Villers (Liège)
1286	Sancho IV

APPENDIX II: GUIDEBOOKS, ITINERARIES[39]

DATE	TITLE/AUTHOR

12th century:
c. 1150   Book V, *Liber Sancti Jacobi*

13th century:

14th century:
[late]   *Itinéraire en vers anglais du chemin de Londres à*
          Compostelle, Jerusalem et Rome
[late]   *Da Venexia per andar a meser San Zacomo de Galizia*
          per la via da Chioza
[late]   *Itinéraire d'Avignon à Compostelle*

15th century:
1417   *Voyaige*   Nompar II Caumont
1425 (?) "Here Beginneth"
          Viaggio de Venezia a S. Giocomo di Galicia
1477   *Itinerario da Firenze a Santiago di Compostella*
[late]   *Itinéraire de Bruges*

16th century:
1523   Robert Langton
1535 [1621] *Chemin de monsieur sainct Iacques en Galice*
c. 1535   *Le Chemin de Paris a Compostelle et combien il y a de*
          Lieues de Ville en Ville
1585   *Nouvelle Gvide des Chemins*   Nicolas Bonfons

APPENDIX III: NARRATIVES OF A PERSONAL
PILGRIMAGE[40]

DATE	AUTHOR/NATIONALITY/TITLE

12th century:
c. 1150   Book V, *Liber Sancti Jacobi*

13th century:

14th century:

15th century:
1446-8   Sebastian Ilsung/Austrian
1456   William Wey/England
          Itinerarium
1466   Leo von Rozmital/Germany
          Ritter-Hof-und Pilger-Reise durch die Abendlande
1472   Francesco Piccardi/Italian
          Il viaggio al Santo Sepolcro ed a S. Jacopo
1483-6   Nicholaus von Popplau/Polish
1488   Jehan de Tournai/France
1491   Mardiros, Bishop of Arzendján/Armenia
1494   Hieronomus Münzer/Germany
1495   Herman Künig von Vach/Germany
          Die walfahrt vnd Strass zu sant Jacob
1498   Arnold von Harff/Germany

16th century:
1502   Philip the Fair/France [written by Antonio de Lalaing]
          Voyage de Philippe le Beau en Espagne
1550   Bartholomeo Fontana/Italian
          *Itinerario o vero viaggio . . . seguendo poi per ordine
          di Roma fino a Santo Iacobo in Galitia*
1581   Erich Lassota de Steblovo/German
          Tagebuch

NOTES

[1] The beginnings of the cult of Santiago are shrouded in time, time warp, and forged documents. Van Herwaarden ("Origins") is one excellent source for tracing the written record of the growth and importance of the cult.

[2] A lack of documentation in the article leads us to be wary of the claim. See Taliani (1: 129-32).

[3] Vázquez de Parga mentions that the discovery of Iria, but the reference comes from a twelfth-century manuscript, so again the evidence is tangential (1: 40). Cantera alludes to an Arab poet named Algazel and two papal legates named Reynalda and Zanelo, or Janelo, in the latter part of the ninth century. There is only the slimmest reference to them in third-person documents. See the Appendix I to this Introduction for a brief list of names through the thirteenth century.

[4] See Vázquez de Parga's Spanish synopsis of the original Latin reference (1: 41). English translation is ours.

[5] Two English-language translations of the "Guide" have recently become available. See Melczer, whose translation appeared in 1993, and Shaver-Crandell and Gerson, whose translation, part of their larger project including a Gazetteer, just arrived in 1995.

[6] Shaver-Crandell and Gerson speak of only twelve copies of the *Pilgrim's Guide* in manuscript form (24).

[7] The nature of the author's commentary in the *Guide* has proved a fertile field for commentary. See the extensive bibliography in Melczer.

[8] For the numbers and contents of the various manuscripts of the *Pseudo-Turpin*, see Hämel. He cites 139 Latin editions in "manuscritos latinos." The number of subsequent versions goes far beyond 100.

[9] Originally unavailable to the general public, and published only as her dissertation at the University of London in 1964: "Jacobean Pilgrims from England from the Early Twelfth to the Late Fifteenth Century." The Xunta de Galicia has recently (1994) republished the work with the same title.

[10] See Appendices II and III for lists of early itineraries and narratives on the Route to Compostela.

[11] See Wey. An early edition was published in 1867; a more recent and accessible translation of the section on Wey's pilgrimage to Compostela is by Hogarth.

[12] See his "A Pilgrimage for Religion's Sake."

[13] See his short article, "Le pèlerinage après le moyen âge." Cordero Carrete has transcribed a license dated 1638 which allowed pilgrim Robert Puchin to beg for alms during his pilgrimage to Rome. The document was written by the *penitenciario* of the Compostela Cathedral ("Peregrino mendicantes").

[14] Publication of Albani's journal with the accompanying watercolors was made in 1993. Until its appearance, we had no reference either to Albani or the existence of such an important tome.

[15] For these and other pilgrims, see Dunn and Davidson, *The Pilgrimage to Santiago.*

[16] See María Teresa García Campello, "Enfermos y peregrinos en el Hospital Real de Santiago durante el siglo XVII," as one example of several studies of this nature.

[17] Neither the Gil nor the Jaspar book are available in the United States. We have relied on the various references to the works to intuit that they are personal narrations. We also have some, scant, evidence of other pilgrims, such as may be found in an article by A.F. Ozanan, "Un pèlerinage du Pays du Cid, 1852" published in 1872. While we have not located this article, references to it indicate that the narration apparently deals with a pilgrim on the way to Compostela, but who got sick in Burgos and returned to Paris, without having completed the pilgrimage. Fuentes Noya describes the 1897 Holy Year, who attended, and what celebrations there were.

[18] The bull "Deus Omnipotens" confirms the tradition of the legend of St. James' being buried in Compostela.

[19] For the period between 1800 and 1899, the Dunn and Davidson bibliography lists 146 publications. Antonio López Ferreiro and José Villaamil y Castro, both connected with the Compostela Cathedral, were responsible for 31 of that number, one of which is López Ferreiro's 15-volume history of the Compostela Cathedral.

[20] Of the 146 publications (see previous note), 10% were written in the English language.

[21] These stories have been studied in detail by Walker and Adams.

[22] The Pórtico was so entrancing to the British that a full-sized cast was made in 1866 and placed in the architectural court of the South Kensington Museum.

^{23} What are lacking are easily-accessible statistics on numbers of pilgrims and their origins for the years 1900-1950. The journal *Compostela* did offer counts of pilgrims, especially for the Holy Years 1954, 1965, and some for 1971.

^{24} This estimate of numbers if based on personal experience and conversations with persons involved in the pilgrimage in Roncesvalles and the Compostela Cathedral. We do not have, nor do we know of any statistics published for the years 1900-1990 that carefully count the numbers of pilgrims on foot to the shrine.

Both Dunn and Davidson have walked the pilgrimage several times. Davidson first hiked the route in 1974 in a study abroad program directed by Prof. David M. Gitlitz, who had been moved to organize the program after reading Starkie's book. Several small towns closed their businesses when our group of eight hiked through to ask us questions, and some of the older women asked us to take their prayers to the Saint. When we arrived at the Cathedral, we had some trouble finding the Cathedral archivist for the *Compostela* certificates. His book listing pilgrims for that year had fewer than fifty names, and it was already after the Saint's feast day. In 1979, Davidson and Gitlitz co-directed the program, and Dunn was a student on that pilgrimage. The organist at Roncesvalles, don Javier Navarro (who still receives pilgrims there), walked with us on our first day in Spain (we had crossed over from St-Jean-Pied-de-Port) in order to mark the route for any others who would come through. He was adamant to maintain the "old" Route, even to the point of crossing through private property. There was evidently more pilgrimage traffic in 1979, but, with the increasing prosperity of Spanish farmers who now drove motorscooters to work along paved roads, many of the old trails were overgrown and we thought we'd need a machete to make it through.

In 1986 Dunn made another pilgrimage with students from Creighton and Nebraska-Lincoln Universities. By then don Elías Valiña Sampedro's long-standing efforts to revive the pilgrimage were showing real results: in Galicia Dunn watched as he personally helped mark the route with heavy concrete steles, each with a shell and a kilometer-reading of how far away from the goal the pilgrims stand.

In 1987 Gitlitz and Davidson once again hiked, this time using the Somport pass. We were a curiosity, but not the oddity of the previous decade. By the time we got to Galicia, it was obvious that we were not alone. We met up with several church youth groups, and their priest leaders were not cassock-wearing. We joined in several outdoor, California-style prayer meetings. The hospitality, however, was nearly the same: that is, we depended on small *hostales*, and in the very small villages, the kindness of the residents in their allowing us to sleep in their porches or barns.

What a difference in 1993! 99,000 pilgrims, with whom we hiked, sweated, showered at the *autonomía*-organized *refugios,* and wondered at the rebirth of an ancient tradition, with all of its carnivalesque and human aspects. In these twenty years I feel that I have witnessed and participated in the rebirth of the phoenix.

25 See the Dunn and Davidson bibliography.

26 Valiñas died in 1989. From 1985 he had been the Comisario Coordinador del Camino. By 1993, a stele had been erected outside of the church in O Cebreiro in his honor.

27 See, for example, Juanjo Alonso, *El camino de Santiago en mountain bike,* and Juan García Hourcade and Elías Serra Martínez, *En camino, a los cuarenta.*

28 We know of two works, with lovely photos, and/or with drawings and maps published in Japanese in the last ten years: Munchiro Ikeda's *El Camino de Santiago en España hoy (Guía del peregrino y Visita al románico español)* and Akira Kotani, *El camino de Santiago.*

29 This is a fairly complete list of these published works on personal pilgrimages. The dates here are the date of publication of the book-length narratives:
1985: Robin Neillands; 1987: Laurie Dennett, Eleanor Munro; 1989: Ada Alvey, Ellen Feinberg, Bert Slader, and Paul Graham, Carlos Paternina and Adrian Wright in a group; 1990: Jerome Bertram, Robin Hanbury-Tenison; Dennis Nykiel [unpublished manuscript used in high school classrooms], Karen Whitehill; 1992: Neil Curry, William Dalrymple; 1994: Jack Hitt, Bettina Selby, Edward Stanton. Prof. Lee Hoinacki's description of his pilgrimage in 1993 will appear next year. For all but Hitt, Hoinacki, Nykiel, and Stanton, see the Dunn and Davidson bibliography for full annotations.
The pilgrimage as tourist phenomenon has received spotted attention in the U.S., as well. Articles in popular travel journals have appeared since the 1930s through this month's *house beautiful* [sic], in which William Bryant Logan has written about his cycling-pilgrimage from León. His trip, apparently organized by Camino Tours in Houston Texas, put him in contact with several people from various parts of the world as they pedalled to Compostela.

30 In our research we rejected another 500 titles as being purely touristic.

31 We do not wish to exclude anyone purposely from this list, which is meant as only suggestive of the broad scope of titles, interests, and nationalities involved. This set of names is completely casual and non-scientific: it comes simply from a scan of one shelf in Davidson's office. Other lists of names and titles in this paragraph are, similarly, meant as examples only. See the Dunn and Davidson bibliography for full titles, bibliographical data, and annotations.

32 The list of organizations and accompanying newsletters changes often. One list is in the Dunn and Davidson bibliography (10-12).

Peregrino occasionally prints information from the confraternities and gives information about new publications.

[33] For the music, see Helmer.

[34] The photographs with accompanying essays were published in 1991.

[35] In 1993 several of the towns along the Route in Spain also ⁓⁓⁓⁓⁓⁓⁓⁓⁓⁓⁓⁓⁓⁓⁓⁓⁓⁓⁓⁓⁓⁓⁓⁓⁓⁓⁓⁓⁓⁓⁓⁓⁓⁓⁓⁓⁓⁓ pilgrimage-motif T-shirts burgeoned.

[36] The information was compiled at the University of Dayton. Address: http://www.udayton.edu/mary (*Providence Journal-Bulletin* (17 Sept. 1995): A7. See "Virgin Mary."

[37] One CD-ROM already exists on the Camino, meant to offer touristic information about such things as hotels (see "Camino de Santiago"). Italica Press (New York) is in the process of creating another CD-ROM, focusing on the historical and artistic aspects. (MAC, ISBN: 0-934977-58-5, Windows, ISBN: 0-934977-59-3).

[38] These lists of pilgrims' names, narratives, and itineraries from the eleventh through the thirteenth centuries have been gleaned through several years of intense reading in facilities in the United States and Europe. We offer them here as a schema of the information that is becoming available through research in diocesan and parochial libraries and publications of hitherto unknown materials. This is not an exhaustive list, nor is it immutable. See Dunn and Davidson, *Pilgrimage to Santiago,* for bibliographic information.

[39] We consider "Guidebooks" and "Itineraries" those works whose content is a rendering of basic travel information about the Route to Compostela.

[40] We classify as "Narrative" a document that describes a pilgrimage, or trip, to Compostela and whose account contains more than basic information of distance and accommodations.

Competing Triacastela Bars Offer Pilgrims the Necessary Stamp for the Pilgrim's Passport, July 1993

The Pilgrimage to Compostela in the Middle Ages

CHAPTER 1

The Cult of Saints and Divine Patronage in *Gallaecia* before Santiago

Alberto Ferreiro

The fourth through the sixth centuries were a time of growing up, in terms of ecclesiastical culture, in the western provinces of the late Roman Empire. In the midst of the Germanic migrations and settlement there arose major ecclesiastical centers at Lérins (France), Braga (Portugal), Toledo (Spain), and Tours (France) among others. We also witness in these unsettling times the emergence of Augustine, Gregory the Great, and Cassiodorus who equaled intellectually the great Greek theologians of the eastern provinces of the Mediterranean. While the East held a virtual monopoly on the most prestigious pilgrimage centers, in the West the See of Tours surfaced as one of the most popular pilgrimage sites, attracting devotion even in the faraway eastern provinces. The cult of St. Martin of Tours (372-97) procured a significant place in the Iberian Peninsula, notably in what are now northwestern Spain and northern Portugal in the ancient province of *Gallaecia* [Galicia] (see map, page 16).

The task of this essay is two-fold: first, to examine the literary evidence, as found in Gregory of Tours (539-94), Peninsular sources, and others, on the diffusion of Martin's cult in Galicia; second, to attempt to explore in what ways the cult of St. Martin was a precursor to—or paved the way for—the rise of devotion to Santiago in Galicia. I will end our discussion with some thoughts on why the patronage of Martin was abandoned, or set aside, in Galicia-Asturias for that of Santiago in the eighth and ninth centuries. It is not my purpose here to delve into investigating the authenticity of Santiago's remains and tomb at Compostela, or the origins of the cult in pre-eighth century Galicia, nor to his alleged preaching in Galicia. Much ink has been devoted to those questions and continues to be, but I will defer such controversies to others.[1] In the final analysis, no one has been able to establish in the affirmative the veracity of any of these questions. As my friend and colleague, Don Eugenio Romero Pose, of San Martín Piñario (Compostela), said to me as we strolled one evening in front of that great Cathedral in Compostela, "It's all a matter of faith, you either *believe* [italics mine] Santiago is buried here, or you do not." Not all matters on the cult of saints in Galicia are left up to assent of faith. We are on much surer historical ground on the patronage of saints in Galicia before Santiago and that story is the focus of my efforts in this essay.

Throughout the entire Roman era Galicia was anything but a remote backwater province on the edge of the Empire. The deep Romanization of Galicia, not at all reversed by the Germanic migrations, is well documented by archaeological and literary remains.[2] Galicia's orientation towards Lusitania, greater Iberia, and the Mediterranean is only a partial view of its economic and cultural contacts. Steady and somewhat extensive relations existed between Galicia and its neighbors to the North in what are now Ireland and France.[3] The northern connections likewise were not severed by the Germanic migrations to and settlement of Galicia in the fifth century. In fact, economic, political, and cultural activity between Galicia and Merovingian France actually intensified well into the late seventh century. The entry of the cult of Martin of Tours in Galicia was the direct result of these contacts in the middle of the sixth century. Devotion to Martin of Tours in Galicia and a shrine in his honor at Braga was in part the work of his namesake, Martin of Braga (520-79).

Long before an actual shrine was established at Braga to honor Martin of Tours, his fame and reputation had already preceded him. Hydatius, Bishop of Iria Flavia in Galicia (390-470), in his *Chronicon*, which covers events in Iberia from 378 to 469, bears witness to the popularity of Martin's cult in Iberia (1-36).[4] Hydatius' comments, characteristic of the *Chronicon*, are very brief, but no less valuable for the information they provide. The passages are indicative of what aspects of Martin's character attracted devotion to him in Galicia and throughout western Christendom.

Hydatius, in the first reference, mentions Martin of Tours alongside another great luminary of the Church, Ambrose of Milan (15). There are perhaps two underlying reasons for this association. Ambrose of Milan's reputation, to be sure, did not need any legitimization; it was Martin's own stature that was further enhanced as he was aligned by Hydatius with such an eminent ecclesiastic. More to the point, however, both Ambrose of Milan and Martin of Tours were contemporaries of Priscillian, and they together opposed this heretic.[5] In the same passage, Hydatius praises Martin's virtuous life as a model for emulation, and the miraculous signs associated with his ministry. Miracles and extraordinary feats of faith were believed to be the visible stamp of sainthood and apostolicity.[6] After his death and burial at Tours devotees reported frequent miracles, which in their turn galvanized devotion to Martin and pilgrimages to Tours. In a second passage,

Martin of Tours is mentioned within the context of the Priscillianist heretical controversy that had unfolded in Galicia and in Gaul (15). Hydatius, then, introduced the most authoritative voice against Priscillian: Pope Damasus, the successor of Saint Peter. Ambrose of Milan is invoked again as an opponent of the sect while in Gaul Martin of Tours is said to have echoed the condemnation. Hydatius' main purpose in the entry, it seems, was once again to laud the reputation and influence of Martin of Tours.

Priscillian was an ascetic with extraordinary oratory skills who attracted a significant following of men and women. He and his followers were accused of Gnosticism, promoting apocryphal literature, and questionable sexual liberties.[7] Priscillian made a sincere attempt to gain official approval for his teachings from Pope Damasus and Ambrose of Milan, but was rebuffed by both (Sulpicius 101). Apparently, Priscillian likewise sought the endorsement from the pre-eminent ecclesiastic in the Gallic church, Martin of Tours. I believe that within Hydatius' *Chronicon* all three ecclesiastics were intended to convey the *auctoritas* of the church: Pope Damasus, as successor of St. Peter, symbolized apostolic censure; Ambrose of Milan, the great scholar-theologian, represented the authoritative learned voice of the Church; and, Martin of Tours, while not learned nor directly apostolic, seemed to have represented the saintly holy man at the grassroots level. What emerged was a three-tiered rejection by the Church, and Martin of Tours occupied a significant place within Hydatius' purposes.

The third and final reference shifts to Martin's reputation after his death. Hydatius, while extolling the literary career of Sulpicius Severus, (c. 360-c. 420), singled out the *Vita sancti Martini* as his most enduring contribution to posterity (16-7). The passage is compelling evidence that this hagiography from Sulpicius' pen was one of several sources that propagated the fame of Martin of Tours, even into a remote province like Galicia on the fringes of Christendom. Hydatius' testimony does not suggest, in the least, that any shrines in honor of Martin of Tours existed at that time in the Iberian Peninsula. While we cannot rule out completely the possible introduction of shrines in Hydatius' lifetime or soon thereafter, they most assuredly proliferated in the not too distant future.

The earliest witness to a shrine dedicated to Martin of Tours in Galicia, for that matter in all of Iberia, dates from the middle of the sixth century. The documentation of this momentous event did not originate from within the Iberian Peninsula: it came not surprisingly from the pen of Gregory of Tours. Gregory, as Bishop of Tours, made it one of his principal agendas to promote the cult of St. Martin.[8] The entry of Martin of Tours' cult into Galicia and subsequent proclamation was in part the work of Martin of Braga, who carried out a lengthy and fruitful missionary career within the kingdom of the Sueves of Galicia. Before immersing ourselves into Gregory of Tours' account on this activity, some background is called for on Martin of Braga and the Sueves.

Of the several Germanic tribes who vied for a permanent settlement in the Iberian Peninsula, the lot, so to speak, fell upon the Sueves to occupy what is now Galicia and Northern Portugal.[9] The principal bishopric in Galicia was at Braga, and the new overlords established their capital there. To date, the archaeological and literary evidence about the Sueves is still rather scarce. What we do have permits us to reconstruct a coherent yet sketchy understanding of their history.[10] While the Suevic kingdom expanded dramatically in the fifth century, it was checked and nearly destroyed altogether by the Arian Goths, who in that era ruled in Gaul and were themselves attempting to carve out an even larger kingdom.[11] In the second phase, the Suevic kingdom flourished until 585, when the Arian Goths led by Leovigild—who had been expelled from Gaul by the Franks in 511 but now ruled most of Iberia—destroyed completely the Sueves. According to Isidore of Seville the Sueves, from beginning to end, ruled Galicia for almost 177 years (*Historia Gothorum* ch. 92).[12]

Throughout this entire period the Sueves maintained an inconstant relationship with the Church. The Suevic kings converted to or rejected both the Arian and Catholic forms of Christianity at various stages, that is, until Martin of Braga arrived in 556. Within this ambivalent religious climate a well-organized church thrived and developed, which exercised significant influence upon Galicia in general and more directly on the Suevic kings. Although many clerics and laity were responsible for this success, the contemporary sources from Gaul and Iberia unanimously identify Martin of Braga as the main catalyst for effecting a permanent and enduring conversion of the Sueves and greater Galicia to Catholic belief.[13]

The precious little that has survived of Martin of Braga's literary output does not justly measure his influence in the Middle Ages.[14] The three major sources containing biographical information on Martin of Braga are Gregory of Tours, Isidore of Seville, and Venantius Fortunatus. We, of course, should not lose sight of Martin's own works which corroborate numerous details in these sources.[15] Succinctly, the following is all that we know about Martin of Braga. Like Martin of Tours, the Bishop of Braga was born in the same province of Pannonia (present-day Hungary). As in the case of the Bishop of Tours, Martin travelled West and there flourished as a missionary. Prior to his westward move, Martin of Braga ventured to the East (presumably Constantinople). He visited the Holy Places (Jerusalem, etc.), and became so learned that, according to Gregory of Tours, "he was second to none" (*Liber historiarum* 37). Isidore of Seville credits Martin of Braga with the conversion of the Sueves, with the help of the Suevic King Theodemir, out of Arianism to the Catholic faith. He is further praised for founding numerous monasteries and writing a variety of pastoral and theological works, some of which survived in abundance in the Middle Ages (*Historia Gothorum* 302-3).[16] Gregory of Tours, however, in his *De virtutibus sancti Martini* (1. 11), relates the only account concerning the arrival of Martin of Braga to Galicia with the relics of Martin of Tours and the establishment of the first Martinian shrine in the Iberian Peninsula.[17] Insofar as the hagiographical element is concerned in Gregory's account, the narrative bears all of the earmarks of the genre. One miraculous event after another occurs, and they serve the high purpose of demonstrating the authority of Martin of Tours.

Gregory tells of a King Chararic (550?-8?) of Galicia who sought a miraculous cure for his son, apparently afflicted with a life-threatening illness, and who remains nameless in the narrative. As Chararic sought the divine intervention of Martin of Tours there was one major obstacle to be surmounted before the king could obtain the desired cure. Chararic was an Arian Christian and it was widely known God did not heal unrepentant heretics, nor could bishops of the Arian church effect cures. Gregory firmly believed this and made every attempt to promote his views.[18] Gregory lamented that Galicia suffered a plague of leprosy of epidemic proportions. Gregory's invocation of leprosy is all too obvious: so long as Chararic remained an Arian, along with his people, his son would not only remain ill, but the entire region would continue to suffer from leprosy. Leprosy was a metaphorical reference to the spiritual leprosy of heresy. God was punishing Chararic's heresy by allowing his son to become ill and visiting upon the people of Galicia a plague of leprosy, so Gregory would have his readers believe. And believe they did! Curiously, Gregory never indicated outright that Chararic's son suffered from leprosy, and we are left to assume that he was very likely afflicted with the dreaded disease. Chararic in desperation inquired of those around him about the shrine at Tours, the miracles reported there and as to what faith, Arian or Catholic, Martin adhered to in his own lifetime. Chararic decided to send envoys to Tours laden with gold and silver, equal to the weight of his son, as an offering to Martin. When this strategy failed and his son remained ill, Chararic resorted to a new tact. He once again sent envoys to Tours—this time to obtain a relic, and he declared his intent to build at Braga a shrine in Martin's honor and to abjure the Arian heresy. When the messengers reached the shrine at Tours, miracles in abundance were unleashed, prisoners' chains miraculously fell off, and when the pilgrims returned to Galicia Chararic's son was already healed. If that were not enough, leprosy had disappeared altogether from Galicia. But there is more. Providentially, Martin of Braga and Chararic's envoys, who brought with them relics of Martin of Tours, arrived at Galicia on the same day and at the same port of call, although both had commenced their journeys from different points of departure. At the end of the narrative Gregory of Tours proclaimed that Martin of Tours became the *beatus patronus* [blessed patron] of Galicia. Gregory of Tours in his *Libri historiarum* added an additional note: Martin of Braga is said to have written verses in honor of Martin of Tours on the southern portal of the church (37). [19]

Whether fact or fiction, we must keep in mind that in Gregory's day the account circulated as gospel truth throughout Gaul and beyond into the Iberian Peninsula.[20] Fortunately, Gregory's account concerning the initial entry of Martin's cult into Galicia is not the only source that we possess on these developments. Venantius Fortunatus and Martin of Braga are powerful reliable voices that unquestionably affirm the presence of the cult of Martin of Tours in Galicia, and they confirm Gregory of Tours on this critical point.

Venantius Fortunatus (ca. 530-600), Bishop of Poitiers, is best known for his numerous poems dedicated to those whom he admired.[21] One of his poems, "Ad Martinum episcopum Galliciensiem" (5.2), was written to an Abbess Radegund, who is praised for her adoption of the Rule of Caesarius for a community of nuns at Poitiers.[22] Martin of Braga played a major role in the development of this community of female ascetics at Poitiers via letters to Radegund. Unfortunately, none of the letters have survived. Martin's involvement was one of his numerous monastic activities in Gaul and Galicia; the poem by Venantius is a tribute to Martin of Braga's missionary deeds. There is much in the poem that bears directly on the question of Martin of Tours' cult in Galicia.

Venantius recalled first the evangelism of Martin of Tours in Gaul, then proceeded to proclaim Martin of Braga a successor of the apostles, and specifically a new apostle of Galicia (*Carminum libri V*, 17-8). Just as Martin of Tours had been the apostle of Gaul, now Martin of Braga had a similar calling in Galicia. Venantius also echoed the well-known fact that both Martins originated from the province of Pannonia. They are also extolled for their defense of the Catholic faith and their triumphs over heresy and paganism (George 68-9). Finally, Martin of Braga's ministry in Galicia, where he spent about thirty years as bishop, is noted by Venantius. Most of these details are found in varying degrees in Gregory of Tours and even much later in Isidore of Seville. In the case of Isidore, however, the information on Martin of Tours is completely absent.

The poem by Venantius on Martin of Braga has in times past been cited as a proof text for the earliest origins of devotion to Santiago in Galicia.[23] Only the most imaginative exegesis of the poem could yield such an interpretation. Careful and restrained scholarship has decisively demonstrated that mention of Santiago (James the Elder) with the other apostles served as a rhetorical vehicle to confirm the apostolicity of both Martins, and has nothing to do whatsoever with an alleged apostolic succession of Martin of Braga from Santiago. Venantius affirms that both Martins have been bestowed with the virtue of Peter, the doctrine of Paul, and the aid of the apostles James and John ["Qui virtute Petrum praebet tibi, dogmata Paulum, Hinc Iacobi tribuens, inde Iohannis opem" (19-20)]. Venantius' poem is valuable for its testimony on the introduction of devotion to Martin of Tours in Galicia and Martin of Braga is rightfully associated with these events.[24]

The most compelling evidence for the cult of Martin of Tours in Galicia comes from the writings of Martin of Braga in the form of two short poems. The first is twenty lines in dactylic hexameters, "In basilica"; the second, "Epitaphium eiusdem," is six lines in dactylic hexameters.[25]

"In basilica" needs to be examined in light of Gregory's comments concerning Martin of Braga's devotion to Martin of Tours. In his *De virtutibus s. Martini* Gregory testified that Chararic "in honorem beati Martini fabricavit miro opere eclesiam" [built a church in honor of Martin of Tours] (Barlow 299). In the *Libri historiarum*, Gregory praised Martin of Braga for "[v]ersiculos qui super ostium sunt a parte meridiana in Basilica sancti Martini, ipse composuit" [having written verses in honor of Martin of Tours, which were posted on the southern portal of the church] (Barlow 300). There has been a mistaken assumption by some scholars that the verses Gregory identified in the *Libri historiarum* were composed and posted in the church at Tours.[26] The problem in the past has been the tendency of some scholars to isolate Gregory's narratives from these other sources rather than viewing them as a consistent testimony that support and enhance one another. Thus the poem "In basilica" needs to be included in any analysis of Gregory's narrative on Galicia. "In basilica" devotes the better part of its subject matter to the nearly universal spread of devotion to Martin of Tours. The latter part of the poem proclaims that the Sueves could now honor and worship at this new shrine of Christ, where miracles abound. It ends with the affirmation that now both Gaul and Galicia could claim him as their patron (Barlow 282). Recall that Gregory of Tours made a similar declaration of patronage in his account of Chararic's conversion to Catholic doctrine and adoption of Martin of Tours as patron [protector] of Galicia (VM 1.11.63-5, Barlow 300).[27]

In the brief "Epitaphium eiusdem" we find yet another significant reference to Martin of Tours. The first four lines provide biographical information corroborated by Gregory of Tours. It identifies his birthplace as Pannonia, his lengthy travels [westward], and his final settlement in Galicia ["Pannoniis genitus, transcendens aequora vasta, Galliciae in gremium divinus nutibus actus" (Barlow 283)]. In the last two lines Martin of Braga associated himself with Martin of Tours, again identifying the latter as patron: "Teque, patrone, sequens famulus Martinus eodem Nomine, non merito" [28] (Barlow 283).

There is yet one final reference to the shrine at Braga dedicated to Martin of Tours in Gregory's work. In the *De virtutibus s. Martini* (4.7), Gregory recorded the arrival in Galicia of legates who came to see King Miro (570-83) of the Sueves. Gregory did not name the site, but it is undoubtedly Braga, since he identified the church there as the one built in honor of Martin of Tours by a predecessor [Chararic]; and as previously mentioned in the first book of the same work (1.11). It is noteworthy that Miro, like Chararic, was perceived as a guardian of this shrine. We need to note that Gregory did not specify by name any of the Suevic kings who had ruled between Chararic and Miro. There also ruled, for example, the kings Ariamir (558-61) and Theodemir (561-70) who led the Sueves after Chararic and before Miro.[29] Some scholars have boldly identified Theodemir as the unnamed son of Chararic in Gregory's account. We cannot with absolute certainty designate Theodemir as the son in question, yet Ariamir would certainly be the most likely candidate.[30] What is of greater importance here is that, beginning with Chararic, the kings of the Sueves at Braga adopted Martin of Tours as their patron and protector. Braga may have been the first center of devotion to Martin of Tours in Iberia, but not the only one in existence in Gregory's lifetime.

In the *Liber in gloria confessorum* (ch. 12), Gregory recounted a story about the Visigoth Arian king Leovigild (569-86) and a shrine of Martin of Tours located at an unidentified monastery somewhere between Sagunto and Cartagena. Leovigild's army, according to Gregory, was in the habit of destroying the holy places of Catholics.[31] When Leovigild's men approached the monastery the resident monks fled in terror. The elderly abbot who was known for his holiness stood his ground and refused to leave. When one of Leovigild's men raised the sword to slay him, the soldier fell over backwards and died on the spot. Upon seeing such a display of God's power, the Arian Visigoths fled horrified and in disarray. Leovigild, who was not present, received the news of these events and was himself humbled. Leovigild ordered his men to restore the stolen goods to the monastery, the abbot returned, and the community continued to flourish once again. Gregory's message here is that Martin of Tours was directly responsible for sparing the abbot's life and restoring to the monastery its stolen property from the ravages of the Arian Visigoths under Leovigild, the arch-enemies of Catholics everywhere.

This leads us to the final question as to what saintly patronage meant in this era, specifically for the Sueves who adopted Martin of Tours. The patronage aspect in regard to Martin of Tours in Gregory's work and saints in general is one that has received increased attention by modern scholars.[32] What has gone virtually unexplored up until now is the patronage of Martin of Tours in Catholic Galicia in relation to the Sueves' chief enemies and nemesis, the Arian Visigoths.

Let us return, then, to the main narrative for Galicia, *De virtutibus s. Martini* (1.11), to glean out the patronage element in that work. Martin of Tours provided healing only to those who became members of the true flock of God, and the litmus test was confession of Nicaean Trinitarianism. So long as Chararic remained an Arian by confession, his son would not be cured, and the whole of Galicia would remain ravaged by leprosy. Once Chararic confessed Catholic orthodoxy, the child was healed and leprosy disappeared *in toto* from Galicia, never to return. Gregory of Tours believed that God punished heretics such as Chararic, but, through his servant Martin of Tours, a way of escape was provided by grace. The ultimate purpose of miracles, whether they were ordinary events believed to be the result of Providence or truly extraordinary manifestations, was to bring people to Catholic belief. In all of Gregory's works the miraculous held a central position, in both the *Libri historiarum* and the *Libri miraculorum*. As Walter Goffart notes on this crucial point, "It makes little sense, then, to distinguish the *Wonders* as hagiography from the *Histories*" (152). The patronage of Martin of Tours meant protection from the wrath of God—i.e., military conquest by enemies or epidemics—and deliverance from doctrinal error. Martin of Tours was a divine instrument that God used to draw people into the Catholic faith.

There are other aspects to patronage to be considered, however. The story in the *Liber in gloria confessorum* regarding Leovigild and his men brings to the surface more benefits from Martin's patronage. The anonymous abbot of the monastery was protected by Martin of Tours for his faithfulness to God and to his shrine. The Arian Goth was slain by God [Martin of Tours] instantly and the fear of God extended all the way to the Arian Goth, Leovigild. This story bears some resemblance to an incident reported by Sulpicius Severus in his portrait of Martin of Tours. While Martin of Tours rejected the doctrinal errors of Priscillian, he also vehemently opposed the Emperor Maximian's threats to execute Priscillian for heresy. Martin of Tours was able to restrain the wrathful hand of Maximus, but soon after his own death the Emperor carried out the execution of Priscillian.[33] In the case of Leovigild, Martin of Tours prevailed against the Arian heretics and provided powerful protection in a decisive way to a faithful Catholic.

The patronage of Martin of Tours carried apostolic authority and ensured success in missionary activity. Conversion to Catholic Christianity was at the heart of all missionary efforts. Conversion stories of people from all social levels are legion in Gregory's *Libri historiarum* and the *Libri miraculorum*. In the *De virtutibus s. Martini* (1.11), the conversion of Chararic and of his people in Galicia is the highlight of Gregory's narrative. Martin of Braga's own success as bishop and pastor was visible fruit of his devotion to the patronage of Martin of Tours. This explains why Martin of Braga was compared to Martin of Tours by Venantius Fortunatus, and Martin of Braga likens himself in this regard to the bishop of Tours, as we have noted above. This point is brought home when Martin of Braga was hailed by Venantius Fortunatus as the apostle of Galicia, as was Martin of Tours for Gaul.

There still remains a final question to consider: What else did the Suevic kings hope to gain from the patronage of Martin of Tours? The most significant aspect of patronage for the Suevic kings in Galicia would have been protection during times of war. To highlight this benefit of patronage in Gregory's narratives we have to turn to those not directly concerned with Galicia. A well-known example revolves around the conversion of Clovis to the Catholic faith, a work in which Martin of Tours had an important role. Clovis' victory over the Arian Goths was the result of Clovis' own faithfulness to the Catholic Church and especially as a result of his appeal to Martin of Tours.[34] Is there any reason to doubt that when the Suevic kings went into battle against the Arian Visigoths, they too called upon their patron Martin of Tours to bring them success against the chief enemy of the faith? In this sense, Martin of Tours became a precursor to that greater patron yet to come, Santiago, who supplanted Martin of Tours in Galicia and eventually all saints in the entire Peninsula, as patron of the Reconquest.

The displacement of Martin of Tours by Santiago was due to the greater religious political reshuffling of Galicia and Gaul from the sixth through eighth centuries. The first event, though not a radical change for the cult of St. Martin, was the destruction of the Suevic kingdom by Leovigild in 585. We have already seen that Gregory of Tours attributed to Leovigild a certain amount of reverence toward the cult of Martin of Tours. In 589 king Reccared, Leovigild's second son who had converted to Catholicism, officially extirpated Arianism and proclaimed all of Iberia Catholic at the Third Council of Toledo.[35] Surely these changes provided the framework for the greater proliferation of the cult of St. Martin of Tours in the Iberian Peninsula. It was the Muslim Conquest of Iberia in 711 that proved to be the major catalyst for the advent of the cult of Santiago and the diminishing role of Martin of Tours. Equally important was the establishment of the Carolingian

Empire north of the Pyrenees, and the rise of the small and ambitious kingdoms in the north of Spain as a result of the Muslim Conquest.[36]

Within the kingdom of Asturias under Mauregatus (783-88), Alfonso II (791-842), and Alfonso III (866-910) we witness the search for and the need of a new patron. This search, in part, was influenced not only by the Muslim threat in the South; it was also due to changes in the Carolingian Empire in the North. The Carolingians, too, were in need of their own royal patron to protect the emerging empire under Charlemagne. In these closing paragraphs I intend only to highlight what is relevant to our study and do not in any way wish to minimize unduly the complexity of this era and related topics.

We do well to heed at the outset Roger Collins' judicious precautionary comments about the emergence of the Asturian kingdom, that we should not anachronistically interpret this era from the later perspective of the Reconquest (*Arab Conquest* 165). Such restraint is especially applicable in regard to the rise of the Santiago cult in the regions of Galicia-Asturias. Important developments are attested to in our sources. What we do not find is an instantaneous full-blown adoption of Santiago; but a process that definitely accelerated in the next two centuries. The *Chronicle of Alfonso III* does not breathe a single word about Santiago and the writer had numerous opportunities to mention the patronage of the new saint. The *Chronicle* identified a variety of shrines, among them: one dedicated to Mary (ch. 10), a basilica to the Holy Cross (ch. 12), basilicas to Jesus and the 12 apostles, another to Mary, and a church in honor of St. Julian and Baselissa (ch. 21); and towards the end we are informed that Ordoño I (850-66) was buried in the church of St. Mary (ch. 28). In chapter 14, however, it is said that Alfonso I (739-57) "built many basilicas."[37] This could be implicitly a reference to a possible shrine dedicated to Santiago since reports of discovery of his bones and burial place did occur firmly in the reigns of his predecessors Mauregatus and successor Alfonso II. The fact remains, however, that under Alfonso III the development of the cult of Santiago seems to have still been a slow-going process.

The eighth-century hymn "O Dei verbum patris," it is believed, was written in the reign of Alfonso II as a homage to his predecessor, Mauregatus.[38] The hymn refers explicitly to Santiago as defender of Christendom and as the helpful patron "patronus vernulus" of Mauregatus. Under Alfonso II the discovery of Santiago's bones and burial site was reported in Galicia. The bishop of Iria Flavia Theodemir was called upon to look into the matter and he confirmed the authenticity of the claims. Since Galicia had already been subjugated by the Asturians earlier in the reign of Silo (774-83) that meant Martin of Tours entered Asturias as patron of the newly-combined kingdoms.[39]

Some scholars have interpreted this series of events under Mauregatus and Alfonso II as attempts by the Asturian monarchy to appropriate Santiago as their own patron and to free themselves from the increasingly overbearing Frankish influence. Alfonso II took the further step at the Council of Oviedo (821) to restore the Asturian church in a move to establish its own ecclesiastical identity in the North.[40] Although deeply challenged, the cult of St. Martin of Tours still continued to hold a prominent place in Galicia-Asturias and in the Carolingian Empire.

Political and religious contacts between Asturias and the Carolingians seem to have been particularly frequent. In his *Vita Caroli Magni* Einhard reports that Alfonso II regularly sent envoys and letters to Charlemagne (768-814) and there is not any reason to doubt the account (44-6; see also Collins, *Arab Conquest* 215-6). Alcuin of York, Charlemagne's main scholar, in a letter to Beatus of Liébana specifically recalled the numerous pilgrims from Asturias who travelled to Tours to pay homage to St. Martin at his shrine (Collins, *Arab Conquest* 215-6).[41] There is one last controversial document that has been rejected as apocryphal, but one that nevertheless dates from the ninth to early tenth centuries (Sánchez Albornoz, *Orígenes* 3. 586-7). Regardless of its true authorship and precise dating, it is still testimony to the degree of interest by the Carolingians in both Santiago and Martin of Tours. The document is a letter dated 906 allegedly directed to Alfonso III from the canons at Tours who inquired asking him about the authenticity of Santiago's tomb, the means of the relics' arrival in Galicia, and other related questions.[42] Once the cult of Santiago emerged in Galicia there was increasingly considerable curiosity by the Carolingians and for good reason. It has been pointed out that French influence on the elaboration of Santiago's cult was significant and should not be underestimated (van Herwaarden 17-8).

The Carolingian interest in Santiago was driven by their own quest to procure patrons for the royal court. If devotion to Martin of Tours was threatened in Galicia-Asturias by the rising Santiago cult, it was equally challenged in the Carolingian Empire, but from still another saint. In the seventh century, St. Denis was adopted by the Franks along with Martin of Tours. The Carolingians seemed to have had a collectors approach to patronage of saints. In spite of these changes, however, Charlemagne and Louis the Pious continued to invoke Martin of Tours as principal patron of their army, and before battle they swore oaths over Martin's *cappa* [cape] and even carried it into the battlefield (Farmer 33-4). Carolingian inquiries about Santiago were probably interpreted by the Asturians as machinations to appropriate Santiago as their own. It perhaps explains why the Asturians moved so quickly to authenticate Santiago's relics and tomb in Galicia, and make him their patron. These events facilitate our understanding as to why Martin of

Tours was abandoned by the Asturians, breaking a tradition dating back to Chararic, as the chief patron saint of the newly emerging kingdom. Martin of Tours very likely was gradually perceived to be principally a Gallic patron saint somewhat exclusively for the Carolingians, a saint doubtlessly worthy of veneration by pilgrims, but not as principal patron for the Asturians. Furthermore, the Asturians had the added agenda of finding a powerful patron to match the Muslim patron, Muhammad.

As the Reconquest unfolded in the medieval centuries Santiago was transformed into the formidable opponent of Muhammad earning him the nickname Moor Slayer (Matamoros). As Muslims and Christians went to war one with another they invoked their respective patrons. The epic *El Poema de Mio Cid* dramatically expresses this ideology: "The Moors called on Muhammad and the Christians on St. James" (1. 36. 61).[43] As the pilgrimage site at Santiago de Compostela developed into a major shrine, the cult of Martin of Tours also continued to grow throughout the Iberian Peninsula and especially along the pilgrimage route to Compostela in the North. But in Galicia both Martin of Braga and Martin of Tours faded in their roles as chief patrons under the looming shadow of Santiago, as did eventually all other saints in Iberia.[44]

The remaining essays in the casebook are a treatment of the significant role of Santiago de Compostela in medieval Iberia and greater Europe continuing even to the present day.

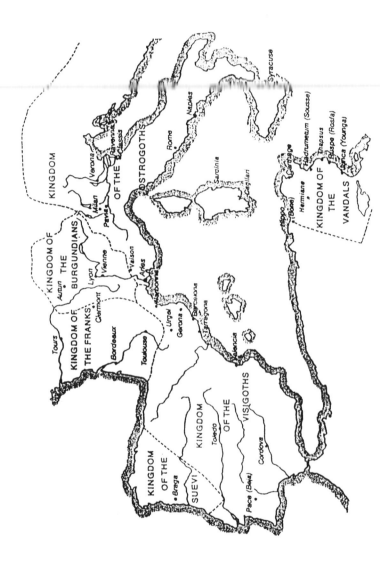

Fig. 1.1 *Centers of Ecclesiastical and Lay Culture* circa 533

NOTES

[1] The bibliography on Santiago de Compostela is enormous and continues to grow. Consult the annotated bibliography on the pilgrimage to Compostela by Dunn and Davidson. For questions on the origins of devotion to Santiago I offer only a select few studies which contain copious documentation from the original sources: Duchesne is an important foundational article. Pérez de Urbel, "Orígenes del culto de Santiago," offers further critical research of the sources and related problems. An excellent brief survey that covers well into the twelfth century is in Oliveira, "Lendas apostólicas," (specifically on Portugal 20-7). A treatment of the medieval documentation concerning the rollos of Santiago le in Costa. Eloiduy in "La tradición Jacobea," provides alternative interpretations on key documents. Sánchez Albornoz, "En los albores," is a meticulous treatment by an eminent scholar, which focuses on the era of Mauregatus. Sánchez Albornoz, Orígenes, offers a panoramic view of the topic with extensive documentation. Casariego is a somewhat romanticized but useful study. Van Herwaarden at present offers one of the best studies in English. Engels is a concise summary of modern scholarship, diverse perspectives, and continuing controversies. Guerra Campos gives an updated study on these matters.

[2] The two most detailed works to date regarding the romanization of Galicia are those by Torres Rodríguez, La Galicia romana and Tranoy, La Galice romaine, both extensively documented. I draw your attention also to the journal Gallaecia published by the Department of Prehistory and Archaeology at the University of Santiago de Compostela, which publishes the very latest on archaeology, especially from the Roman era. See also the most recent collection of essays on Roman and Germanic Galicia, Galicia: da romanidade á xermanización.

[3] For Ireland and Spain [Galicia] see Hillgarth, "Visigothic Spain." He has updated his views in, "Ireland and Spain." For alleged Irish monastic influences see Ferreiro, "A reconsideration of Celtic tonsures." For contacts with Merovingian Gaul see Lewis. The most detailed study in general is by Rouche, L'Aquitaine and by the same author "Les relations transpyrénéennes." An important foundation article is Orlandis, originally published in Annales de la Faculté de Droit et des Sciences Economiques de Toulouse 18 (1970). An in-depth study on Gregory of Tours and his knowledge of Hispania is Teillet. Insightful, too, is Saitta.

[4] An excellent critical edition is Tranoy, Hydace. A translation with limited apparatus is in Campos, Idacio. Professor Richard Burgess, University of Ottawa, has a critical edition in English forthcoming with Oxford UP.

[5] Our chief source for Martin of Tours and Priscillian is Sulpicius Severus' Chronicle. See the Latin edition in Corpus scriptorum ecclesiasticorum latinorum, vol. 1. On Sulpicius and Martin of Tours see Fontaine; for Priscillianism see Stancliffe and Van Dam, Leadership (88-

114). Van Dam, *Leadership,* also discusses Martin of Tours (119-40). Corbett, "Changing perceptions" offers material on Sulpicius Severus (238-42).

[6] We are deeply indebted to Peter Brown for his seminal work on this topic, *The Cult of the Saints.* Within the collection of his previously published essays, *Society and the Holy,* the most relevant essays are "The Rise and Function of the Holy Man in Late Antiquity" (103-52), and "Relics and Social Status in the Age of Gregory of Tours" (222-50). A broader and fascinating study is in Winstead.

[7] For Priscillianism see Chadwick, *Priscillian of Avila,* Ferreiro, "Jerome's Letter," and Stancliffe.

[8] For the growing pilgrimage to Tours in Gregory's era and for an inventory on routes see Lelong. A broader survey of the cult of Martin of Tours in the early Middle Ages is in Ewig and in Pietri, "Le pèlerinage martinien." A very important study that documents thoroughly all of the religious monuments mentioned by Gregory is Vieillard-Troiekouroff (304-29, 428-32, 448-53). An essential study on Tours is Pietri, *La ville de Tours,* on Tours in Gregory's day (247-334, 403-9). For patronage consult Corbett, "The saint as patron," as well as *Praesentium signorum munera,* focusing on Martin of Tours in both works. Corbett treats Gregory of Tours in "Changing Perceptions." Relevant, with a wider agenda is Winstead. Van Dam brings to the surface Gregory's use of Martin to oppose Arianism in "Images of Saint Martin," especially at 13-4. Farmer views Martin as a vehicle to bring "consensus out of disorder" (28). Goffart cautions that Gregory of Tours promoted numerous saints and not just devotion to Martin of Tours (134). Also, Van Dam, *Saints* (68, 78-9, 137, and 141).

[9] Several studies have been devoted to the Sueves, but none adequately address the sources and related problems. Díaz Martínez at the University of Salamanca and I intend to fill this void in a future booklength monograph. For now consult Reinhart, Hamann, and Torres Rodríguez, *El reino de los Suevos.* The only studies in English that deal substantially with the earlier history of the Sueves are those by Thompson, "The end of Roman Spain." They are all reproduced conveniently in his *Romans and Barbarians.*

[10] Aside from the works cited in the previous note, there is a growing bibliography on the Sueves too extensive to reproduce here. For a collection of the literature consult Ferreiro, *The Visigoths in Gaul and Spain,* especially 525-86, which includes bibliography on Hydatius, Martin of Braga, and others.

[11] See Isidore of Seville (279-80). An English translation without commentary is by Donini and Ford, Jr. Wolf provides notes and commentary, but unfortunately does not include Isidore's sections on the Vandals and Sueves (12-27 and 81-110).

¹² The destruction of the Sueves is found in Gregory of Tours, *Liber historiarum. Monumenta Germaniae Historica. Scriptorum rerum Merovingicarum* (1.1.6.43) [hereafter MGH], and Isidore of Seville, *Historia Gothorum* (ch. 92. 303). An English version is in Thorpe (375-6). For the remainder of this study I will be using the MGH edition. See also on the demise of the Sueves, John of Biclar, *Chronica* (217). The only English edition is that by Wolf (1-11 and 61-80). An important study on the complexities of the Suevic monarchy is Díaz Martínez.

¹³ The chief sources are: Gregory of Tours, *Liber historiarum* (5.37), *De virtutibus s. Martini* (594-6) [hereafter, VM], Isidore of Seville (ch. 91). See the critical edition of *De viris illustribus* (ch. 22) by Codoñer Merino and Venantius Fortunatus, *Carminum Libri,* "Ad Martinum" (101-6).

¹⁴ There has never been a comprehensive treatment on the extensive difusion of Martin's works in the Middle Ages. Two examples of the type of research that has been done thus far are Haselbach and Martins.

¹⁵ [See Note 12 above.] The standard edition for Martin of Braga is Barlow. Comprehensive bibliography is in Ferreiro, *Visigoths* (555-69). Studies on his missionary work are Thompson, "Conversion," Ferreiro, "Missionary labors," "St. Martin of Braga's policy," as well as "St. Martin of Braga and Germanic Languages" and "Early medieval missionary tactics." See also Beltrán Torreira.

¹⁶ Isidore identified Theodemir as the Suevic king under whom Martin of Braga carried out his missionary activity. He mentioned him once again in the *De viris illustribus* (ch. 22, "Floruit regnante Theodemiro rege Suevorum"). Gregory of Tours never referred to Theodemir in any of his commentary on the Sueves.

¹⁷ English translations of this section of the *Life of St. Martin* are in McDermott (159-61) and Van Dam, *Saints* (211-3).

¹⁸ Winstead correctly observes, "The issue of Arianism, a persistent concern of the *Libri historiarum,* is treated at length" (7). See also her remarks at 6-7. Teillet remarks that for Gregory all of the Goths were reprobate Arians and he treats them thusly in his works (371-6). Two incidents illustrative of the Arian-Catholic debates are in *Liber historiarum* (2.3), and in *Liber in gloria confessorum* (13 and 14) [hereafter GC]. An English translation is by Van Dam, *Gregory of Tours.* Also relevant is Van Dam, *Saints* (96-7 and 106-9).

¹⁹ In this article I will not engage the challenges some scholars have leveled on the historicity of this text. Thompson has been the most vocal opponent in rejecting the entire story as hagiographical fiction devoid of any historical value. A careful analysis of the text and questions raised by

Thompson in "The Conversion" has been accomplished in a separate study, see Ferreiro, "Braga."

[20] Two outstanding studies on the cults of Martin of Tours and Martin of Braga in Spain are those of Fernández Alonso and García Rodríguez, which includes a consideration of liturgical texts (336-42, 372-6 and 397-403).

[21] Of interest are both articles by Brennan. The most recent critical study is by George.

[22] According to Brennan, "The career" (64, n. 68), Venantius never met Martin of Braga. On this particular letter consult Moralejo Laso, Blomgren (especially 117-8), George (67-9). The poem to Martin of Braga is reproduced in Barlow (294-8).

[23] The main exponent arguing that the poem refers to Santiago is Elorduy, "De re Iacobea" (335-60), who, after painstaking paleographical argumentation, fails to persuade. Duchesne rejected such an interpretation in a much earlier study (147-8). See also Pérez de Urbel, "Orígenes" (12-3), and Moralejo Laso (18-24).

[24] Barlow includes the poems (282-3) and an analysis of them with paleographical information (276-81).

[25] The poem [*Carminum libri* (1-20)] and Gregory of Tours' information [*Liber historiarum* (5.37) and VM (1.11)] provide consistent testimony on this major point.

[26] Barlow's comments (276) are convincing. George mistakenly believes the verses were posted at Tours (68). Barlow suggests that the verses may have been placed in the monastery at Dumium, near Braga, founded by Martin of Braga (280, n. 5).

[27] An insightful discussion is found in Lambert (6-10), who also cited Sidonius Apollinaris as yet another voice that proclaimed Martin of Tours patron of Galicia in *Carmen Carm* [(5. 474); reproduced in Lambert's article, 9].

[28] "And you (my) patron, I am not worthy to follow (as successor), the servant Martin of such renowned fame" (translation mine).

[29] Theodemir is found only in Isidore, *Historia Gothorum* (chs. 90-1) and *De viris illustribus* (ch. 22).

[30] See Oliveira (313).

[31] An overview of these events is in Collins, *Early Medieval Spain* (41-58).

[32] See the works cited in Note 8 above.

[33] For Priscillian's execution see Chadwick and Stancliffe.

[34] The narrative in the *Liber historiarum* begins with Clovis' open disgust against the Arian Visigoths: "Igitur Chlodovechus rex ait suis: Valde molestum fero, quod hi Arriani partem teneant Galliarum" (2.37.1-2). The narrative is replete with references to appeal to St. Martin's patronage in Clovis' campaigns. After the successful victory, Clovis presented himself at Martin's church in Tours to give thanks (2.38). Brennan notes that Gregory called Clovis the "new Constantine" (LH 2.31, cited in "Image" 7). For a general overview of Gregory and Clovis, see Wood (270). Van Dam cautions not to overestimate Clovis' devotion to Martin of Tours (*Saints* 22-3, 28).

[35] A thorough consideration of the Third Council of Toledo is found in the collection of essays from the international congress entitled *Concilio III de Toledo XIV Centenario 589-1989*,ed. R. Gonzalves [Toledo 10-14 May 1989]. On the theological significance consult in the same volume, Ferreiro, "*Linguarum diversitate.*"

[36] A thoughtful treatment of this era is by Collins, *The Arab Conquest,* who is currently working on a follow-up volume that will cover the period from 797-912.

[37] For an English edition of the *Chronicle of Alfonso III*, see Wolf (46-60, and the text, 159-77). I am using his edition for this essay.

[38] Jan van Herwaarden has accomplished a convincing study of the hymn with much needed correction of previous scholarship (17 and 7-18). He even provides a reproduction of two versions of the hymns from the Madrid and London manuscripts (30-2). For previous discussion on the "O Dei verbum patris" see Pérez de Urbel, "Orígenes" (16-9), and Elorduy, "Tradición Jacobea" (339-46), as well as Sánchez Albornoz, "En los albores," and Casariego (37-43). A detailed discussion on Asturias appears in Sánchez Albornoz, *Galicia histórica* (377-548).

[39] For the conquest of Galicia by the Asturians see Collins, *Arab Conquest* (164-5), the *Chronicle of Alfonso III* (ch. 18) and van Herwaarden (23).

[40] Van Herwaarden (18). A discussion of the Asturian church from a political-economic perspective is by Fernández Conde.

[41] For the Beatus and the Santiago cult, see van Herwaarden (7-23).

[42] The authorship of the letter has always been suspect and the consensus seems to be that it is indeed apocryphal, but that it does date to the ninth and tenth centuries. Duchesne suspected the letter to be apocryphal (178, n. 1). David empathically rejected its Alphonsine element in "Notes Compostellanes 1" (187). Pérez de Urbel accepted the letter as authentic in "Orígenes" (26-8), as did Elorduy, who reproduced the pertinent passages in the documents in "Tradición Jacobea" (336-8). Guerra Campos refers to the letter without any critical apparatus (158).

[43] I have used the translation by Hamilton and Perry. There are two more references to Santiago in the poem, "With the dawn the Cid advanced to the attack (shouting his battle cry): 'In the name of the Creator and the Apostle St. James, strike them hard, knights, with all your might; for I am the Cid, Ruy Díaz of Vivar!'" (83). And, "'Bishop Jerome will say mass for us and give us absolution; then we must ride out to the attack in the name of God and of the Apostle St. James'" (111). There is one instance where Doña Jimena and five noble ladies pray to St. Peter and God the Creator: "'Thou who dost rule us all, help my husband, the Cid Campeador'" (35). Pérez de Urbel considers the anti-Muhammadan element as a catalyst that gave rise to the cult of Santiago in "Primeros contactos." Guerra Campos rejects these arguments (157-8). On Santiago as patron of war, see Casariego (18-24).

[44] Several studies on the cults of Martin of Braga and Martin of Tours have been done. What has not been accomplished is a detailed study that demonstrates precisely which ecclesiastical structures in Galicia and Portugal were exclusively dedicated to either saint and which of them might have had dual patronage. The following studies provide the documentation of these structures, most still in existence today, that would facilitate such a survey. See David, "Saints Patrons"; Chaves; and Oliveira, "Culte de Saint Martin." A recent publication on the Hispano-Mozarab psalter, which covers a good portion of Spain and reveals the wide diffusion of the cult of Martin of Tours in the Iberian Peninsula, is *Memoria Ecclesiae II*. Within the volume, the essay by Cal Pardo (177-86) is directly relevant to Martin of Tours and Martin of Braga. See his comments concerning further research on the precise identity of patronage (185). On the cult of Santiago in Portugal, Alberto Veira Braga is still useful though general. Santiago also had many shrines established outside of Spain in Northern Europe; one sample is found in Couffon.

For the mutual liturgical influence between Gaul and Hispania and the presence of Martin of Tours in Iberian texts, consult Salmon or Vives, *Oracional Visigótico* (384-7). On liturgical sources see Vives, "Santoral Visigodo," and Vives and Fábrega, "Calendarios." On toponyms of Martin of Tours, see Piel, "Nomes" (325 and 401). For Martin of Tours, see González as well as Piel, "Coteifes Orpelados."

CHAPTER 2

The Geography and History of Iberia in the *Liber Sancti Jacobi*

Colin Smith

What impressions of the Peninsula did the intending pilgrim to Compostela have as he and she set out in the mid-twelfth century (that is, at a time when the great enterprise was becoming most popular) from homes in France, Britain, Germany, Italy, and from many more remote areas? We cannot know with any precision, but by informed and careful conjecture something approaching the mental map typical of the time can be built up. The key text is obviously the *Liber Sancti Jacobi* as known to us in its prime surviving version, the *Codex Calixtinus* of the Cathedral of Compostela. That this was intended to be copied, in whole or in parts, and its contents publicly divulged and diffused in all sorts of ways throughout the western Christian world cannot be doubted, as is shown both by the plainly propagandistic pleas and statements scattered about in its text and by the very large quantity of diverse surviving manuscripts that derive from it (or in certain cases from texts that antedate their entry into the CC, on which see below).

The spiritual benefits of the pilgrimage were unquestioned and presumably obvious to all. While the Apostle's tomb was the main objective, lesser shrines along the way should be visited in the hope of further benefits, even if in the text (Book V of the LSJ, the *Pilgrim's Guide*) we find an altogether undue proportion of these to be French rather than Spanish. In any community a few noblemen, priests, soldiers, administrators, and merchants who were accustomed to travel and to the ways of foreign lands would have faced the task with equanimity, daunted only perhaps by an awareness of the great distance to be covered but consoling themselves with the thought that at least they (in some cases) possessed horses and would be attended by servants. But for the great majority of simple folk who had probably never before left their native provinces or dioceses, and whose idea of pilgrimage would have been formed by annually visiting the shrine of the locally-venerated saint, much reassurance would have been necessary. In terms of the mid-twelfth century, the pilgrim's parish priest could presumably give this with some confidence: the pilgrim would be with others, often of his own community, with mutual support, and along the road the dozens would become hundreds and then thousands; the authorities, royal and local, had by this time improved the roads and provided bridges, and the great monasteries were generous with their provision of hospitals. The safety of the pilgrims was to an extent (to what extent?)[1] guaranteed by the punishments prescribed by ecclesiastical and royal authorities for any who might molest or cheat or attack them, and selected pilgrims might enjoy the special protection of St. James, as in many of the miracles in Book II of the LSJ. Many may have expected to make the pilgrimage the tourist trip of a lifetime and to become duly devout only at the end of it, a matter of enlivening the months of wearisome walking by seeing a superior class of bear-baiting or cock-fighting, listening to exotic lyrics from Provence or pulsating new rhythms by musicians from Muslim lands, attending a performance of the latest *chanson de geste*, or even, despite warnings,[2] indulging in a little light-hearted dalliance away from the constraints of home. Probably nothing in their intellectual formation would have disposed them to take much of an interest in the often (to us) magnificent scenery they would traverse, or in the picturesque diversity of the peoples they would encounter: the ghastly ethnological details given in Book V of the LSJ about the Basques and Navarrese are offered as dire warnings about the risks of associating with them in any way. As for food, our common pilgrim would not have been able to afford any gastronomic delights, but the fish would (as now) have been abundant and cheap, though sometimes to be avoided even when fresh,[3] and Riojan wine and many other varieties would have been agreeable. In Compostela itself there would be further risks,[4] but the atmosphere would be reassuringly cosmopolitan and doubtless French at least would be widely understood. For confession in the Cathedral, then as now, priests commanding the different tongues would have been on duty. Despite all this, the risks were great, as detailed by the very extensive Sermon 17 of Book I of the LSJ. Wine in excess produces drunkenness and this generates all manner of evils, from argumentativeness up to brawling and lust (ff. 84r-84v); false hosts offer accommodation with a kiss of greeting as traitorous as that of Judas (f. 84v) and will cheat the pilgrim; prostitutes accost the solitary pilgrim in the woods between the Miño bridge and Pazos (f. 85v); pretended confessors are everywhere, "religioso abitu induti" [dressed in clerical garb], imposing ludicrously inflated penances for sins and extracting payment for up to thirty masses (f. 86v). The devil in human guise, the tempter, is everywhere. Naturally we do not know what diffusion these dire accounts may have had, but one has the impression from them that mere survival was a worthy objective. For those returning home, the scallop shell pinned to the clothing could be worn with pride in a truly immense achievement: it is probably only moderns who draw attention to its folkloric and pre-apostolic associations with Venus and erotic cults.

"Yspania" would have had already a few resonances in addition to the religious one, at least for the educated priests and the informed (but still generally illiterate) noblemen and merchants and soldiers. The clergy would have had some idea of the Muslim world, as encountered by the West in the First Crusade (centered upon the capture of Jerusalem in 1099) to the Holy Land and as presented in preaching designed to win support for the Second Crusade in the years leading up to 1147. Most propaganda seems to have presented the Muslims as the devil's agents concerned to attack and undo God's work in Christian lands and in the individual soul. Fundamental parts of the LSJ— especially Book IV, the *Historia Turpini*, and the spurious epistle of Pope Calixtus (II)—were designed to encourage the clergy to preach the need for men to go and fight the infidel in Spain, following the example of Charlemagne (Saint Charlemagne from 1165), Roland, and the Franks, spiritual benefits of martyrdom being promised to those who died on such campaigns. A few of the clergy would have been aware already of the quality of Muslim learning, specifically in Toledo where under its second Archbishop and Primate, the Gascon Raimundo (1125-52), a school of translators working from Arabic into Latin was active. It may also have been known that Gerbert d'Aurillac, later Pope Sylvester II (999-1003), had studied with the learned Arabs somewhere in Spain, and had absorbed together with advanced mathematics some notions of the blacker arts, knowledge of these assisting him in his election as Pope. Among the Cluniac monks in all countries, some awareness of the special relationship of their order with the Leonese royal house and of Cluniac monastic communities in northern Spain, several being on the pilgrim roads, can be assumed. At one time the very genesis and composition of the LSJ were held to be attributable to Cluny.[5]

Among the nobles and soldiers, the myth of Charlemagne as the great Christian warrior and patriarch of the West was already extensively known before the *Historia Turpini* carried the claims to new heights. The chronicler Adhémar de Chabannes in 1028 portrayed him as the conqueror of all Iberia, and the prime version of the *Chanson de Roland* (about 1100?), that preserved in the "Oxford" manuscript, said much the same[6] and would have been early known in its original language throughout France, Norman England, and northern Spain. By the mid-twelfth century some churches already had representations—sculptures, and later, stained glass—of these Frankish heroes in saintly guise.[7] Not all impressions were derived from the doubtless exaggerated depictions of poets and ecclesiastical craftsmen. The tales of the immense booty resulting from the conquest of Muslim Barbastro in 1064 by Norman adventurers seem often to have been true enough, and more must have been told by the French nobles and their armies who fought on the Ebro in the campaign which culminated in the capture of Saragossa in 1118. At this time the promise of material benefits—movable booty, prisoners both attractive and saleable,[8] even *châteaux en Espagne*—must have weighed beside the promise of spiritual rewards with the nobles and their retinues in France and more widely. For the more courtly among the ambitious nobility, there might be further rewards in the royal service, since Alfonso VI of Leon-Castile had four times taken French wives, and the Burgundian connection formed when the cousins Henry and Raymond of Burgundy married his daughters and became Counts respectively of nascent Portugal and of Galicia was to be very important. It may have been no accident that it was the name of Pope Calixtus II (1119-24), Guy de Bourgogne of the same family and uncle of Emperor Alfonso VII (1126-57) of Leon-Castile, that was appropriated in order to give authority to the LSJ. He had earlier been a monk at Cluny and then (from 1088) Archbishop of Vienne to which Turpin was said in the *Historia Turpini* to have retired in order to recover from wounds received at Roncevaux and where he later wrote this memoir.

The question of the diffusion of knowledge of the LSJ as represented by the *Codex Calixtinus* of Compostela is a complicated one. The best recent opinion—that of Professor Díaz y Díaz—is that in any case certain parts of what we know as the collective but hardly unified LSJ as represented in the CC had been composed independently and earlier, being edited together with newly-composed parts when Aymeri Picaud (about whose role Professor Díaz y Díaz is very guarded) compiled the LSJ and carried it to Compostela for presentation to the Cathedral. Examples of such materials are Book IV, the *Historia Turpini*, and probably Book II, the collection of miracles of the Apostle, spuriously attributed to Pope Calixtus. The prologue to Book II states that the miracles had been collected variously in Galicia, Gaul, Germany, Italy, Hungary, Dacia, and even in "lands beyond the three seas" (f. 140r); also that they had been assembled from both written and oral sources. One does not have to believe in the literal truth of such statements nor in the precise dates and personal names of protagonists that are often cited, but at least it is likely that in this case the compiler of the LSJ was doing no more than gathering and editing existing materials from many places. All this means that some diffusion of pre-existing materials in France and from France has to be allowed for. In the case of the *Historia Turpini*, the monastery of St-Denis in Paris had at least as much of a hand in the operation as the monastery of Cluny, its prime interest being not in Spain nor in support for campaigns there but rather in the elaboration of the Charlemagne myth.[9] In any case the production of the whole was less of a purely French matter than has usually been claimed since Compostela itself was involved at least in parts, although even there Frenchmen were to be found as canons of the Cathedral and in other offices.

We know that the CC was copied in large part and that the resulting text was sent by the scribe Arnault du Mont to the Abbot of Ripoll in Catalonia in 1173. Before this or soon after, at least one other copy was made and further copies were made from this for diffusion in France; this kind of text is known as the *Libellus*, surviving today in a number of manuscripts. At some still early stage the *Historia Turpini* was considered detachable, or was already separately available in France where it had originated, and its text circulated in numerous copies, of which today at least 139 survive. Many of these are bound up with such key Charlemagne texts as Einhard's *Vita* and the new *Vita Karoli* of the later twelfth century. Such manuscripts would have been made for the clergy and for chroniclers.[10] There are in addition vernacular French translations of which the earliest seem to be those made by Nicholas de Senlis for Count Hugh de Saint-Pol in 1200 and by Master Jehan for Count Renauld of Boulogne in 1206. These would mostly have been made for the use of noblemen. In the fourteenth century substantial parts of the text were translated into Galician as the *Miragres de Santiago*. The whole process of diffusion plainly responds to, and was an essential part of, the enormous upsurge of enthusiasm for Charlemagne from the middle years of the twelfth century.

The diffusion of the diverse materials of the LSJ and the *Libellus* can then be considered in stages. Book I, consisting of the 17 sermons on Jacobean themes and various liturgical texts and hymns, was clearly for use by the clergy in their preaching on the Saint's special feasts, and for the improvement of church offices. Book II, consisting of the 22 miracles of the Saint, provided attractive materials for the same sermons, for reading in monastic refectories, and for any other interested person, just as saints' lives and other hagiographic texts were very widely known and used for instruction and entertainment. The technical materials of Book III, to which the latest "official" version of the *Translatio* of the Apostle's remains from Jerusalem to Compostela was added, were of concern chiefly to the Cathedral of Compostela and to the authorities of the city, since they were the ultimate justification of the cult and of the pilgrimage. Book IV, the *Historia Turpini*, has already been discussed in this regard. Book V, the famous *Pilgrim's Guide* to the route and shrines, presents a problem, in that while it seems to be the part which would most immediately concern the intending pilgrim, it was not—so far as is known—copied and diffused separately as was the *Historia Turpini*, being available only in the original CC and in the *Libellus* copied directly and indirectly from this. While it is valuable to us as a record, its influence must therefore have been limited.

We know something more about at least the intended propagation of the *Liber Sancti Jacobi*. Most of Aymeri Picaud's claims may be dismissed as mere hype of the kind used by modern advertisers. He says (f. 184v) that his text had already been enthusiastically received in

Rome (not surprisingly in view of the attribution to Pope Calixtus II and the supporting letter fathered upon Pope Innocent II) and had been copied there, and that other copies had been made already in Jerusalem (its Patriarch William figuring beside Diego Gelmírez, Archbishop of Santiago de Compostela, as joint dedicatees of the work), and in Gaul, Italy, and Germany, Frisia, and "precipue" [especially] at Cluny. Near the end of the text (f. 192r) we find the spurious letter of Pope Innocent in which he confirms the veracity of Pope Calixtus' work, the codex in turn being authenticated and praised by a chancellor, six cardinals, and a bishop, all named and all presumably resident in Rome. More credible are the pleas made in the epistle attributed to Calixtus. This now figures as an appendix to Book IV, but was originally intended to serve as an introduction to Books I, II, and III. This details the sufferings of the people of Spain, the need to help them with a crusade on the model of the expedition led by Charlemagne and Archbishop Turpin, and the spiritual benefits awaiting those who respond to the call, these benefits equalling those promised to soldiers going to fight in the Holy Land.[11] The epistle concludes by exhorting priests to preach this crusade in synods and councils, and to address congregations in similar terms; there will be spiritual rewards for those copying the letter and carrying it from church to church, and it is to be read out on all Sundays from Easter to St. John's Day. The attribution of the epistle to Calixtus is of course spurious, the text presumably being the work of Aymeri Picaud, but this kind of exhortation must reflect a kind of contemporary reality or it makes no sense at all: that is how things were done, that is how propaganda campaigns were launched and carried forward.

The outline history of Spain conveyed to the pilgrim by chapter 1 of the *Historia Turpini* is a complete fabrication designed solely to add lustre to the myth of Charlemagne. The Apostle by his preaching converted the Galicians, but for their sins they lapsed after his return to the Holy Land, and remained unbelievers until Charlemagne's time. Among his immense conquests there figured Angliam (England) and many other lands. In a nightly-recurring dream the Emperor saw the Milky Way stretching westward toward Galicia, where the remains of the Apostle lay unrecognized. As he pondered the meaning of this, St. James appeared to him in a vision to explain that the Milky Way was a celestial pointer to his tomb and that Charlemagne's duty was to liberate the road to it from the Muslims (Sarraceni and Moabitae) and to become the first of the pilgrims along it. Charlemagne in consequence assembled his army. In chapter 2 the attack on Pamplona succeeds only when, after the Emperor prays to Christ and to St. James, the city's walls fall. As in the *chansons de geste*, the Franks spare any Muslim who converts but slaughter the rest. Charlemagne continues his conquests, finds the Apostle's tomb, proceeds to El Padrón and plants his lance in the sea as a sign that he has gone as far as man could. Meanwhile, Archbishop Turpin rebaptizes the backsliding Galicians, but again, those unwilling to convert are killed or enslaved. The chapter ends with the sentence "Deinde iuit per totam Yspaniam a mari usque ad mare" (f. 3r) [Then he went throughout Spain from sea to sea]. However, in chapter 6, after the Emperor had left Spain apparently secure and had returned to Gaul, "Quidam paganus rex Affricanus nomine Aigolandus" [a certain pagan African ruler by name Aigolandus] recovered the land, this requiring Charlemagne to undertake a second campaign (chapter 8). Aigolandus is eventually tracked down near Sahagun (whose church and abbey are built by Charlemagne's order) and the resulting battles are indecisive; Aigolandus retires to the region of Leon, the Emperor to Gaul. In a third campaign (chapter 9) the armies clash again in Gascony on the Garonne river. For a fourth mighty campaign Charlemagne gathers 134,000 men, the captains being listed at length (chapter 11). During a truce the leaders of the opposing armies—one camped on each side of the pilgrims' road outside Pamplona—parley. A ludicrous theological debate (chapter 12) ensues, conducted in Aigolandus' Arabic, which Charlemagne, having learned the language in his youth when he spent some time in Toledo (as in the *Mainet* poem), speaks well enough. After losing a battle the Muslim commander agrees to accept baptism, in accordance with his earlier promise, but at the sight of thirteen poor men at a table in the Christian camp among so many brilliantly accoutered knights and robed clergy, refuses it and condemns Christianity. In another battle Aigolandus is killed (chapter 14), and after further incidents the Emperor confronts near Nájera the giant Ferracutus, "of the lineage of Goliath," who has come from Syria with 20,000 Turks from Babylon (chapter 17). Roland, the new David, fights the giant in single combat, followed, after a truce, by a course of Christian instruction from Roland, both providentially being able to speak Spanish. The superior of the two faiths is to be determined by further single combat, which Roland naturally wins. Charlemagne then advances upon Cordova (chapter 18) and after a final victory pacifies the whole country and divides it up into fiefs for his followers according to their nation of origin. In last place "Terram Gallecie Franci inhabitare noluerunt, quoniam aspera illis uidebatur" [The Franks were unwilling to dwell in Galicia, since it seemed to them to be wild]. In chapter 21 we find that Charlemagne's efforts were not over. When in Pamplona on his way to Gaul, he had to deal with "two Sarracen kings resident in Saragossa," Marsirus and his brother Beliguandus, which then leads into a strongly variant version of the Roncevaux story. In chapter 22 the author Archbishop Turpin, surviving the fight in the Pyrenees, is in Vienne recovering from his wounds, and recounting how the Emperor has decorated his palace at Aix-la-Chapelle (Aachen) with scenes from the Spanish campaigns and representations of the seven liberal arts, on which there follows a strange disquisition, with additional notes on necromancy, pyromancy, etc.

The impression given by all this to the previously uninformed person who read (or heard a reading of) the *Historia Turpini* is one of the immense superiority of the Franks and their empire, that is of its descendant Francia, as Turpin anachronistically (with a twelfth-century public in mind) remarks in chapter 22. The inhabitants of the Peninsula are depicted as likely to have been fickle in their faith: thus before Charlemagne's first conquest of the Peninsula (chapter 3), "Quasdam tamen ex prefatis urbibus alii reges Galli et imperatores Theutonici ante Karolum magnum adquisierunt que postea ad ritum paganorum conuerse sunt, usque ad eius aduentum" [Certain of the aforementioned cities taken by other rulers of Gaul and by German emperors converted later to the faith of the pagans, up to the time of his coming]. The native population seems docile and unmilitary, unable to help itself in the Christian cause, and at no point in any of the Emperor's campaigns do Peninsular knights or militias join his forces. There is one grudging sentence, following that just quoted, about local efforts made in the Christian cause: "Et post eius necem multi reges et principes in Yspania Sarracenos expugnarunt" [And after his (Charlemagne's) death, many kings and princes in Spain attacked the Saracens]. Even here, such commanders are said merely to be "in Spain" rather than native Spaniards. The conclusion is that had it not been for Charlemagne's efforts, the whole Peninsula would still be "pagan," that is, Muslim. In any case there might remain pockets of "paganism," as when at the start of chapter 21 the completeness of the Emperor's cleansing of the Peninsula is emphasized, but in the next sentence it is discovered that Marsirus and Baliguandus have in some way—not specified—managed to hold out in Saragossa. However, in the Middle Ages most were unaware of the total lack of basic historical truth in this text, and of the glaring anachronisms involved: if in the time when "Turpin" was writing his text in the late eighth century we have mention of Turks (chapter 20), we also have "Moabitae" in chapter 1, this being the name applied in Spain to the Almoravids from North Africa who began to dominate Al-Andalus from about 1090.[12] For most of the rest of the Middle Ages the *Historia Turpini* was taken as a true record, entering French historiography and causing a grave distortion there (Short, 127-52). Geoffrey of Monmouth's elaborate fiction *Historia regum Britanniae* of 1136, equally famous in its day and for long after, similarly disturbed the course of historiography in Britain.[13] What is even more surprising than the acceptance of the *Historia Turpini* on its home ground in France is the fact that nobody in Compostela seems to have uttered a word of protest or correction, even though any moderately informed person there must have known the account to be false and, moreover, a denigration of native Spaniards in ways outlined above. It was left to the anonymous author of the *Historia Seminensis*, writing in the city of Leon, to pour scorn on the fiction in a famous passage.[14] Presumably in Compostela the text of the whole LSJ was mulled over in anguished sessions of the Cathedral Chapter—which included a number of French canons—and it was resolved that any doubts should be silenced because in general the whole enterprise was likely to be so beneficial to the shrine, to the clergy, and to the city. Indeed Compostela at some stage contributed to the fraud, by inserting chapter 19 into the *Historia Turpini*. In this, Charlemagne ordains that all powers ecclesiastical and civil in the Peninsula should be subject to the see of Compostela, that there should be no bishop of Iria Flavia (long a bone of contention), that all should pay an annual tithe to Santiago de Compostela, and that this should be reckoned an apostolic see of equal status with Rome and Ephesus, since St. James deserved equality with the Apostles Peter and John. It is here that the contemporary—that is, twelfth-century—interests of Compostela are most nakedly expressed, with Archbishop Diego Gelmírez and his clergy using the cover of Charlemagne and of "Turpin's" words to make moves in the various power struggles in which they were involved.

Charlemagne is further depicted as a builder and reformer of churches. In chapter 5, with gold received from the "reges et principes Yspanie" [the kings and rulers of Spain], presumably here Muslims, the Emperor spent three years extending [augmentauit] the Cathedral of Compostela, appointed the bishop and canons according to the rule of St. Isidore, and provided bells, vestments, books, and ornaments "decenter" [of seemly sort]. The implication is again that the native church authorities had been too idle or too poor to provide a proper setting for the Apostle's shrine. Despite this, in Compostela the fiction of Charlemagne's largesse was still maintained in the late fifteenth century, and even long after that.[15] With surplus Spanish gold the Emperor built many other churches in his realms, of which a number are detailed in the same chapter.

In chapter 3 we embark upon the geography of the Peninsula, presented as a very extensive list of "urbes et maiores uille" [cities and larger towns] which Charlemagne captured.[16] In part it serves as a mere *étalage d'érudition*, but its prime intention was to emphasize and authenticate in detail the extent of Charlemagne's achievement. While the Emperor's predecessors from Clovis onward had conquered parts of Spain, he alone (with the help of God and St. James) completed the task. A few places were cursed by the Emperor and left "usque in hodiernum diem" [until today] uninhabited: Lucerna, Ventosa, Capparria, Adania. It was "Lucernam urbem munitissimam que est in ualle uiridi" [Lucerna, a very strongly fortified city, which lies in the green valley (or in Valverde)], the "Luiserne" of French epic that had resisted the Franks the longest. This air of unreality, most manifest at the end of chapter 3, in fact pervades all of it, since very little by way of system can be made out. One can pardon a twelfth-century author writing in France his ignorance about the state of the Peninsula in Turpin's time in the late eighth, but some approximation to basic truths about Iberia in his own time could be expected. Even notions of political geography are extremely vague. Iberia about 1140-50 consisted, starting in the west, of the kingdom of Portugal (independent from 1139, formally recognized by Leon in 1143), Leon-Castile ruled by the Emperor Alfonso VII, Navarre (newly independent from 1134), Aragon which after the union of 1137 included Catalonia, and Muslim Al-Andalus, ruled from North Africa by the Almoravids up to 1146 and thereafter by the Almohads. Yet according to chapter 3 of the *Historia Turpini*, after a first group of place-names in northern Portugal and Galicia announced as being "in Gallecia," all the rest are listed without further division as "in Yspania." The author seems unaware that Galicia was simply a region within the kingdom of Leon-Castile, that the independent kingdoms of Navarre and Aragon existed, and even worse, that a powerful Muslim state still covered a huge territory in the south and east. After the list of "urbes et maiores uille" conquered by Charlemagne there comes a confused sentence in which various "tellus" [lands] are mentioned, and here we do indeed find "tellus Alandaluf" (sic), "tellus Portogallorum," etc., but confusion continues because there is not only a "tellus Alandaluf" but also a "tellus Maurorum," and all these are mentioned only to insist that they "bowed to the rule of Charlemagne." The compiler also seems to think that the "tellus Serranorum" (for "Serracenorum" [of the Saracens]) is distinct from the "tellus Maurorum." As for "Yspania," elsewhere in the *Historia Turpini* it is variously used to mean "the whole Peninsula," "Muslim Spain, Al-Andalus," and "Christian Spain except Galicia." In chapter 1 it is apparently used to mean "Castile," since the way to the west shown to Charlemagne by the stars passes through Gascony, Navarre, "Yspaniam," and Galicia. In chapter 7 of Book V (the *Pilgrim's Guide*) also, we find that the "Yspani" are the Castilians: after Navarre, "sequitur tellus Yspanorum, Castella uidelicet et Campos" [there follows the land of the Hispani, that is to say Castile and Tierra de Campos]. When the designations are paired, "Yspania" means "Muslim Spain" and "Gallecia" "Christian Spain." The reasons for the extreme prominence of Galicia throughout—Leon, Castile, and the other political entities being hardly mentioned—can be conjectured and are not quite so absurd as might be thought; nor was such a misconception (that the kingdom of Leon was called "Galicia") confined to the present text.[17]

The most startling features of the long list of town names in chapter 3 are that Christian lands are not separated from Muslim ones, and that the compiler passes from the Peninsula to North Africa without being aware that he is doing so, even including "Besertum" far to the east (= Bizerta, in modern Tunis). He is apparently aware that there is sea at least at the western end of his list, since he mentions "Septa que est in districtis Yspanie ubi maris est angustus concursus"

[Ceuta, which is in that region of Spain where there is the narrowest coming-together of the sea(s)] (i.e. at the Strait of Gibraltar).

The spelling of the names, announced as being given "uulgo" [in their vernacular forms], is in the CC as reproduced by Whitehill and in other manuscripts derived from it often wildly erroneous, to the extent that some items cannot now be identified. To judge by the nature of some deformations, both oral and written sources were used, some forms seeming explicable only by allowing for the defective memories of non-Hispanic individuals rather than by copying errors. The claim to be stating vernacular names is not fully maintained, since a number of learned latinized forms appear: "Aurenas" [Orense], "Tuda" [Tuy], "Brachara" [Braga], "Seguncia" [Sigüenza], "Emerita" [Mérida], "Ouetum" [Oviedo], "Legio" [Leon], "Pampilonia" [Pamplona], "Gerunda" [Gerona], "Aurelia" [Oreja], and so on. This indicates reliance upon a tradition of ecclesiastical documents in which ancient learned (and sometimes pseudo-learned) forms of names were maintained. The exceptional note attached to mention of "Accintina" [Guadix] where St. Torquatus' olive-tree miraculously flowered and produced mature fruit annually on his feast-day is drawn nearly verbatim from the text of a martyrology.

That the compiler used a rough map or set of itineraries for some sections of his list is an interesting possibility. There are several clues to this. First, a map on which the Mediterranean hardly existed as a broad sea (perhaps being compressed to a narrow strip and not named or marked as water) and was represented as sea only at the western end in the reference to Ceuta above, would lead the compiler to think that the North African places he mentions were to be placed in some southward extension of the Peninsula. Second, while "Maioricas insula" [Majorca island] is correct, the compiler's eye failed to register the fact that this "insula" label should have embraced "Euicia" [Ebesus, Ibiza] and "Formenteria" [Formentera] also; he lists them as if they were settlements. Third, and most glaringly, he failed to recognize that "Godiana" [Guadiana] on his map was a river, and he listed it among the towns. Fourth, some of the comments he adds occasionally to mention of towns could well have proceeded from brief legends of the kind traditionally entered on maps. Examples of these are "Talauera que est fructifera" [Talavera, rich in fruits/produce], "Segouia que est magna" [Segovia, an important place], "Petroissa in qua fit argentum obtimum" [Los Pedroches (province of Cordova) where excellent silver is mined].

In other cases, however, it seems that a gloss of the kind made marginally in manuscripts was involved. This might concern the ancient name of a well-known place, as in "Sarragocia que dicitur Cesar Augusta" [Saragossa, also known as Caesar Augusta], or be a rhetorical flourish of the etymological kind, as in "Medinacelim id est urbs excelsa" [Medinaceli, which means lofty/noble city], from the notion that the second element was Latin "caelum, celum" [sky, heaven], whereas it is really the Arab personal name Selim. In respect of the "Sarragocia" example, it may be noted that the compiler could have had access to some text in which names of the Roman period were given beside modern vernacular designations, since he includes in his list—as though they were separate places, at a distance from each other—both "Yspalida" and "Sibilia," the ancient name for Seville being "Hispalis."[18] One such gloss is especially notable: "Osqua in qua nonaginta turres numero esse solent" [Huesca, in which there are towers to the number of ninety]. Huesca was taken by the Christian forces in 1096, after a famously lengthy siege in which the Aragonese under King Pedro I had been helped by several French bishops and lords and their forces. It was already known in Frankish tradition because the town figured in a campaign of 797 in Charlemagne's time, recorded in the *Annales Regni Francorum*.[19] It may have been a combination of these factors which led the forger of the crusading epistle fathered upon Pope Calixtus (Whitehill 347) to select Huesca for special mention in his appeal: "Quot sanctorum martirum, episcoporum scilicet abbatum et sacerdotum ceterorumque Christianorum, corpora iuxta urbem Osquam, et in campo laudabile, et in campo letorie, ceterisque mediis finibus Christianorum Sarracenorumque ubi bella fuere inhumata requiescunt, nullo sermone fas est explicari" [How many bodies of holy martyrs—bishops, priests, abbots, and other Christians—lie in honoured cemeteries at Huesca, or lie unburied in other Christian or Saracen lands where there were battles, cannot be properly told by any reasoned discourse]. To these conjectures another should be added, a particular reason why a French compiler working in collaboration with Compostela should mention Huesca with such prominence: Compostela Cathedral received as a gift a very substantial property in Huesca shortly after its capture, in 1098. The matter of the ninety towers might seem an epical exaggeration, but may have had some justification.[20]

In a few places it seems that the information on which chapter 3 of the *Historia Turpini* was based came from memories of military campaigns. Huesca has already been mentioned, and other places in the foothills of the Aragonese and Catalan Pyrenees would also have been well-known from the recent French military endeavours. The concentration of place-names in the upper Ebro region surely reflects the campaign which culminated in the conquest of Saragossa in 1118, in which French troops had fought alongside the Aragonese. The names along two north-south routes in what is now New Castile, one stopping at Toledo and the other, more easterly, also stopping near the Tagus, might show memories of roads followed by recruits and town militias as they moved to join royal forces at Toledo, a frontier city at times in the first half of the twelfth century and the base from which raiding expeditions set out into Al-Andalus. One cannot conjecture the compiler's source for his knowledge of places in Muslim territory.[21] His extraordinary error in writing Al-Andalus with final "-f," not once but several times, shows that any source was not very immediate, and that nobody in Compostela was consulted about the proper form of this and other names.

The dates at which the geographical information, such as it is, was gathered, or became available to the compiler, seem from what has been said above to fall in the 1120s and 1130s. There is nothing novel about that. One speculates, however, that two further details may be relevant. Among the principal cities of the Peninsula as they were in the twelfth century, Lisbon obviously should have been mentioned but is omitted. This seems to show that the text was put into final form before 1147, when the city was captured by the Portuguese substantially aided by the fleet of English and German crusading forces who were sailing to the Holy Land and were briefly diverted into this worthwhile and brilliantly successful operation. The conquest would have been early celebrated in Compostela and abroad: lack of mention of Lisbon seems to provide a *terminus ante quem* of 1147. The second possibly relevant argument concerns chapter 4 of the *Historia Turpini*, which is—very surprisingly—devoted to the statue which guarded the entrance to the harbour of Cadiz. The author leads into the matter by saying that "Ydola et simulacra que tunc in Yspania inuenit penitus destruxit, preter ydolum quod est in terra Alandaluf, quod uocatur Salam Cadis" [Charlemagne completely destroyed the idols and images which he found in Muslim Spain, except for the idol in the land of Al-Andalus, which is called Salam Cadiz]. Of this, "Tradunt Sarraceni quod ydolun istut Mahummet quem ipsi colunt, dum adhuc uiueret, in nomine suo proprie fabricauit" [The Saracens say that this idol, Muhammad, whom they worship, made in his lifetime specially in his own name]. Further, Muhammad sealed within it by his magical arts "demoniacam legionem quandam" [a certain legion of devils], their purpose being so to strengthen it that it could never be pulled down. It is hard to say whether such appalling notions resulted from the writer's ignorance or from his prejudice.[22] In fact the huge statue, perhaps erected in late antiquity, seems to have represented Hercules with his club. This club is erroneously taken by the compiler, as it was by others favoured with a nearer view, to be a large key ("clauem ingentem") having symbolic importance: "Que scilicet clauis, ut ipsi Sarraceni aiunt, a manu eius cadet anno quo rex futurus in Gallia natus fuerit, qui totam terram Yspanicam Christianis legibus in nouissimus temporibus subiugauerit" [The aforementioned key, as the Saracens themselves say, shall fall from his hand in the year in which a future king shall be born in France, who in times still to come shall make the whole of Muslim Spain subject to Christian rule]. The statue was dismantled in 1145 by the local Muslim ruler when in need of funds, since it had been assumed—so bright was it—that it was of gold; but it turned out to be of gilded bronze. Of this, Meredith-Jones observes that "Mais nous savons, d'autre part, que la statue tout entière, avec ses colonnes, fut abattue en 1145. Il en résulte qu'avant cette date la Chronique de Turpin avait déjà été compilée" [But we know, on the other hand, that the complete statue, with its columns, was knocked down in 1145. It is clear from this that the Chronicle of Turpin had already been compiled before this date] (292). This is altogether too simple-minded, and medievalists know many examples of prophecy-by-hindsight. That the compiler devotes a whole chapter to the subject is in itself suspicious. One purpose was naturally to give Charlemagne a reputation as a destroyer of infidel idols; another was to predict that a French successor to his throne would imitate him and complete the Reconquest of Iberia. It seems plain enough that, contrary to Meredith-Jones' view, this chapter was composed because there was news in France (via Spain, presumably) of the "fall" of the key with the complete statue. There is a near-proof of this in one detail. The statue is said by the *Historia Turpini* to be "de auricalco obtimo" [made of best-quality aurichalcum (better and more classically orichalcum, of Greek origin, then in Latin mistakenly associated with "aurum," gold)]. This is defined as "mountain copper . . . a metal resembling gold, a form of brass or similar alloy": that the statue was in fact made of this and not, as had been thought, of gold can only have been revealed after it was demolished. On these two arguments—about the omission of Lisbon and about the statue—one might suggest the years 1145-47 as those in which the compilation (not the gathering of very diverse materials nor the writing of its parts) of the *Historia Turpini* was concluded.

Our intending pilgrim in the mid-twelfth century, left badly confused by the authorities about the religious history, the political and physical geography, the cities, and much else in the Peninsula, might of course have been further disturbed by what was conveyed by the *chansons de geste*. Most of those that deal with Spain seem to belong to the second half of the twelfth century and the early thirteenth, but the first (for us) surviving version of the *Chanson de Roland* undoubtedly circulated widely soon after 1100. In this, Charlemagne has a prophetic dream about the dangers which his army would face when advancing into Spain. First, dire natural phenomena threaten:

Carles guardat amunt envers le ciel,
Veit les tuneires e les venz e les giels,
E les orez, les merveillus tempez,
E fous et flambes i est apareillez
Isnelement sur tute sa gent chet . . . (lines 2532-36)

[Charlemagne looked upward to the sky, and saw thunderstorms, gales, and frosts, storms, appalling tempests, thunderbolts and flames being prepared there, soon to fall over all his men].

The native fauna are equally threatening:

> En grant dulor i veit ses chevalers,
> Urs e leuparz les voelent puis manger,
> Serpenz e guivres, dragun e averser,
> Grifunz i ad plus de trente millers
> N'en i ad cel a Franceis ne s'agiet . . . (lines 2541-45)

[He saw his knights in great distress, Bears and leopards are trying to eat them, Serpents and vipers, dragons and daemons, and more than thirty thousand griffons, there is none that does not launch itself against the French].

Well, this was poetry, the *jongleurs* were condemned by the Church as liars, and Charlemagne was a long time ago: but our pilgrim might have retained impressions from this powerful verse. Such impressions would have been reinforced by the Church itself if the pilgrim heard materials from Book II of the *Liber Sancti Jacobi* recited or used in a sermon. In this, Miracle 22 relates the awful experiences of a seafaring Barcelona merchant whose devotion to the Apostle was judged (on a mere technicality) insufficient, and who suffered in consequence captivity in the widest possible variety of infidel lands. "Calixtus" (to whom the writing of the miracle is, as in many cases, attributed) records that he met the man after his release in the year 1100 "inter Stella et Grugnum" [between Estella and Logroño], on the pilgrim road, and heard his tale. After finally being released from his chains, thanks to the Apostle's intervention, in Almeria, he had made his way to Christian lands, still facing many perils both human and especially faunistic: "Multa etiam agmina leonum, ursorum, leopardorum et draconum illum gradientem per deserta loca deuorare appetebant, sed uisa catena, quam apostolus tetigerat, procul ab eo recedebant" [Many lines of lions, bears, leopards, and dragons tried to devour him as he made his way through wild places, but on seeing the chain which the Apostle had touched, they drew back to a distance from him]. It would be all very well for a preacher to explain such references as symbolic only; our pilgrim might retain some woefully exaggerated impressions of Peninsular wildlife, for even symbolic interpretations must start from some basis in reality.

Let us hope that the pilgrim, despite all the misinformation, exaggeration, and mendacious propaganda conveyed by these so powerfully authoritative texts, travelled with a firm enough faith and reached his destination unharmed.[23]

NOTES

[1] It was not a matter only of safety on the road. In the Cathedral of Compostela itself, "[s]o many pilgrims arrived, by night and day, that violent collisions between them were not infrequent, the more so as it was a point of national honour for Germans, French, and Italians to seize the place nearest the tomb of St. James in the night vigils. Violent deaths of pilgrims within the Cathedral were so common that in 1207 Pope Innocent III agreed that church offices need not be suspended on these occasions" (Hillgarth, I: 145). In Book I, Sermon 17 of the LSJ, there is mention of battles between French and Gascons to secure favoured places at a shrine of St. Egidius, leading to woundings and in at least one case to a death (f. 83r).

[2] In Miracle 17 of Book II, a youth from near Lyon committed fornication and omitted to confess the sin before setting out on the pilgrimage, whereupon the devil (claiming to be the Apostle) tempted him into an awesome self-mutilation. This is perhaps better known in the variant form recounted by Berceo in the eighth of his *Milagros de Nuestra Señora*, in which the sinning pilgrim is a monk of Cluny, no less. The erring pilgrim is decently anonymous in No. 26 of the Alphonsine *Cantigas de Santa María*.

[3] Chapter 6 of Book V of the LSJ contains such warnings, as it does also about rivers and streams whose water should not be drunk. Perhaps there was pollution even in those days. The writer uses strong terms, evidently from personal experience.

[4] At the end of the description of the peoples of northern Spain in chapter 7 of Book V, we read that "Galleciani uero genti nostre Gallice magis, pre ceteris gentibus Yspanicis incultis moribus, congrue concordantur, sed iracundi et litigiosi ualde habentur" [The Galicians are, among the other uncultured peoples of Spain, those who most closely resemble our own French, but are considered extremely prone to anger and argumentative]. The sermon mentioned in Note 1 above details at length the dangers which beset pilgrims in Compostela.

[5] This was the view of Bédier in particular. Discussion of it may be studied via the index in Díaz y Díaz.

[6] In the famous opening laisse of the poem, the Emperor has conquered all of Spain "as far as the sea" except for Saragossa.

[7] According to Lejeune and Stiennon, the earliest representation seems to be that of scenes from the epic sculpted on the lintel of the cathedral of Angoulême, dated to about 1120-30.

[8] On the conquest of Barbastro, see Smith, *Christians and Moors in Spain*, I (Warminster: Aris & Phillips, 1988), text 17, pp. 84-7. Among the spoils, the Norman leader Robert Crespin alone was said to have taken away

1,500 young women and 500 cartloads of furnishings, ornaments, clothing, and coverings.

[9] This is powerfully argued by Keller, "Changes" (150-73, especially 165-8). The existing poem was reworked, the Baligant episode and others being added, by a monk of St-Denis in the years 1147-9 when Abbot Suger of the monastery was Regent of France. See further Keller's paper "Song."

[10] See Meredith-Jones (1-32); Díaz y Díaz, Primera parte, esp. 45-8, with references to lists of manuscripts compiled by Hämel, de Mandach, and others.

[11] For a translation of part of this crusading epistle by "Calixtus," with comments about the problems involved in defining what was properly a "crusade" from the Spanish point of view, see Smith, I, text 33, pp. 162-5.

[12] The use of this term shows that the author drew upon some Latin text of Hispanic origin. It appears from the early twelfth century, but is specially prominent and frequent in the *Chronica Adefonsi Imperatoris* about the reign of Alfonso VII of Leon-Castile up to 1147. The author of this may well have been Arnault, Bishop of Astorga from 1144 until his death in 1152 or 1153, and much in the royal service. He was French, and one speculates that some contact between the author of the *Historia Turpini* and the bishop or his entourage may have produced the reference to the "Moabitae" (though the author was far from understanding who they were).

[13] The thought occurs to one that the early diffusion of Geoffrey's work of 1136 in Norman England and France prompted composition of the *Historia Turpini*. If Geoffrey created Arthurian myth in large measure and enhanced the glories of the throne of England/Britain, the aim of the *Historia Turpini* was to embellish the myth of Charlemagne and dignify the French throne of his successors.

[14] The composition of the *Historia Seminensis* (generally but incorrectly called *Silense*, "of Silos") is usually dated to 1110-20, but some have thought it later. An argument for a later date—mid-twelfth century— may be based on the passage in section 18 on p. 130 of the edition by Pérez de Urbel and Ruiz-Zorrilla. In this, the writer limits the objectives of Charlemagne's expedition of 778, correctly, to Pamplona and Saragossa, adds that he withdrew when "as is the way with the Franks, he was bought off with gold," and went home. The added scorn is in the final sentence of the section: "Anelebat etenim Carolus in termis illis citius lauari, quas Grani ad hoc opus delitiose construxerat" [Charles was keen to wash himself as soon as possible in the hot baths which for this purpose he had luxuriously built at Aix]. It is not likely that earlier texts (such as that of Adhémar de Chabannes, 1028) from France about the near-complete conquest of the Peninsula by Charlemagne were known in Spain, and it is not likely that a learned monk in Leon would trouble to react to the poetic fiction of the

vernacular *Chanson de Roland*. He would, however, feel obliged to condemn the claims made in the *Liber Sancti Jacobi*, a serious work in Latin prose stamped with the authority of the popes. The argument seems to be clinched by the fact that the *Historia Turpini* (chapter 22) says that after his exertions in Spain and return to Aachen, Charlemagne there "balneos sedule calidos, limpha sed calida et frigida temperatos in eadem uilla parauit" [he carefully had built in that same city hot baths, supplied with water both warm and cold]. It is this reference which the *Seminensis* writer ironically took up, replacing the Emperor's restoration of socially pleasurable Roman baths by the need for a bath in which to wash off sweat and dust. For Spaniards, at least as a literary topos, bathing for either purpose could seem unmanly: according to one chronicler, after the defeat at Uclés in 1108 Alfonso VI ordered all the baths in his realm to be destroyed because their use was making his knights effeminate.

[15] The Austrian doctor Hieronymus Münzer, who toured the Peninsula in 1494-95, was told in Compostela that Charlemagne had built the Cathedral with the proceeds of spoils from his campaigns. The *Historia Compostellana* composed up to 1139 under the direction of Gelmírez had been more guarded, recording only that the Cathedral was begun in Charlemagne's time. Ambrosio de Morales in his *Viaje* (1575) recorded in a straight-faced way that "hacíase en Compostela aniversario muy solemne por Carlomagno el día 6 de julio [. . .] porque dicen que hizo grandes bienes y males a aquella Santa Iglesia" [a most solemn anniversary for Charlemagne was celebrated each 6 July . . . because they say that he did much good, and harm also, to that Holy Church] (128). He went on, however, to express surprise that the Emperor, who died in 813 (better: 814), had done anything at all for the shrine, since the Apostle's body was not found until 835. Elsewhere Morales condemned the *Codex Calixtinus* as mendacious and said it should be removed from the Cathedral (after a time, probably in 1619, Book IV—the *Historia Turpini*—was indeed excised from the CC and kept separately from it).

[16] Identifications have been attempted from Dozy onward. A very helpful study is that of Meredith-Jones (267-87).

[17] The very fame of the shrine and the popularity of the pilgrimage to it in the twelfth and thirteenth centuries, and beyond, form one obvious reason. I study others in a paper, "Galicia, todo un reino," currently in press for a Spanish homage volume.

[18] This kind of gloss might be a rhetorical topos of the kind taught in the schools of the period. It is notable, as an extension of the suggestion made in Note 14, that the *Chronica Adefonsi Imperatoris* indulges in the same: "Sibiliam vero, quam antiqui vocabant Hispalim" [Seville, which the ancients called Hispalis] (section 35); "quandam civitatem opulentissimam, quam antiqui dicebant Tuccis, nostra lingua Xerex" [a certain extremely rich city, which the ancients called Tuccis, in our tongue Jerez] (section 37).

[19] In MGH.SS. I: 183. In 799 and 800 the same text says that the Arab ruler of Huesca sent gifts and the keys of the city to the Emperor, promising to surrender it to him when the time was right.

[20] Reilly says of the city in 1096 that "Contemporary Muslim accounts relate that it had 9 gates in its walls and 90 towers bolstering them. The 90 towers may be hyperbole, but a consideration of its extant ground plan suggests that it may well have had 9 gates" (113).

[21] Places mentioned in chapter 3 are helpfully set on a map of the Peninsula and North Africa by Meredith-Jones (268-9).

[22] That Muslims make and adore images, and that they worship Muhammad, were gross errors all too deeply ingrained in hostile Christian attitudes and campaigns of disinformation over a long time. The author of the *Historia Turpini* has simply adopted these, his most obvious contemporary source being the *chansons de geste* such as the *Roland* itself. There is much of interest on this question in the paper by Bennett.

[23] Alberto Vàrvaro in his excellent study associates the *Historia Turpini* intimately with French epic and asks how the authors could be so ignorant and confused about their neighbouring country. The question may not, however, as Vàrvaro says, be properly posed, since it is rather a question of a genre which created a geographical (and, one adds, a historical) "space" in which elaborate fictions and myths could be developed. The world of courtly Romance was to do the same in the later twelfth century, also at first in France. One might then compare the world of the epic Western, story and film, in America, and even the other-worlds of Tolkien and Mervyn Peake.

CHAPTER 3

Music and the Pilgrimage

Vincent Corrigan

Because it was reputed to hold the relics of St. James the Greater, the Cathedral of Santiago de Compostela became a religious center of high importance in the Middle Ages, and pilgrims from all parts of Europe and the British Isles flocked to Compostela. The Cathedral boasted a rich and complex liturgy for the feasts of St. James, in which music played an important part, and pilgrims may have chosen their travel dates to coincide with the most elaborate liturgies. These liturgies, which formed the focal point of the pilgrims' experience at Compostela, are recorded in the first book of a twelfth-century manuscript known as the *Codex Calixtinus* (hereafter CC). The author, who styles himself Pope Calixtus, says that the manuscript contains everything necessary for the Saint's feasts. Indeed, all of the special texts for St. James are included in the manuscript. Moreover, all of the music, which 'Calixtus' credits to himself, is found there as well. It is this music that the people of the time associated with pilgrimage, and this music that the author took such pains to record. It did not exist on its own, however. The rituals formed the context in which the music was heard, and the avenue through which it can be understood.

LITURGIES

The rituals were of two types. The Divine Office was a series of eight services that spanned the entire day. Matins was the longest, taking place sometime between midnight and 3:00 A.M. It was followed immediately by Lauds, begun before dawn, so that the sun rose during the service. The next four took place at roughly three-hour intervals during the day: Prime (6:00 A.M.); Terce (9:00 A.M.); Sext (12:00 Noon); None (3:00 P.M.). Vespers was performed in the late afternoon, and Compline in the evening before retiring. Matins, Lauds, Vespers, and Compline are the most significant ones musically, while the remainder, the Lesser Hours, are much shorter. The Mass, the other important ritual at the Cathedral, commemorates the Last Supper. The High Mass for the day was celebrated after Terce, and another Mass could, if necessary, be performed after Prime.

In both the Office and the Mass certain texts and melodies are repeated from one service to the next. These passages, known as the Ordinary, would have been familiar to everyone, and would not have needed special preservation. Others, referred to as the Proper, change from one feast to the next, and would need special care. The CC preserves, for the most part, the Proper items for all of the services for St. James.[1]

CALENDAR OF FEAST DAYS

Because the first book of the CC is a liturgical document, it is organized around the calendar of feasts. This is true both for the texts and the music, and a knowledge of the feasts of the Saint is basic to an understanding of the musical organization of the manuscript and the role music played in the experience of the pilgrim.

The CC specifies dates in the old Roman way, by counting backwards from certain fixed points. There are three such points: Kalends, Ides, and Nones. Kalends was the first day of the month and was fixed. Ides, roughly around the middle of the month, was a moveable date. It fell on the 15th day of March, May, July, and October, and on the 13th day of the other months. Nones was reckoned as the 9th day before Ides. Because of this its placement too was variable, the 7th of March, May, July, and October, and the 5th of the other months.

In the counting system, the reference point itself stood as number one, *Kalendas Augusti* standing for the first day of the month (*I Kalendas Augusti*). The day before the reference point was 2, the day preceding that, 3, etc., the reverse of our system. Thus *II Kalendas Augusti* is equivalent to July 31, the day before Kalends of August. The same process is used for the other points.

The following table shows dates and feasts listed in the first book of the CC:

Feasts of St. James in the CC

VIIII	Kalendas Augusti	July 24	Vigil of St. James
VIII	Kalendas Augusti	July 25	Passion of St. James
VII	Kalendas Augusti	July 26	2nd day within the Octave St. Josia, Martyr
VI	Kalendas Augusti	July 27	3rd day within the Octave
V	Kalendas Augusti	July 28	4th day within the Octave
IV	Kalendas Augusti	July 29	5th day within the Octave
III	Kalendas Augusti	July 30	6th day within the Octave
II	Kalendas Augusti	July 31	7th day within the Octave

			Octave of the Passion celebrated[2]
	Kalendas Augusti	Aug. 1	Octave of the Passion of St. James
			St. Peter in Chains
V	Nonarum Octobris	Oct. 3	Miracles of St. James
III	Kalendas Ianuarii	Dec. 30	Election and Translation of St. James
	Nonas Ianuarii	Jan. 5	Octave of the Translation celebrated

STRUCTURE OF *CODEX CALIXTINUS*

The music to be used for these feasts is found in three different places in the CC.[3] The first and longest section, running from f. 101v to f. 139v, contains all of the monophonic music—the chants—for the Offices and Masses for the Saint's feast days. This section serves the triple function of an antiphonary (music for the Office, ff. 101v-113), a gradual (music for the Mass, ff. 114-130), and a troper (optional music, ff. 130-139v). The second section (ff. 185-190v), a supplement to the main body of the manuscript, is really a continuation and extension of the troper, devoted almost exclusively to polyphonic music. This too is divided into three sections: one for tropes, the second for Office movements, and the third for Mass movements. Finally, there are two oddments at the end of the manuscript. These were added later and one of them, *Dum Pater familias*, uses a notation unrelated to that of the rest of the manuscript.

Antiphonary, ff. 101v-113

The antiphonary opens with the Office Hours for the feast of the Vigil (ff. 101v-105v), beginning with Matins and continuing throughout the day until Compline. For all of the Office Hours, only propers, those texts and melodies specific to the feast, are given. Anything of a more standardized nature (ordinary portions, psalm formulas, recitation tones, etc.) is omitted.

The Matins service is short, using only three psalms under one antiphon and three responsories. Those texts with music added are given in the following table:

Matins for the Vigil
Invitatory: *Regem regum/Ps. Venite exultemus*
Hymn: *Psallat chorus*
Antiphon: *O venerande Christi*
  Ps. Confitemini Domino et invocate
  Ps. Confitemini II
  Ps. Confitemini III
Verse: *Ora pro nobis*

Responsory: *Redemptor imposuit Simoni/Ascendens Ihesus*
Responsory: *Vocavit Ihesus Iacobum/Sicut enim tonitrui*
Responsory: *Clementissime Deus/Exue nos a viciis*
Verse: *Imposuit Ihesus Iacobo*

Antiphons for Lauds with their psalms follow on ff. 102v-103. The hymn for Lauds, *Sanctissime O Iacobe*, is not provided with music. However, the verse following it, *Iacobus fuit magnus*, does have notes written above the syllables of the text, but without a staff.

Lauds for the Vigil
Antiphon: *Imposuit Ihesus Simoni/Ps. Miserere mei Deus*
Antiphon: *Vocavit Ihesus Iacobum/Ps. Domine refugium*
Antiphon: *Sicut enim tonitrui/Ps. Deus Deus meus*
Antiphon: *Recte filii/Ps. Audite celi*
Antiphon: *Iacobus et Iohannes/Ps. Laudate dominum de celis*
Chapter: *Iacobus Dei et domini*
Hymn: *Sanctissime O Iacobe*
Verse: *Iacobus fuit magnus*
Antiphon: *Ascendens Ihesus in montem/Ps. Benedictus*
Prayer: *Vigiliarum sacrarum*

The lesser hours (Prime, Terce, Sext, None) are compressed on ff. 103-103v. Only essential pieces are given, and then in staffless neumes. The antiphons that are used in these services have already appeared in Matins and Lauds, and so the absence of precise notation does not pose a problem. However, the three responsories, *Ora pro nobis* for Terce, *Imposuit Ihesus Iacobo* for Sext, and *Occidit autem Herodes* for None, are new.

Lesser Hours for the Vigil
Prime
    Antiphon: *Imposuit Ihesus*
Terce
    Antiphon: *Vocavit Ihesus*
    Chapter: *Iacobus in diebus suis*
    Responsory: *Ora pro nobis/Ut digni efficiamur/Gloria Patri*
    Verse: *Imposuit Ihesus*
Sext
    Antiphon: *Sicut enim*
    Chapter: *In vita sua*
    Responsory: *Imposuit Ihesus Iacobo/Nomina Boanerges/*
            Gloria Patri
    Verse: *Occidit autem Herodes*
None
    Antiphon: *Recte filii*
    Chapter: *In omni ore*

Responsory: *Occidit autem Herodes/Fratrem Iohannis/*
Gloria Patri
Verse: *Iacobus fuit magnus*

The antiphonary continues on ff. 103v-105 with the five antiphons of First Vespers for the feast day. The staff reappears, eliminating any ambiguity in the notation. The responsory *Dum esset* is not written out completely. Rather, it is indicated by an incipit, and its complete notation is given later on f. 107v. Furthermore, a polyphonic version exists on f. 187v and could have been performed here.

Felix per omnes is given completely here, and it is also to be sung at Lauds and Second Vespers for the Feast. In those sections (f. 111, 112v) *Felix per omnes* is indicated with a textual incipit only; no musical notation of any sort appears. The verse *Ora pro nobis* has staffless neumes above the text. The concluding prayer *Deus qui presentem* is written under a staff without notes. The remark "ut supra" indicates that the whole text can be found earlier in the manuscript, but in fact the prayers for the hours are entered only on f. 116v, after the Mass for the Vigil.

First Vespers
Antiphon: *Ad sepulchrum/Ps. Laudate pueri*
Antiphon: *O quanta sanctitate/Ps. Laudate dominum omnes gentes*
Antiphon: *Gaudeat plebs Gallecianorum/Ps. Lauda anima*
Antiphon: *Sanctissime apostole Iacobe/Ps. Laudate dominum*
  quoniam
Antiphon: *Iacobe servorum spes/Ps. Lauda Iherusalem*
Chapter: *Inmisit inquit*
Responsory: *Dum esset/Sicut enim tonitrui*
Hymn: *Felix per omnes*
Verse: *Ora pro nobis*
Antiphon: *Honorabilem eximii/Magnificat*
Prayer: *Deus qui presentem*

The Office of the Vigil concludes with Compline (ff. 105-105v). Again the concluding prayer, indicated "ut supra," is found on f. 116v.

Compline for the Vigil
Antiphon: *Alleluia Iacobe sanctissime/Ps. Cum invocarem*
Hymn: *Psallat chorus*
Chapter: *Tu autem in nobis*
Verse: *Custodi nos domine*
Antiphon: *Alma perpetui/Nunc dimittis*
Prayer: *Deus qui hanc noctem*

Since the celebration of the liturgies for the feast day had already begun with First Vespers, no particular major heading for the section devoted to Matins for the Feast is needed (f. 105v-111). None of the music used in this section was found earlier, and thus everything is written out in full. Even the verse *Iacobus fuit magnus*, which had been given staffless neumes in Lauds for the Vigil, is here written in notes on a staff.

This section covers more than Matins for the feast, however. It becomes the repository for all antiphons responsories to come. Thus, only the first nine antiphons, those in which the psalms are indicated, are sung at Matins for the Feast. The last four stand apart. Three of them have no psalms and their texts are drawn, not from the Gospels, but from the Ecclesiastical History of Eusebius. The remaining one, on a text by Calixtus, may have been intended to precede the canticles at a monastic Matins service. Similarly, only the first nine responsories are sung at Matins. This is shown by the presence of the doxology at the end of the third, sixth, and ninth responsories. The final three are intended for other feasts, probably as the last of a group of three responsories. These features say something about the nature of the Matins ceremony at Compostela: it was secular, not monastic, but with sufficient additions that a monastic service could be constructed.[4]

Matins for the Feast
Invitatory: *Venite omnes Cristicole/Ps. Venite exultemus*
Hymn: *Iocundetur et letetur*
Antiphons (ff. 105v-107)
> *Ihesus dominus vidit/Ps. Celi enarrant*
> *Venite post me/Ps. Benedicam dominum*
> *Iacobus et Iohannes/Ps. Eructavit*
> *Ihesus vocavit Iacobum/Ps. Omnes gentes*
> *Eduxit Ihesus/Ps. Exaudi Deus deprecationem*
> *Dixerunt Iacobus et Iohannes/Ps. Exaudi Deus orationem*
> *Ihesus autem/Ps. Confitebimur*
> *Iam vos delectat/Ps. Dominus regnavit exultet*
> *Herodes rex misit/Ps. Dominus regnavit irascantur*
> *Videns Herodes*
> *Regis vero facinus*
> *Statim percussit Herodem*
> *Iacobe magne* (at the canticles)
Responsories (ff. 107-111)
> *Salvator progressus/At illi*
> *Dum esset/Sicut enim vox tonitrui*
> *Accedentes ad Salvatorem/Ihesus autem/Gloria Patri*
> *Cum vidissent/Et conversus*
> *Iam locum celsitudinis/Iam vos delectat*
> *Confestim autem/Statuto autem/Gloria Patri*

Hic est Iacobus/O quam venerandus
Misit Herodes/Hic Iacobus
Huic Iacobo/Tristis est/Gloria Patri
Cum adpropinquaret/Viso hoc miraculo/Gloria Patri
Iacobe virginei/Tu prece continua/Gloria Patri almo
O adiutor/Qui subvenis/Gloria Deo Patri
Verse: *Iacobus fuit magnus*

The music for antiphons at Lauds (ff. 111-111v) is also new and given in full. After the fifth antiphon, a marginal note indicates the Chapter, responsory, the hymn *Felix per omnes*, and the verse *Ipse est directus*. A later hand has squeezed the music to a responsory, *Ora pro nobis*, onto the bottom of f. 111v. However, this is not the same music as that used in the upcoming lesser hours, and so probably was not sung at the lesser hours for the Vigil.

Lauds for the Feast
Antiphon: *Inmisit inquit/Ps. Dominus regnavit*
Antiphon: *His qui obtulerat/Ps. Iubilate Deo*
Antiphon: *Ducti sunt/Ps. Deus Deus meus*
Antiphon: *Cum ducerentur/Ps. Benedicite*
Antiphon: *At Iacobus/Ps. Laudate dominum de celis*
Chapter: *His qui obtulerat*
Responsory: *Ora pro nobis/Ut digni efficiamur/Gloria Patri*
Hymn: *Felix per omnes*
Verse: *Ipse est directus*
Antiphon: *Apostole Christi Iacobe/Ps. Benedictus*
Prayer: *Gloriosissimam sollempnitatem*

The lesser hours for the feast are presented in the same compressed format used before (ff. 112-112v). Again staffless neumes sit above the syllables of the antiphon texts, and they show that, for the most part, the same music is used here as in Lauds. The chapter *Cum ducerentur* also carries neumes that are identical to the antiphon at Lauds. I suspect that this is an error, since the Chapter should be sung to a recitation formula. No other Chapter has such music added to it. The responsory *Ora pro nobis*, however, is different, and an alternate to it, the responsory *Iacobe servorum spes* is new and written out in full. This responsory and the alternate responsory given for Sext, show that all of these short responsories, including those without music listed before, were sung to the same music, with adjustments made for the texts. The melismatic *Ora pro nobis* is exceptional.

Lesser Hours for the Feast
Prime
Antiphon: *Inmisit inquit*

Terce
  Antiphon: *His qui obtulerat*
  Chapter: *Cum ducerentur*
  Responsory: *Ora pro nobis/Ut digni efficiamur/Gloria Patri*
  Verse: *Imposuit Ihesus*
  Alternate Responsory: *Iacobe servorum spes/Suscipe*
                                   servorum/ Gloria Patri
  Verse: *Imposuit Ihesus*
Sext
  Antiphon: *Ducti sunt*
  Chapter: *At Iacobus*
  Responsory: *Imposuit Ihesus Iacobo/Nomina Boanerges/*
                     Gloria Patri
  Verse: *Occidit autem Herodes*
  Alternate Responsory: *Iacobe pastor/Lapsis manum/Gloria*
                                   Patri
  Verse: *Occidit autem Iacobum*
None
  Antiphon: *Cum ducerentur*
  Chapter: *Iacobus vicit turbas*
  Responsory: *Occidit autem Herodes/Fratrem Iohannis/Gloria*
                     Patri
  Verse: *Imposuit Ihesus*

Second Vespers (f. 112v) continues in the same abbreviated
notation, since all but one of its antiphons (*O lux et decus Hyspanie*)
have been given earlier. The responsory *O adiutor* does not use the
formula of the other short responsories, but the melismatic setting
given on f. 110v. As an option, the polyphonic version given on f.
188, together with the prosa *Portum in ultimo*, could replace the chant.

Second Vespers
Antiphon: *Inmisit inquit/Ps. Dixit dominus*
Antiphon: *His qui obtulerat/Ps. Laudate pueri*
Antiphon: *Ducti sunt/Ps. Credidi*
Antiphon: *Cum ducerentur/Ps. In convertendo*
Antiphon: *At Iacobus/Ps. Domine probasti me*
Chapter:*Vocavit Ihesus Iacobum*
Responsory: *O adiutor*
Hymn: *Felix per omnes*
Verse: *Ipse est directus*
Antiphon: *O lux et decus Hyspanie/Magnificat*
Prayer: *Deus qui diem festum*

The antiphonary concludes with Compline for the Feast (ff. 112v-
113). The only music notated for the service is a series of staffless
neumes above the words of the antiphon *Alleluia Iacobe Sanctissime*.

None is really needed, because this service is identical to the one written on f. 105.

Compline for the Feast
Antiphon: *Alleluia Iacobe Sanctissime/Ps. Cum invocarem*
Hymn: *Psallat chorus*
Chapter: *Tu autem in nobis*
Verse: *Custodi nos domine*
Antiphon: *Alma perpetui/Nunc dimittis*
Prayer: *Deus qui hanc noctem*

Graduale, ff. 114-130
The Graduale portion of the manuscript begins with the complete propers for the Masses of the Vigil and of the Feast. Many of the proper items were spoken and have no music. Other proper sections were sung by means of recitation formulas, and these of course are not written out. Other items had quite elaborate musical settings, and these are recorded with their melodies.

Vigil Mass (Mass 1), ff. 114-116v
Introit: *Iacobus et Iohannes dixerunt*
Tract:*Vocavit Ihesus/Et imposuit*
Gradual: *Nimis honorati sunt/Dinumerabo eos*
Tract: *Iacobus in vita sua/Ipse est directus*
Offertory: *Certe dum filii Zebedei/ Iam locum celsitudinis*
Communion: *Ego vos elegi*

Mass for the Feast, ff. 116v-122
Processional Hymn: *Salve festa dies*

Mass 2, ff. 118-122
Introit: *Ihesus vocavit Iacobum*
Gradual: *Misit Herodes rex manus/Occidit autem Iacobum*
Alleluia: *Sanctissime apostole Iacobe*
Alleluia:*Hic Iacobus valde*
Alleluia:*Vocavit Ihesus Iacobum*
Alleluia with Prosa: *Gratulemur et letemur*
Offertory: *Ascendens Ihesus/Et enim*
Communion: *Ait Ihesus Iacobo/Si mens vestra appetit*

These are the only two masses whose propers are notated entirely. Following them are abbreviated entries for ten other Masses: a *Missa pro peregrinis* which contains no musical entries, seven Masses for the days within the octave, and Masses for the Feast of Miracles and the Feast of the Election and Translation. The musical portions of the proper are indicated by an extremely efficient abbreviation system. Only the opening of the introit *Ihesus vocavit Iacobum* is given, this being sufficient to cue the entire proper of the Mass for the Feast. In the case of the Mass of St. Josia, the incipit *Michi autem nimis* refers to a standard Introit now used for the feast of St. Andrew.[5] The prosa *Clemens servulorum*, also for the feast of St. Josia, is written out in full, presumably because it is used only here.

Other Masses, ff. 122v-130

Mass 3—"for Pilgrims" ff. 122v
Mass 4—2nd day in octave and St. Josia, ff. 122v-123v
Prosa *Clemens servulorum*
Mass 5—3rd day in octave, ff. 124-124v
Mass 6—4th day in octave, ff. 124v-125v
Mass 7—5th day in octave, ff. 125v-126
Mass 8—6th day in octave, ff. 126-126v
Mass 9—7th day in octave, ff. 126v-127v
Mass 10—Octave, sung after Prime, ff. 127v-128
Mass 11—Feast of Miracles, ff. 128-128v
Mass 12—Feast of the Translation and Election, 129v-130

Monophonic Troper, ff. 130-139v

The monophonic troper of ff. 130-139v is devoted to liturgical accretions, texts that enhance the liturgy, rather than ones essential to it. The section begins with five relatively short works, a trope for the *Benedicamus Domino*, for use at the end of the Office Hours, and four settings of Latin poems called conductus. Three of these works carry the refrain *"Lector, lege, et de rege, qui regit omne, dic: Iube, domne [benedicere]"* [Reader, read, and tell about the king who rules over all: Your blessing please], showing that they belong before the readings at Matins. Also, two of these conductus are polyphonic. A second voice, written in red ink, has been added to *Iacobe sancte* and *In hac die* (The same hand added a third voice to *Congaudeant catholici* on f. 185, again in red ink).

The longest work in the troper is the farced Mass of Fulbert of Chartres, farced in the sense that it is stuffed with text. Directions indicate that this Mass can be sung on any feast of the Saint. It contains a mixture of Ordinary and Proper movements. The *Kyrie* can be found in Mass 12, while the *Gloria* and *Agnus Dei* belong to Mass 4.[6]

Monophonic Tropes

Exultet celi curia, f. 130—Benedicamus Domino Trope
Iacobe sancte, f. 131—Conductus
    Lector lege—Invocation before readings at Matins
In hac die, f. 131v—Conductus
    Lector lege—Invocation before readings at Matins
Resonet nostra domino, f. 132—Conductus

Lector lege—Invocation before readings at Matins
Salve festa dies, f. 132—Conductus
Mass 13—Farsed Mass of Fulbert of Chartres, ff. 132v-139v
    Ecce adest nunc
    Introit:*Ihesus vocavit Iacobum/Reges terre*
    Kyrie XII: *Rex inmense*
    Gloria
    Versus:*Qui vocasti super mare*
    Epistle:*Cantemus Domino/Lectio libri ecclesiastice ystorie*
    Sanctus:*Osanna salvifica*
    Agnus Dei: *Qui pius ac mitis es*
    Benedicamus Domino: *Regi perhennis glorie*

Polyphonic Troper, ff. 185-190v

The polyphonic troper occurs at the end of the manuscript, as an addendum after Book Five, commonly called the *Pilgrim's Guide*, and constitutes an extension of the earlier collection of tropes. There is a three-fold division of the music in this section that mirrors the division in Book One. The section opens with a collection of tropes (ff. 185-187v) much like those on ff. 130-132v. This is followed by polyphonic settings of Office responsories (ff. 187v-189v) and of Mass movements (ff. 189v-190). The polyphonic music concludes with three two-voice settings of the *Benedicamus Domino* without any added text.

The tropes on ff. 185-187v emphasize the *Benedicamus Domino*. This acclamation occurs at the end of certain Masses, but it is most often associated with the Office where it is used as the concluding prayer. Six of the texts incorporate the phrase *"Benedicamus Domino"* into their last lines and thus show themselves to be tropes. One of them, *Regi perhennis glorie*, is used monophonically at the end of Fulbert's farced Mass (f. 139), and thus the setting on f. 187, based on the same melody, serves as an alternate version in that Mass. The remaining five were probably intended for performance at the Office Hours. The music to two of these works appears with different texts in a group of Aquitanian manuscripts: *Ad superni regis decus* carries the text *Noster cetus psallat letus* in three manuscripts, while *Gratulantes celebremus festum* is given the text *Ad honorem sempiterni regis* in one. Both Karp (*The Polypohony* 2: 49, 91, 162, 197, 208) and van der Werf (*Oldest Extant Part Music* 2: 12, 109) give transcriptions and details of transmission. Of the two other works in this section, *Iacobe sancte* had appeared earlier on f. 131, one of two pieces with a second voice written in red ink. Now the two voices are placed on different staves and written in the same black ink. Only *Annua gaudia* has no obvious relation to either the Office Hours or the Mass.

Congaudeant catholici occupies a special place in the history of medieval music. Like the other pieces in the addendum it is notated in black ink on two staves. However, someone has added another voice, in red ink, to the lower staff. This has convinced many that *Congaudeant catholici* is a three-part work, the first such work in the history of Western music that we possess. Its attribution to Albertus of Paris, where three-part composition was cultivated later in the century, has made this idea even more appealing. As early as 1931 Peter Wagner suspected that the work was a two-part composition with two options. The notation does not agree with any three-part notation we know, and the harmonic language is at odds with contemporaneous ideas of consonance and dissonance. Thus it is safest to assume that *Congaudeant catholici* is not a three-part work, but two different two part works notated in a very efficient manner.

Polyphonic Tropes
Nostra phalans, f. 185—Benedicamus Trope (?)
Congaudeant catholici, f. 185—Benedicamus Trope
Gratulantes celebremus, f. 185v—Benedicamus Trope
Ad superni regis decus, f. 185v—Benedicamus Trope
Annua gaudia, f. 186v
Iacobe sancte, f. 186v—Conductus (before readings)
Regi perhennis glorie, f. 187—Benedicamus Trope for Mass 13
Vox nostra resonet, f. 187v—Benedicamus Trope

Four of the responsories from the first section of the CC are set polyphonically: *Dum esset, Huic Iacobo, Iacobe virginei*, and *O adiutor*. In these cases, however, the setting is not that of the simple discant style, but the more elaborate organal style, in which the chant melody is given in prolonged notes as the lower voice, above which moves a florid second voice. This was the newer style of polyphony in the twelfth century.

In the chant portion of the CC the responsory *Dum esset* appears twice. It is written out in full as the second of the nine responsories at Matins for the feast (f. 107v). In this position it should not contain the doxology *Gloria patri*, and none is written into the manuscript. It is also indicated by an incipit at First Vespers, as the responsory between the chapter and the hymn, and here the doxology is appropriate (f. 104v). Since the polyphonic version contains the doxology written under the syllables of the verse, it should be performed at First Vespers, not at Matins.

Huic Iacobo is the last of the nine responsories at the Matins service for the feast day carried out in the cathedral, and a polyphonic setting would be fitting at such a significant point.

Iacobe virginei poses something of a puzzle. It is the eleventh of the twelve responsories contained in the first section of the CC, where an inscription attributes the text to the *Magna Passione*. However, unlike its neighbors, it does not appear in any of the liturgies in the first section of the manuscript. Furthermore its text comes, not from the *Magna Passione*, which itself was not an appropriate source for responsory texts, but from the even more inappropriate "Veneranda dies," Calixtus' sermon on pilgrimage for the feast of the Translation and Election, Dec. 30 (Whitehill 176). Perhaps this polyphonic setting was intended as the ninth responsory at Matins for that feast, or as the responsory at either of the Vespers services. Apparently a prosa, *Festa digne,* was to accompany *Iacobe virginei,* but no trace of it remains in the CC, either in the monophonic section or in the polyphonic troper.

O adiutor, the last responsory in the Antiphonale, is indicated by a brief incipit as the responsory at Second Vespers, and functions in this service as *Dum esset* did at First Vespers. Like *Iacobe virginei* it carries a prosa, *Portum in ultimo,* although this is not indicated in the first section of the manuscript. The prosa itself is set polyphonically, making *O adiutor* the most elaborate of the polyphonic pieces in the manuscript.

Polyphonic Responsories

Dum esset/Sicut enim, f. 187v—1st Vespers
Huic Iacobo/Tristis est, f. 188—9th responsory at Matins for feast
Iacobe virginei/Tu prece continua, f. 188
O adiutor/Qui subvenis and Portum in ultimo, f. 188—2nd
    Vespers

There are four polyphonic Mass sections in the manuscript. Two of them are settings of Ordinary texts, those texts which remain constant throughout the year. *Rex inmense* is the Kyrie trope for Fulbert's Mass, and is given in its monophonic version on f. 134. *Cunctipotens genitor* is not indicated for any of the Masses in the CC, but it was very popular, appearing in many sources, and may have been an option in any of the Saint's Masses. The two Proper settings are intended for the Mass of the feast day.

Polyphonic Mass Movements

Rex inmense (Kyrie XII), f. 189—Kyrie Trope for Mass 13
Misit Herodes/Occidit autem Iacobum, f. 189—Gradual for Mass 2
Alleluia/Vocavit Ihesus, f. 189v—third Alleluia for Mass 2
Cunctipotens genitor (Kyrie IV), f. 190—Kyrie Trope

Of the three *Benedicamus Domino* settings, two are based on chant melodies that can still be found in modern chant editions.[7] The first is used to conclude First Vespers of solemn feasts, while the second is used as an alternate chant at Second Vespers. The third setting is based on a chant line that is not as distinctive as the other two; it may have been used for the minor Office Hours or on week days outside of the feast and vigil.[8] Oddly enough, this section of the manuscript concludes with a monophonic work, *Ad honorem regis summi* (f. 190v).[9] Its text refers to the 22 miracles of St. James, and the work may have been added to the addendum when the Feast of Miracles was added to the first book.

Oddments, ff. 192v-193
Two pieces were added after the CC was completed. The first, *Alleluia in Greco* (f. 192v), is identical to the *Alleluia Vocavit Ihesus Iacobum* in the Mass for the Feast, but with the text translated into Greek. The final work, *Dum Pater familias* (f. 193) is the only piece in the manuscript that looks like something the pilgrims themselves might have sung. It may also have been used as a teaching tool to assist the memorization of Latin cases.[10] In any event it would be nice to know what this piece sounded like. But there is a problem. It uses a notation wholly unrelated to the music in the rest of the manuscript. There is no staff, and the note symbols are different. As a result, the piece cannot be transcribed with any certainty, and performances that one hears are entirely conjectural.

ATTRIBUTIONS IN THE MANUSCRIPT
One of the most remarkable features of the CC is the presence of attributions. Normally, musical compositions in the 11th century are blanketed in anonymity. However, in both liturgical section and the appendix, names of real people are attached to the various pieces. Of course it is never certain that these individuals are responsible for the words, the music, both, or neither. Yet they give some idea of the date of the manuscript and the cities thought to be important in its development.

Manuscript Attributions
Aymeri Picaud of Parthenay-le-Vieux (d. 1141): *Ad honorem regis summi*
Airardus of Vezelay (?-?): *Annua gaudia*
Albericus, Bishop of Bourges (fl. 1137-41): *Ad superni regis decus*
Albertus of Paris (fl. 1147-80): *Congaudeant catholici*
Anonymous doctor of Galicia: *Regi perhennis glorie*
Anselmo: *Exultet celi curia*
Aton (Ato, Hatto), Bishop of Troyes (fl. 1123-45):
Nostra phalans
Dum esset/Sicut enim
Huic Iacobo/Tristis est
Iacobe virginei/Tu prece continua
O adiutor/Qui subvenis
Portum in ultimo
Misit Herodes/Occidit autem Iacobum

Bishop of Benevento: *Iacobi sancte, tuum repetito*
Calixtus (reigned 1119-24): Masses and Offices for St. James
Droardus of Troyes (?-?):
   2 *Benedicamus Domino* settings ff. 190-190v
Fortunato, Venantius, Bishop of Poitiers (ca. 530-610):
   Salve festa dies
Fulbert, Bishop of Chartres (fl. 1007-29):
   In hac die
   Kyrie Rex inmense
   Psallat chorus
   Sanctissime O Iacobe
   Ecce adest nunc
Goslenus, Bishop of Soissons (fl. 1126-52):
   Gratulantes celebremus
   Alleluia/Vocavit Ihesus
Gualterius de Chateaurenault:
   Regi perennis glorie (organal voice only)
   Cunctipotens genitor (organal voice only)
   Benedicamus Domino (f. 190)
Guillermo, Patriarch of Jerusalem (fl. 1130-45):
   Clemens servulorum
   Felix per omnes
   Iocundetur et letetur
Johannis Legalis: *Vox nostra resonet*
Roberto, Roman Cardinal=Roberto Pullen, Archdeacon of
   Rochester, later Cardinal and Chancellor at Rome (d. 1146):
   Resonet nostra Domino

Only one of these men is known to have been a musician: Albertus of Paris, to whom *Congaudeant catholici* is assigned, was Cantor at Notre-Dame Cathedral for over thirty years.[11] Many of these persons are associated with cities along the two pilgrimage routes issuing from Paris and Vézelay. Particularly striking is the importance of Troyes in this list (nearly half of the polyphonic works come from there), and of its bishop Ato (credited with seven works).

EDITIONS, TRANSCRIPTIONS, AND RECORDINGS
The music of the CC first came to scholarly attention through the work of Guido Dreves in 1894. Dreves (223-33) gave transcriptions of fifteen pieces from the manuscript, eleven of them from first section and the remaining four from the appendix. For over thirty years this was the only edition of the music to be had, and Dreves' versions formed the basis of all scholarly work on the music for a generation. In 1931 Peter Wagner published all of the monophonic and polyphonic music in the CC in modern chant notation. This was followed in 1944 by Walter Muir Whitehill's edition of the complete manuscript, which included a facsimile of the musical portions together with Germán Prado's

transcription into chant notation. Finally, José López-Caló has published color facsimiles of the polyphonic music and of *Dum Pater familias*.

Transcriptions of the music into modern notation were limited for much of this century to isolated pieces, usually from the polyphonic repertory. Recently, however, complete editions have begun to appear. The polyphonic music has been edited by Theodore Karp (*Polyphony*), López-Caló, and Hendrik van der Werf (*Oldest Extant Part Music*). Paul Helmer has published a performing edition of one of the Masses, and I am working on an edition of Matins for the feast day.

Like modern editions, until recently recordings of the Calixtine repertory were limited to exerpts from the polyphonic music. Now one can find recordings devoted to the CC alone, including Fulbert's farced Mass,[12] or which place its music in the context of pilgrimage[13] or the history of Spanish music.[14] It is not yet possible to find complete recordings of the Office, but it would seem to be only a matter of time until this lack is remedied.

MUSICAL SIGNIFICANCE OF THE MANUSCRIPT
Outside of the editions of Wagner and Prado, relatively little scholarly work has been done on the chants for the services. An exception is Hendrik van der Werf's "The Composition *Alleluya Vocavit*." Most of the research has concentrated on the twenty two-part compositions in the appendix, and the goal has been to relate these works to the development of polyphonic music which is such a distinctive characteristic of Western Art Music.

The early history of Western polyphony is usually divided into three large periods. In the earliest, a single note in one voice is matched by one note in another voice, a style later known as discant. This style, described as *punctus contra punctum* (from which derives our term "counterpoint") flourished from the late ninth through the late eleventh centuries. A second kind of composition, melismatic, sustained-tone, or organal style, was added in the early twelfth century. The notes in the lower voice were sustained, sometimes to great length, while the upper part contained extensive, elaborate melismas. Finally, in the late twelfth century, a school of polyphony at Notre-Dame Cathedral in Paris used measured rhythm in both parts, devised a notational system to express that rhythm, and expanded the number of parts from two to three.

The CC thus falls among the immediate forerunners to the Notre-Dame School of the late twelfth century, and contains examples of all contemporaneous styles of polyphony. Note-against-note polyphony, while not of central importance in the manuscript, appears here and there in many compositions for individual lines of text or for short sections of pieces. The discant setting of *Congaudeant catholici* is the longest example of note-against-note writing in the manuscript (Fig. 3.1).

Sometimes a small cluster of notes in one voice was set against one or two notes in the other. This type of polyphony, cultivated in northern Spain and southern France in the early twelfth century, is related to discant style and can be seen in the alternate version of *Congaudeant catholici* preserved in the manuscript (Fig. 3.2).

The melismatic style also appears in the CC and is used for liturgical texts of the Mass and the Office. It is visually distinctive because of the significantly greater number of notes on the top staff (Fig. 3.3).

The nature of the rhythm in these pieces is a very controversial issue. Many writers have embraced the idea that the rhythm of the polyphonic music was as unmeasured as was the chant. Some recent studies, however, have begun to explore possible relationships between the CC and the rhythm of Parisian music later in the century ("modal rhythm").[15] The first version of *Congaudeant catholici* shows one possible rhythmic reading. To date no consensus has been reached on this topic.

CONCLUSION
An idea of the magnificence of the liturgy and the effect it might have had on the pilgrim can be gotten by considering Matins for the Feast. This service, which took place in the earliest hours of the morning, is without question the most extensive and elaborate of the rituals for the Saint, with a performing time of approximately three hours.

Matins Service for the Feast
Introduction
Opening Prayers
  Pater noster
  Ave, Maria
  Credo in Deum
  Domine, labia mea
  Deus in adiutorium
  Gloria Patri
Invitatory: *Venite omnes Cristicole*
Psalm 94: *Venite exsultemus*
Hymn: *Iocundetur et letetur*
1st Nocturne
Antiphons and Psalms
  Antiphon 1: *Ihesus dominus vidit*

Psalm 18: *Celi enarrant*
Antiphon 1 repeated
Antiphon 2: *Venite post me*
Psalm 33: *Benedicam dominum*
Antiphon 2 repeated
Antiphon 3: *Iacobus et Iohannes*
Psalm 44: *Eructavit*
Antiphon 3 repeated
Versicle: *Ora pro nobis*
Pater noster
Absolution: *Exaudi, Dominus*
Lessons and Responsories
Blessing 1: *Adsit nobis*
Lesson 1
Responsory 1: *Salvator progressus*
Blessing 2: *Bonam nobis*
Lesson 2
Responsory 2: *Dum esset*
Blessing 3: *Cui Iacobus*
Lesson 3
Responsory 3: *Accedentes ad Salvatorem*
2nd Nocturne
Antiphons and Psalms
Antiphon 4: *Ihesus vocavit Iacobum*
Psalm 46: *Omnes gentes*
Antiphon 4 repeated
Antiphon 5: *Eduxit Ihesus*
Psalm 60: *Exaudi Deus deprecationem*
Antiphon 5 repeated
Antiphon 6: *Dixerunt Iacobus et Iohannes*
Psalm 63: *Exaudi Deus orationem*
Antiphon 6 repeated
Versicle: *Imposuit Ihesus*
Pater noster
Absolution: *Ipsius pietas*
Lessons and Responsories
Blessing 4: *Det nobis*
Lesson 4
Responsory 4: *Cum vidissent*
Blessing 5: *Eius nos*
Lesson 5
Responsory 5: *Iam locum celsitudinis*
Blessing 6: *Faciat nos*
Lesson 6
Responsory 6: *Confestim autem*
3rd Nocturne
Antiphons and Psalms

Antiphon 7: *Ihesus autem*
Psalm 74: *Confitebimur*
Antiphon 7 repeated
Antiphon 8: *Iam vos delectat*
Psalm 96: *Dominus regnavit exultet*
Antiphon 8 repeated
Antiphon 9: *Herodes rex misit*
Psalm 98: *Dominus regnavit irascantur*
Antiphon 9 repeated
Versicle: *Occidit autem Herodes*
Pater noster
Absolution: *A vinculis*
Lessons and Responsories
    Blessing 7: *Genetricis Iacobi*
    Gospel
    Lesson 7
    Responsory 7: *Hic est Iacobus*
    Blessing 8: *Huius diei*
    Lesson 8
    Responsory 8: *Misit Herodes*
    Blessing 9: *Iacobus dexteram*
    Lesson 9
    Responsory 9: *Huic Iacobo*
Conclusion
Te Deum
Collect
Benedicamus Domino
Fidelium animae

This magnificent service took place, not in the confines of a quiet monastic community, but in a bustling civic cathedral dedicated to the worship of God and his Saint in full public view. It is described in one of the sermons of the CC, "Veneranda dies," for the feast of the Election and Translation.

Nimio gaudio miratur, qui peregrinantum chorus circa beati Iacobi altare venerandum vigilantes videt: Theutonici enim in alia parte, Franci in alia, Itali in alia catervatim commorantur, cereos ardentes manibus tenentes, unde tota ecclesia ut sol vel dies clarissima illuminantur. Unusquisque cum patriotis suis per se vigilias sapienter agit. Alii citharis psallant, alii liris, alii timphanis, alii tibiis, aliifistulis, alii tubis, alii sambucis, alii violis, alii rotis Brittannicis vel Gallicis, alii psalteriis, alii diversis generibus musicorum cantando vigilant, alii peccata plorant, alii psalmos legunt, alii elemosinas cecis tribuunt. Ibi audiuntur diversa genera linguarum, diversi clamores barbarorum loquele et cantilene Theutonicorum,

Anglorum, Grecorem, ceterarumque tribuum et gentium diversarum omnium mundi climatum. Non sunt loquele neque sermones, quorum non resonent voces illorum. Huiusmodi vigilie ibi sedule habentur, alii enim vadunt, aliique recedunt et diversi diversa munera sacrificant. Si tristis accedit quis, letus recedit. Ibi semper sollempnitas assidua celebratur, festivitas sedule agitur, preclara celebritas die noctuque excolitur, laus et iubilacio, gaudium et exultacio, iugiter decantatur. Omnes dies et noctes quasi sub una sollempnitate continuato gaudio ad domini et postoli decus ibi excoluntur. Valve eiusdem basilice minime clauduntur die noctuque, et nullatenus nox in ea fas est haberi atra, quia candelarum et cereorum splendida luce ut meridies fulget.

[One marvels with exceeding joy, who sees the chorus of pilgrims keeping watch around the venerable altar of St. James: Germans on one side, French on another, Italians on another standing in groups, holding burning tapers in their hands, which illuminate the whole church as the sun or rather the brightest day. Each one with his compatriots wisely performs the vigils [Matins] by themselves. They keep awake, some by playing citharas, others lyres, others timpanis, others pipes, others trumpets, others harps, others viols, others Breton or Gallican rotas, others psalteries, others by singing various kinds of music, some lament their sins, others recite psalms, others give alms to the blind. There are heard diverse genera of tongues, diverse shouts of barbarous languages and the prattle of Germans, Angles, Greeks, and of all the other tribes and diverse races of all climes of the world. There are neither languages nor tongues whose voices do not resound. In this way vigils are observed there, some indeed advance and others retire and various people offer various gifts. If anyone approaches with sadness, he withdraws with happiness. Solemnities are continually celebrated there, feasts carefully conducted, magnificent throngs worship day and night, praise and jubilation, joy and exaltation, are sung together. Splendor pervades all days and nights, as though under a continual joyful solemnity to the Lord and to the apostle. The doors of his same cathedral are seldom closed day or night, and it is ordained that night has no place in it, because the splendid light of the candles and tapers shines like mid-day.][16]

This visual brilliance was accompanied by an aural splendor that could be heard nowhere else in the world. For the piigrims it was a profoundly moving experience, the culmination of their arduous journey, the goal they had so long sought.

Fig. 3.1 *Congaudeant catholici A*

Fig. 3.2 *Congaudeant catholici B*

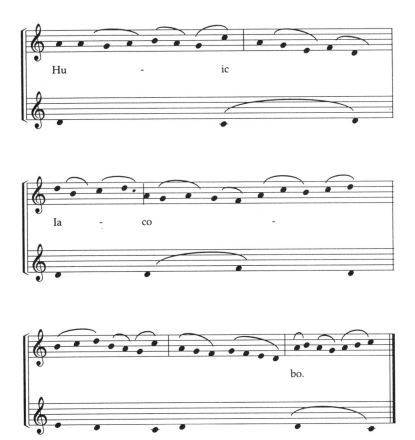

Fig. 3.3 *Huic Iacobo*

NOTES

[1] The CC is the only readable source for this music. The Ripoll manuscript contains the music for the services, but in staffless neumes.

[2] Both the Octave of the Passion and the Octave of the Translation fall on days devoted to other, more significant, feasts. August 1, the Octave of the Passion, is also the feast of St. Peter in Chains, and Jan. 6 is the feast of the Epiphany. In both cases the celebration of the office hours for the octave of James' feasts took place one day earlier, and changes were also made in the schedule and content of the masses. The CC describes these changes:

Octava vero sancti Iacobi II kalendas Augusti cum novem lectionibus sicut in die festo debent celebrari propter festum sancti Petri ad Vincula, quod die octavo festi sancti Iacobi colitur (f. 113) [The Octave of St. James should be celebrated on July 31 with nine lessons as on the feast day because of the feast of St. Peter in Chains, which is observed on the eighth day after the feast of St. James].

Kalendas Augusti. Missa in octavas sancti Iacobi mane post Primam cantanda, quia maior missa hodierna sancti Petri ad Vincula post Terciam hac in die debet iure celebrari (f. 128v) [August 1. The Mass for the octave of St. James is sung early in the morning after Prime, because the high mass of the day, St. Peter in Chains, should properly be celebrated after Terce on this day].

Octave translacionis et electionis sancti Iacobi septimo die scilicet nonas Ianuarii celebrentur, quia octava die nequeunt celebrari propter festum Epyphanie, quod ibi colitur. Matutine vero cum novem lectionibus sicut in die decantentur, et tota missa similiter, excepto quia hoc evangelium debet legi: Sequentia sancti evangelii secundum Matheum. . . (f. 130) [The Octave of the translation and election of St. James is celebrated on the seventh day, namely nones of January (Jan. 5), since it cannot be celebrated on the eighth because of the feast of the Epiphany which is observed there. Matins is sung with nine lessons as on the feast day, and all of the mass is the same, except that this gospel should be read: Continuation of the Gospel according to Matthew. . .] (my translation).

[3] Book V uses a new foliation, because of the reintegration of the Pseudo-Turpin, Book IV, into the CC. However, I will use the old foliation since musicologists are more familiar with it.

[4] The case for a monastic service is made most forcefully by David (1: 16; 2: 155-59). It is refuted by Hohler (43).

[5] Several sources are needed to construct the entire mass proper for this feast: *Graduale* 392 (Introit); *Graduale* 533 (Gradual *Constitues eos* from Mass for Sts. Peter and Paul); CC f. 119v (Alleluia *Vocavit Ihesus* from Mass for the Feast); *Graduale* 534 (Offertory *Constitues eos* from Mass for Sts. Peter and Paul); CC f. 122 (Communion *Ait Ihesus* from Mass for the Feast).

[6] *Graduale* 42*, 15*, 17*. Mass 4 begins with the Kyrie *Cunctipotens genitor*, which is contained in the polyphonic troper. Perhaps it was used as an alternate to *Rex inmense*.

[7] *Antiphonale* 1244, 1245.

[8] Huglo offers in an appendix (150-52) a catalogue of *Benedicamus Domino* chants arranged by mode. The Calixtine tenors are, respectively, numbers 117, 302, and 202.

[9] Some scholars have interpreted the work polyphonically. Prado (2: 84) thought he saw two clefs at the beginning of the third line, and so rendered it in parallel thirds. However, the scribe seems to have had difficulty writing the piece down, one of the clefs is clearly erased, and Prado's idea must be abandoned. Hiley (167-73) gives a different polyphonic reading, but it violates at one point the contrapuntal ideas of the time, and so must also be abandoned.

[10] Using the Latin poetic style known as polyptoton, each verse contains the Saint's name in one of the various cases, and abbreviations for case names appear beside the appropriate verse: Nominative—*Iacobus*; Genitive—*Iacobi*; Dative—*Iacobo*; Accusative—*Iacobum*; Vocative—*Iacobe*; Ablative—*Iacobo*.

[11] The known details of Albertus' life are given by Wright (278-81).

[12] *Codex Calixtinus*, Ensemble Venance Fortunat; *Donnersöhne*, Sequentia; *Missa Sancti Iacobi*, Paul Helmer.

[13] *Camino de Santiago*, Ensemble Frühe Musik Augsburg; *Camino de Santiago I and II*, Thomas Binkley; *The Pilgrimage to Santiago*, New London Consort.

[14] López-Caló; *Mozarabic Chant and the Calixtine Codex*, Choir of the Abbey of Santo Domingo de Silos.

[15] See Stäblein, Karp, and van der Werf. Karp's edition uses measured rhythm throughout.Van der Werf's uses unmeasured rhythm.

[16] Translation mine.

CHAPTER 4

1494: Hieronymus Münzer, Compostela, and the *Codex Calixtinus*

Jeanne E. Krochalis

The fifty-six year old Nürnberg physician Hieronymus Münzer traveled around Italy and Spain in 1494-5 to avoid the plague in his native city. He had three companions: Anton Herward from Augsburg, who spoke Italian and Spanish, and two Nürnberg friends, Kaspar Fischer and Nikolaus Wolkenstein. His strategy worked; he lived until 1508. Spain was new to him, and he made a complete circuit, entering from France, going up the west coast to Barcelona, then down and across Granada, Malaga, Seville, and up through Portugal to Galicia. From Padrón and Compostela, he went down to Salamanca, then northeast to Zaragoza, rejoining the familiar pilgrim's route through Pamplona and Roncesvalles back to France. It took one hundred and forty-six days in all, and the distances and travel time are carefully noted in his Latin account of his journey.[1] His record provides a description of the shrine at Padrón, and the city and church of Compostela as they were in the late fifteenth century. What is of particular interest is that he also saw, and made notes from, a manuscript containing *Codex Calixtinus* texts. He is the first foreigner, and the first layman, whom we know to have done so. An English translation of his description of Compostela and the parts of the pilgrim route he travelled, and his excerpts from the CC manuscript he saw, conclude this article.

Italy he already knew, having done his medical degree at Pavia from 1472-80. He made a return trip to Italy in 1484-5. Though he had not been to Portugal, he knew the Nürnberg-born sailor Martin Behaim (d. 1507), who sailed for Portugal, was interested in ideas of westward voyages to the East, and constructed the first world globe from 1490 to 1492 (Cardini 227).[2] Inspired by the Emperor Maximilian and informed by Behaim, Münzer had written a letter about it to King John II on 14 July 1493, and when he got to Evora he met the king. In Lisbon, he stayed with Behaim's father-in-law; Martin was away in Antwerp. On his travels, Münzer encountered illness, and indeed helped cure a cleric at Scala Dei, but traveled, like the contemporary English physician Andrew Boorde, for pleasure, not for profit.[3]

Münzer was a sociable traveler. He conversed with German merchants wherever he could find them—and even the German who organized the monk's clothes at the abbey of Guadalupe—but was not totally dependent on fellow-countrymen, or his interpreter. He found Spanish closer to Latin than Italian, and easier to understand (Pfandl 132).[4] It seems to have been easy for him to meet important people. At Malaga he met Fray Bernardus de Boil, of Aragon, chaplain to Columbus on his first voyage, and learned about the new islands. Unfortunately, de Boil's descriptions were not among the things Münzer wrote down in detail (Pfandl 69-70). He also met Ferdinand and Isabella and was impressed by their piety as well as their magnificence. In addition to comments on the royal couple in his Itinerary, he wrote a separate description in their praise, taken from the oration of Alfonsus de Ortus, canon of Toledo, at Seville on November 10. This summarizes their military victories and political and spiritual reforms (Pfandl 123-5n.). When he met them, he saw that "[t]he king is of middle height, with a pleasant and smiling countenance, mixed with a certain gravity," and that "[t]he queen is 48 years old, older than the king, of a similar stature, and somewhat plump, with a very charming face" (Pfandl 129-30).[5]

Münzer loved books and was himself a keen book collector.[6] He began collecting books when he was studying for his MA at Leipzig from 1466-70. His one hundred and eighty-five surviving volumes include medical, theological, and historical works, as well as works by humanist authors like Petrarch, Pico della Mirandola, and Marcilius Ficino.[7] But, though he read them, they did not influence his own Latin style. His prose is straightforward, rather than elegant, more medieval than humanist, and sometimes, especially in the compression of *Codex Calixtinus* Book IV, commonly called the *Pseudo-Turpin*, a bit casual in syntax. He has a special fondness for the ablative absolute construction. It is surprising that, for all his love of books, Münzer's surviving manuscript is a copy, not an original. The surviving manuscript of his travels to Spain, Munich Bayerische Staatsbibliothek Clm 431, is a copy made by his friend Hartmann Schedel, best known as the compiler of the Nürnberg Chronicle, for which Münzer drew the map of Germany (Goldschmidt 45). Perhaps because it is in Latin, his itinerary has not been much studied. Also, as Klaus Herbers has remarked, his attitudes are not those of the typical medieval pilgrim, but more those of the Renaissance (26-7).

In general, Münzer was skeptical of marvels, and records only one miracle. His interests were more practical. One of the few hagiographic legends he recounts is of the holy man of Barcelona, who cured the count's mad daughter and, then, bewitched by her beauty, raped her. Appalled by his own deed, he killed and buried her, and fled to the desert for seven years' penance. He returned as a captive in chains, only to have the girl and his six-year-old son cry out from the grave, " John Garin, rise up! Your sins are forgiven you!" The holy widowed queen of Portugal founded the monastery of Montserrat on the site of this miracle (Pfandl 16-7).

Most of Spain he loved. Of Valencia he wrote, "And I believe that there is scarcely such perfect seafood in the whole of Europe!" (Pfandl 20-1).[8] Even more troubled cities did not deter or frighten him. Before King Ferdinand restored order, Seville had been so full of unrest that it was unsafe to wander about at night, and robbers entered the homes (Pfandl 76), but he describes both the cathedral and the mosques in leisurely detail. Dodging Saracen robbers outside Alicante seemed more adventurous than dangerous (Pfandl 33). He found Muslim rituals interesting, and approved of the Saracen pleasure in baths (Pfandl 43). In fact, though he complained from time to time about accommodation in villages, Compostela is the only Spanish city he did not enjoy.

He was interested in architecture and kept comparing Spanish churches to those he knew in Nürnberg. But his greatest enthusiasm is reserved for small decorative objects, among which he included manuscripts, and for the fruits, fountains, and gardens he saw. And at the monastery of Guadalupe he was fascinated by the great copper cooking pots, capable of holding a whole steer at once, and a vessel with channels for hot and cold water. "The cooking of the fathers is superb!" (Pfandl 109).[9]

He noted the presence of scientific or specially beautiful books elsewhere on his travels. Guadalupe had the biggest choir books he had ever seen and the most beautifully decorated missals. It also had a superbly organized library, with thirty-six banks of books, all the volumes well bound.[10] At Barcelona, the library is sandwiched in between the gilded tablets on the twenty altars and the orange trees.[11] But it was the monstrance with ninety-four marks of gold decorated with pearls and gems "which is stupendous to remark" (Pfandl 6),[12] that called forth his greatest admiration. He also commented on the Barcelona great library, with annals kept in booklets, one for each year. If you knew the year, it was easy to find a detailed account of any event.[13] The book which most impressed him is still at Toledo: the great thirteenth-century *Bible Moralisée*, three volumes on uterine vellum, text and gloss written in letters of gold, illuminated with miniatures on historical subjects, with gold and lapis lazuli, all bound in silk, ornamented with gems and pearls.[14]

He saw and talked to scholars, well disposed and garbed, in the library at Salamanca, but was more impressed by the ceiling ornamented with the signs of the zodiac and liberal arts (Pfandl 102).[15]

One might have expected him to note the description of the liberal arts in Charlemagne's palace in the text of the *Pseudo-Turpin*, but it does not appear in his notes from the *Codex Calixtinus*. Astronomy interested him; the Salamanca library contained a book on astronomy, which ignorant men believed to be about magic.[16] He had a pleasant conversation in Madrid with several young sprigs of the nobility who recited Juvenal and Horace, and noted with approval that *humanitas* was on the rise in the younger generation (Pfandl 133). At Zaragoza, in the Franciscan monastery, he found not only ancient books, all on parchment, but eight volumes of Jerome in italic script.[17]

In Compostela, Münzer described the city and its parts. Throughout Europe he must have seen many books, but though he admired the beauty of other books, the Compostela *Codex Calixtinus* volume is the only one from which he copied passages.

Münzer made nineteen summaries from the *Pseudo-Turpin*, beginning with Charlemagne's vision, and ending with the conversion of Altumaior, after Charlemagne's death. Most of these are adaptations rather than direct quotations. The result is an epitome of the entire work, a sort of *Reader's Digest Condensed Books* version of Turpin, leaving out most non-military matters, such as the lengthy debate between the pagan Agoland and the Christian Roland, and the miracle of the lances, which predicts the fate of Charlemagne's soldiers at Pamplona. Magical elements such as Roland's fight with the giant are also omitted. The result is a sober, chronicle-like account of Charlemagne's military struggles in Spain and the final Christian victory.

When he came to consider Book I, Münzer copied none of the liturgy as such, no hymns, verses or responses, and certainly no music. His brief excerpts from Book I seem mostly to be aimed at establishing the evidence for the validity of the early cult of James, and the reason for pilgrims wearing the shell. The two "prayers" he gives are excerpted, with some condensation, from sermons ascribed to Calixtus. Given the lush and hyperbolic rhetoric of these passages, one wonders if his concluding excerpt, on the virtues of the plain style, was copied ironically.

The translation of Münzer's travels, as they concern Compostela and the *Pseudo-Turpin*, follows below. Material from the *Codex Calixtinus* comes where it came in Münzer's text. Pfandl ("Ein unbekannte") has been collated with Hämel. The folio numbers for the *Pseudo-Turpin* extracts are supplied from Hämel's article. Since they differ from the current foliation of the manuscript CC folio numbers are also given. For the extracts from Book I, folio numbers are taken from the detailed description of the manuscript in Stones and Krochalis (vol.

2). The rest of the narrative appears as it is given by Pfandl (93-9 and 143-4). Materials in brackets are my own clarifications. Place names appear in their modern Spanish form; if Münzer's version differs markedly, it is given in the footnotes. If the identification is uncertain, Münzer's form appears in the text and the suggested identification in the footnotes.

THE ITINERARY OF HIERONYMUS MÜNZER

On the thirteenth [of December 1494], setting out eagerly before sunrise, we came to the very ancient town of Padrón, once called Iria.[18] There, on first going into the very ancient church of St. James, we saw a stone column under the high altar, with that very concavity in which the body of St. James is said to have lain.[19] Then we went out to the river bank[20] where [we saw] the ship which brought St. James with some disciples from Judea without oars, who placed the body upon a rock, which accepted the holy body, just as wax flows—as you will find at greater length in his legend; by ascending the mountain[21] beyond the bridge, we even saw the place where he preached to the Gentiles—which is a certain pile of great stones, in the form of a pyramid, and with a flat place on the highest stone, like a chair. We even saw the chapel there, under which is a working fountain which they say blessed James turned into a rock with a blow of his staff. And the water, which we drank, is sweet and soft, and flows well.

Having seen these things, we went sedately for four leagues to the most holy city of Compostela,[22] in which, as they say, the body of Blessed James the greater, son of Zebedee and brother of John the Evangelist, lies entire.

Of the Site of Compostela of St. James

On December 13, we came to Compostela, whose site is circled on all sides by hills. And in the middle another hill rises, as if it were to be situated in the center of the circle. Nor does it have any river, but it does have many good fountains showering sweet water. And it is not large, but it is old, and fortified with a very ancient wall, with many very strong towers. For its land is good, and the gardens of the city are full of oranges and lemons, apples, pears, plums and other fruits. But the people there are porcine—and it has many pigs, which are available in a good market—and [they are] lazy, because they do little to cultivate the land, so that they live mostly on the pilgrim trade. They have good air, and many monasteries both within and without the walls, such as the monastery of St. Dominic,[23] in which a man, a most learned preacher, showed me many things. Item, the monastery of St. Benedict, whose abbot the king in Castile deposed, and had expelled because he had dissipated so much of the [abbey's] goods.[24] Item, the monastery of St. Clare;[25] of the Carmelites;[26] of the Friars minor.[27] The king—may God long protect his life—also plans an Augustinian reform.

On the Church of St. James
The Church of St. James is one of the three principal churches, after Rome, and Ephesus, which has now perished. It was built by Charlemagne, King of the Franks and Emperor of Germany. Afterwards you will hear about his wars; he had it built from the spoils and gifts and booty of the Saracens. And it is a stupendous cruciform work.[28] The length of the nave is one hundred paces, and the length of the arms one hundred and twenty; the width of the arms fifteen, and the width of the nave and the head one hundred and fifty. And it is all made and vaulted with very strong square stones. And it has two side aisles like the church of St. Sebald [Nürnberg].[29] And at the head, chapels in a ring. And that actually is the strongest work. And it has four towers at the four corners, and today the strongest tower is being built.

Image of the Church of St. James
There are twelve chapels around the choir, and the vault at the head of the crossing point is the highest. In the middle of it, a great thurible is swung from side to side of the arms with aromatic smoke.

Pope Calixtus, that singular lover of St. James, wrote a great and diffuse work divided into four books about his deeds, and the redemption of Galicia by Charlemagne. Likewise his [i.e., St. James'] many miracles. And I excerpted the following, in brief bits, while I was at Compostela in the house of a certain chaplain, a most devout man, John Ramus, from his original, as follows. December 14:[30]

On the Apparition of St. James to Charlemagne
1. *[CC f. 163; chapter 1]*[31] Charlemagne, after many labors with the cooperation of God, had put England, France, Germany, Italy et cetera, under the holy imperial rule, and had been zealous against the pagans, and, worn out by his exertion, proposed to take a long rest. But the Apostle James appeared to him in rapt ecstasy at night, saying, "My body lies unrecognized in Galicia, and I marvel that you, having subdued all other territories, do so little to liberate my land, occupied by Saracens. Go, therefore, as quickly as you can. I will be your helper." When James had indeed appeared to him three times, Charles, trusting in the apostolic promise, having gathered his army together, entered Spain, and continued to attack Spain and then Galicia for thirteen years.

2. *[CC f. 165; chapter 2]* First he set siege to Pamplona, ringed about with very strong walls, for three months, and then, having broken through the walls with divine help, he seized it, baptized the pious, and ordered those refusing the faith to be slaughtered. Having heard these things, the Saracens came hurrying to Charles from all sides, offering him tribute, and all Navarre became his tributary. Then, having visited the tomb of St. James, he came to Petronius, today called Padrón, and

fixed his lance in the sea, giving thanks to God and St. James. Truly he regenerated the Galicians, who after the preaching of St. James and his disciples had fallen away from the faith, and were now baptized by Archbishop Turpin. He either had the rebels killed, or took them captives, and then subjugated all Spain to himself.

3. [CC f. 166v; chapter 5] Remaining in Galicia and Spain for three years, Charles ordered the basilica of St. James to be built from the gold which the Spanish kings gave to him, and established a bishop and canons according to the rule of St. Isidore the bishop, and bedecked it [the basilica] suitably with bells, ornaments and other things. On going into France, he made the church of the Blessed Virgin at Aix-la-Chapelle from the rest of the gold. Item, in Aix, a church of St. James. Item, St. James at Toulouse. Item, that [church of St. James] which is in Gascony. Item, St. James of Toulouse, and innumerable abbeys throughout the whole world.[32]

4. [CC f. 166v; chapter 6] However, Charles having returned to France, a certain Saracen[33] king Agoland rose up. With his army, he subjugated all Spain to himself again, having killed the Christians protected by Charles. Charles therefore returned to Spain, with a certain leader of his army, whose name was Milo de Angleris.

5. [CC f. 167v; chapter 8] They found Agoland in the land which is called Tierra de Campos, beside the river Cea.[34] After fighting for a long time in a fierce fight, forty thousand Christians fell, and with them the leader Milo. Charles, however, standing on foot with two thousand foot soldiers, with his unsheathed sword, which is called Gaudiosa,[35] sliced many Saracens in half. Towards evening on that day, therefore, the Saracens and the Christians met each other in the field. On the second day came four border lords from Italy with four thousand warriors in Charles' service. Agoland,[36] hearing this, fled into Limoges, the province next to Betin.[37] Having achieved the victory, Charles returned to France.

6. [CC ff. 168-168v; chapter 9] Afterwards Agoland, having gathered to himself Saracens, Moors, Ethiopians, Pards, Africans, Arabs,[38] and many of their kings, regained the whole of Spain. After a long time, however, Charles, having collected an army, came to Agen and there besieged Agoland for six months. Then Agoland, with his forces, secretly left through a hidden gap in the walls. The city yielded to Charles, and he triumphed in it.

7. [CC ff. 169v-170; chapter 11] But Charles, meanwhile, having been conquered by Agoland, entered France, and gave all slaves their liberty, and began enclosures for convicts, gave punishments to all evil doers, reconciled himself to all his enemies, and collected an army of 134,000 soldiers. And he went into Spain, with those whose names were: Turpin, Archbishop of Rheims, who wrote this history; Roland, leader of the army, count of Le Mans and lord of Blaye and nephew of Charles; Milo, duke of the Angleri;[39] the count of Gembloux;[40] the count of Limoges;[41] Aristagus, king of the Britains; Eugelerus, duke of Aquitaine; Gaudebodus,[42] king of Frisia; Namaan, duke of Bavaria, with ten thousand men; Ogier, king of Denmark, with ten thousand men; Lantbert, duke of Bourges; Samson, duke of Burgundy, with ten thousand men; Constantinus, prefect of Rome, with twenty thousand men; and Charles indeed, having collected an innumerable army, they all entered Spain through Gascony, and gathered at a certain field, twelve leagues broad.

8. *[CC ff. 170v-171v; summary of chapter 12]* Agoland, however, seeing such a great army, came to Charles, and, pledges having been given and a pact initiated, they first conducted a long disputation about each other's faith, and which was better; nonetheless they began a war, [having agreed] that, whoever's faith should be better, to him would come the victory, and whoever was conquered would assume the faith of the victor.

9. *[CC f. 172v; chapter 14]* For the army of Charles was 134,000, and that of Agoland indeed 100,000. Therefore, entering into war, many Saracens fell. The army of Agoland, completely encircled by the Christian army, was therefore cut to pieces. Indeed Arnald, prince of Bellande, rushed in first with his army, and cut down everyone, right and left, until he came to Agoland, who was in the middle, and he struck him with his own sword. Nor did any Saracen evade him, except the king of Seville, and Altumayor of Cordoba, who took flight with a few Saracens. Behold how Charles did battle for the pact for the Christian faith, and killed Agoland.

10. *[CC f. 173; chapter 15]* Having accomplished this slaughter, however, certain Christians eager for spoil, unknown to Charles, left the battlefield by night and gathered up gold and silver for themselves. When Altumayor of Cordoba, lying hidden in the mountains, sought them out, he slew them all at once. And there were a thousand of them.

11. *[CC ff. 177v-178v; chapter 19]* Therefore, Spain having been conquered after many individual battles, Charles came to Compostela, and ordained priests and bishops throughout the cities. And he established that in future, all nobles, princes and bishops of Spain should obey the bishop of St. James.[43] And he wished it to be an apostolic see in the west, just as Ephesus, dedicated to blessed John, once was in the east. For according to the Christian religion, three principal churches are to be venerated: Ephesus in the east, Compostela in the west, and Rome in the center. The first is dedicated to John, the

second to James and the third to Peter. With these, God united his secret[44] places before the rest.

12. [CC f. 178v; chapter 20] As Turpin wrote in the same place, Charles was brown-haired, rosy-faced, attractive and handsome in body, fierce in gaze, eight feet in height with his feet extended to their greatest length,[45] very broad-shouldered, lean-hipped, broad-chested, with large arms and legs, certainly most learned, and a very bold soldier.

Many things might be written about the battle of Roland and his death, which, for the sake of brevity, I have not excerpted.[46]

13. [CC ff. 179-180; chapter 21] Having therefore subdued all Spain, Charles readied himself to go into France. There were, however, in Seville, two Saracen kings, namely Masirus and Beligandus his brother, who had been sent by the emir of Babylon in Persia to Spain. They had submitted to the imperial power of Charles, but in feigned charity. Charles ordered through Ganelon that they undergo baptism, or send tribute. They sent him thirty horses burdened with gold and silver, and forty horses burdened with very sweet wine, for the warriors to drink, and a thousand beautiful Saracen maidens to deflower. Truly, they gave much gold to the traitor Ganelon, so that he would betray the warriors into their hands, which he did. For the traitor returned to Charles with gifts, saying the kings would come into France, and would receive baptism. The warriors truly accepted the wine, but not the women.[47] Charles, therefore, believing Ganelon's words, made ready to return to France via the pass of Cize.[48] From there, having accepted the advice of Ganelon, Charles issued orders to his closest companions:[49] to Roland, count of Le Mans and [count of Blaye and Oliver][50] count of Gembloux, that they form the rear guard with the best warriors and twenty thousand Christians, while Charles went through the Port of Cize with the rest of the army, which was done. But because on the preceding night some were drunk with Saracen wine, and some contaminated from depravity, they perished in death. What more? While Charles went through the pass with twenty thousand and with Turpin and Ganelon, and the other best men formed the rear guard, behold! Marsirus and Beligandus set out in the early morning with fifty thousand Saracens from the woods and hills where they had lain hidden for two days and nights on the advice of the traitor Ganelon, making two troops, one of twenty, the other of thirty thousand. That with twenty thousand began to attack us from the rear, and, our forces being unprepared, all fell as one, from in front and behind, in a varied image of death, except Roland and Baldwin and Theodoric, who, dispersed through the woods, lay hidden, etc.

14. [CC chapter 21, f. 180v; chapter 22] The battle being finished, Roland therefore returning, found a certain dark Saracen, fatigued with the battle, who, by his threatening appearance (and with the help of a hundred Christians) was shown to be Marsirus himself; rushing in to their midst, he killed him. With one hundred dead, and himself gravely wounded with four lances, Roland nevertheless evaded them there. Charles, however, had already gone over the Pyrenean mountains, and did not know what had happened behind his back. Roland, however, worn out with such a great battle, came on foot to the pass of Cize, and, sitting under a certain tree, drew forth his very strong sword, which was called Durendal, that is, strong blow. He said, "O most beautiful sword! Who again will use your strength? How much have I done through you!"

15. [CC chapter 21, f. 181v; chapter 23] And he made[51] a great sound with the horn, which Charles, at a nod from God, heard at a distance of eight leagues. And, wishing to return to Roland, he was forbidden by the advice of Ganelon, who said that Roland sounded the horn in the daytime for very slight cause. So, having made a very beautiful prayer to God in the agony of death, [Roland] journeyed to the Lord. Meanwhile, Baldwin, hastening to Charles on Roland's horse, which he found by chance, soon told him everything in order. Having been hidden in the woods, he had rushed to Roland at the sound of the horn, and, while he was seeking water to refresh Roland, Roland died in his absence.

16. [CC chapter 21, f. 183v; chapter 25] Charles, instantly returning, embraced the dead Roland with a great groan, saying "O right arm of my body, best beard, ornament of the French, sword of justice, inflexible spear, incorruptible shield!" et cetera. "Why do I not die with you?" et cetera.[52]

17. [CC chapter 21, summary of ff. 184v-188; chapter 26] On the next day, therefore, in the morning, they came back to Roncesvalles, to the place of his death, with a great army. They found some dead, some half alive. The king therefore swore by almighty God to follow the pagans wherever he might find them. The day had been prolonged by the sun standing, and therefore he found the Saracens stationed beside the River Ebro,[53] near Seville and eating, and, having destroyed four thousand, returned to Roncesvalles. For, having found the traitor Ganelon, he had him bound and torn apart by four horses.

18. [CC chapters 21-23, fol. 189v; chapter 27] However he had the bodies of the dead preserved, some with myrrh, some with balsam, some with salt, and brought to Arles and Bordeaux, and magnificently entombed there. But the greater part were buried in the place where they fell. Roland was buried in the basilica of St. Romanus at Bordeaux,[54] the king of Brittany was buried at Nantes. Afterwards, Charles went to Arles, where he found the Burgundian army, who had buried their embalmed ones there. After coming to Vienne, the king returned to

Paris, where he gave many privileges to the bishop and church of St. Denis. And he made all Paris, with the province encircling it, free in honor of St. Denis. Therefore what was once called Gaul is now called France, that is free. Afterwards Charles came through Lyons to Aix-la-Chapelle, and commanded a beautiful palace to be built, and endowed a church of the Blessed Virgin.

19. [CC chapter 25, f. 190; Appendix C] However, after the death of Charles there arose a certain Saracen Altumayor of Cordoba, who, having entered Galicia, despoiled the church of St. James in all ways.[55] However, divine vengeance followed; some perished from a flux of the gut, others became blind. King Altumayor having been likewise blinded, pleaded with the God of the Christians, and Saint James, so that if they would restore his sight, he would give a church to the greater ones. Having been restored to health in a fortnight, he gave the church twice over, and withdrew to Cordoba. However, in the passage of time, such great wars and calamities occurred between the Mohammedans and Christians, as you will find widespread in the history of Spain; likewise in the *Fortification of Faith.*[56]

[CC ff. 52v-53; Hämel ff. 47-47v] Saint James[57] first preached in Judea, and then came to Galicia. After remaining there a short while, however, he returned to Judea, and had his head cut off by Herod. All of these things are found more clearly in his legend, which is called *Jacobus.*[58] Although[59] many apocryphal[60] things were written concerning his translation to Galicia, nevertheless, having rejected them all, Calixtus accepted this history, which is called *Jacobus,* as sufficiently authentic.[61]

Pope Calixtus further says, that, when he had been beheaded, his head did not fall to the ground, but [62] he held it in his arms, nor could any persecutor snatch it away by any means. At night, however, his disciples arriving, found his very body kneeling.[63] And they placed his body and head in a deerskin bag, with spices, and, accompanied by an angel, *[f. 53]* transported it across the sea from Jerusalem to Galicia, and buried it at the place in which it is venerated today. And St. James was beheaded in the eleventh year after the passion of the Lord. How indeed queen Lupa of Galicia behaved, you may read in more detail[64] in the history.

[CC f. 71; Hämel f. 62v] **A Beautiful Exclamation**[65]
Rejoice, therefore, Galicia, displayed in such great radiance, having cast out shame at the error of superstitions. Rejoice because, by the arrival of such a great guest you have cast out bestial ferocity, and have placed your neck, heretofore indomitable, under the yoke of Christ. For the humility of St. James has brought you more than the immensity of all your kingdoms. For they have polluted you by sacrifices with tricks;[66]

he has cleansed you in delivering the true cultivation of God. Happy is Spain in the abundance of many things, but happier still in the presence of blessed James. Once you had been glorious for the pillars of Hercules; now indeed more happily supported by the column of James. Hercules enticed you to the devil in pernicious superstition. James linked you to his creator. You spread infidelity by stony columns; here you have acquired gracious salvation for yourself.

Venerating therefore his solemnity, let us conquer the desires of our flesh, lest the impurities of the libido stain us, lest the arrogance of elation puff us up. Let us not be easily inflamed to wrath, nor twisted by envy in malice. Let us struggle that we may be like unto him, if we wish our prayers to be accepted . . . . [f. 73] For neither the savagery of the Jews, nor the arrogance of the Pharisees, has subdued him, nor has the insanity of Herod pulled James back from the true God. Therefore let us not be moved by a superabundance of riches, nor smoothed down by carnal emoluments, nor terrified by the torments of savage rulers, so that we may not follow the offices of such preaching. . . .

[CC f. 76; Hämel f. 66v][67] We believe in [the account of] his translation, however, as I have said above, in that authentic book which is called *Jacobus*, scorning other versions. For here *Jacobus* refers to those things which are necessary for reading, or for singing on festive days. Let us therefore rejoice in James on earth, whom the angels celebrate in the celestial court. . . . *[CC f. 79v; Hämel f. 69v]* Behold, the city of Compostela is made holy through the suffrages of blessed James. For this is the salvation of the faithful, and the protection of those coming into it. O, how awesome is this holy place, in which the holiest members of the Apostle, who touched God in the flesh, are hidden. Therefore the great James glitters in miracles in Galicia, and glitters in other places. . . .

[CC f. 80; Hämel f. 70r] Therefore, let us go as pilgrims on a proper pilgrimage, which is the rooting out of vices, the mortification of bodies, the raising up of virtues, the remission of sins, the penitence of penitents, the way of the just, the delight of the saints, the faith of resurrection, the distancing of hell, and the propitiation of heaven. It diminishes rich foods, restrains the maw of the gut, and tames lust. It represses carnal desire, purifies the spirit, provokes men to contemplation, humbles the lofty, blesses the humble, delights in poverty, hates the counting up of riches of avarice.

On Scallops, That Is, Muschlen. Calixtus[68]

[CC f. 81; Hämel f. 71] There are fish in the sea of blessed James having two shields, [one] on each side, between which, as between two tiles, lies the fish, on the model of an oyster. The tile on top is sculptured like the fingers of a hand. The common people call them

nidulas,[69] the French indeed *crusellas*, the Germans *muschelas*. Pilgrims returning from the threshhold of St. James place them in their caps, both in honor of the Apostle, and as a sign that they have gone themselves in person on such a journey. By the two shields are signified the two precepts of charity, by which the wearer should conduct his life, one always to delight in God above all, and to love his neighbor as himself. He loves God who keeps his commandments, and his neighbor, indeed, who would not do to another what he would not wish done to himself.

[CC f. 81; Hämel f. 71a] O pilgrims of St. James, do not lie with that mouth with which you have kissed his altar! With those feet on which you have indeed taken every step, do not go to places of depravity. With those hands with which you have touched the altar, do not work any evil. If you wish to have the strength and help of his patrons, have St. James as a lover. . . .

The Prayer of St. James. Calixtus[70]
[CC f. 92v; Hämel f. 81v] O blessed James the great, beloved of Christ, olive branch,[71] son of Zebedee, brother of John the Evangelist, who with the Lord dost reign happily in the citadel of heaven, whose famous site is established in Galicia, who brings salvation to his petitioners, grant that those who seek thee, whether there or elsewhere, may receive all healthful things, insofar as they seek Him, or trust in Him for all their necessities, may they be aware of thee as an intercessor, face to face with God in heaven. May you be the guardian of our souls on the day of our departure, o advocate of pilgrims. For you are the ornament of the Spanish, the refuge of the poor, the strength of the weak, consoler of those in tribulation, safety of pilgrims, fisher of souls, eye of the blind, foot of the lame, hand of the dry, safety of sailors, intercessor for those people calling upon you, father of all, destroyer of vices, builder of virtues, we seek you with a humble heart, that you may continuously extinguish the fires of vices.

[CC f. 1] In[72] a humble style indeed, Pope Calixtus wrote these things, so that they should be as clear to the learned as to the unlearned. For he says the outer shell is of too little use, unless the morsel within appears. (It is better) for pure liquid to show more clearly what it has within it, and for the candle to display its light more fully, so that it may shine for all, than to give to some and deny to others.

These[73] things I have excerpted from the great and diffuse work of Calixtus, as I have noted above in the prohemium.[74]

On the Archbishop, Cardinals and Canons and Relics
Calixtus the Pope gave this church many privileges, and today the archbishop is Don Alfonsus, count of Fonseca, a learned man and a

great orator.[75] And he is now sixty years old, and has always incited civil wars. And he has weakened many things in this district of Galicia. The king, however, now guiding the reins of Spain with a stronger hand, called him to Salamanca, as if from exile, and deprived him of his temporal powers, and, his own powers being restored, permitted him to live there. And he [Ferdinand] reformed the whole of Galicia with new laws and institutions. May that most serene king live eternally!

The church has forty-five canons, among whom are seven, ordained by an institution of Calixtus, who alone are permitted to celebrate mass on the high altar of St. James, and they are called cardinals of St. James. [This privilege] is also allowed to the archbishop and other bishops coming here, but to none other. And the benefices of the canons are seventy ducats, excepting occasional benefits.[76]

The king of Castile gave it very beautiful ornaments.[77] King Louis of France, father of that Charles, gave it many things; among the rest, at the end he gave the church three great bells and ten thousand *écus*, which the canons divided among themselves, and for another portion they bought very beautiful ornaments. And the king's insignia, with lilies, is inserted everywhere.

On December 16, which was the third day before the feast of St. Thomas, they had the great feast of St. Fructuosus, bishop, whose body lies there,[78] where they had most beautiful ornaments, with the lilies of the king of France, in a great procession. Item, December 18, which was the fifth day before Thomas, they celebrated the feast of the Blessed Virgin, which the Spanish do.[79] And the name [of the feast] is the feast of the expectation of the incarnation of the Lord. And [they celebrate it] with marvellous solemnity, and a procession, and incense in the middle of the choir, and with golden ornaments made from purest gold, which the King of Castile gave them. And on the reverse was the insignia of the kingdom of Castile and Aragon, all in gold and gems. O how great is that King in his gifts to the churches, and also in their reformation!

On the same feast of the Blessed Virgin, the high altar was decorated with two images of saints, which were of thirty and twenty-five and forty marks of silver gilt. Nevertheless, as they said, the [image of] the Blessed Virgin was the greatest among the rest, made from the purest gold; in her right hand she had a shining sceptre, and in her left the infant, her son, with a superb crown. A cardinal carried it in procession, singing the command for silence,[80] under a veil, which two priests were holding. There was also a very great cross, decorated with gems and gold, which was shown to the pilgrims in the sacristy, under guard. I have a copy of the relics at Compostela on a loose page.[81]

Of the Chapels of the Choir of St. James

Among the twelve chapels circling the choir, the first is that of the King of France, which he had built, and granted two hundred ducats for some years, so that individual hours should be sung in it. The canons, however, taking up the fee, sing the hours only in the main choir. Item, among these twelve chapels, there are seven, which are parishes of all Compostela, where the better members of the parish are buried, and are offered the sacraments. We saw two dead men buried; before the corpse of one they carried a flask full of wine, two bags of bread, two hindquarters of beef, and two of mutton, which belonged to the parishoner, and with this the best garment of the dead man. These are their customs. And it is allowed that they sing the hours and the offices, diligently, in choir, but nevertheless they raise their voices, complaining. And there is such a great clamor of people in the church continually, that you could not believe it. This is their fashion of devotion! It would be worthy of the holiest apostle that he should be venerated with greater reverence. Indeed, he is believed to be buried under the high altar with his two disciples, of whom one is on his right, and the other on his left. No one, however, has seen his body. Even when the King of Castile himself was here, in the year of our Lord 1487, he did not see it. We believe on faith alone, which saves us men.

Of the Departure from Compostela

On December 21, we bid farewell to St. James; we left after breakfast, and went five leagues to the small village Ferreiros, and had bad hospitality. In the morning we rode for nine leagues through Mellid[82] to the small village of Ligonde..[83] Item, 24 leagues to the village of Puertomarín; across the great river to Sarria, a small castle,[84] we came eight leagues. All this district has fertile farmland and is mountainous, but not thickly populated. And the people live largely on pork flesh, and truly in all their doings they are unclean and porcine.

Then on the twenty-fifth, which was the feast of Our Lord's Nativity, we rested for the whole day, and on that day, from a certain pilgrim I had single letters from Jodocus Mayer, the brother-in-law of my brother, which contained information about the great epidemic at Nürnberg.

Then on the morning of the twenty-sixth, we came through mountains and valleys, indeed, up the highest mountain to the village of Cebreiro,[85] which is on the top of the mountain called Malfaber.[86] And they were nine great leagues.

Then on the twenty-seventh, descending from the highest mountain, we came seven leagues through a long valley to the castle called Villafranca [del Bierzo]. The castle is situated in a lovely plain, and the best wines in abundance are born there. And it is adorned with two monasteries of St. Francis and St. Benedict. Three rivers flow together there from the highest mountains of Galicia and provide plenty of sweet, drinkable watering troughs.[87]

Then on the twenty-eighth, leaving Villafranca in the morning, we went eight leagues across that fecund plain and castle, called Ponferrada to the base of the highest mountain, to a village called Ryo.[88] This is however, the highest mountain dividing Galicia from Castile, and is very high. It is called Mons Rasanellus.[89]

On the twenty-ninth day, asending and descending the mountain for eight leagues, we came into Castile at a small village called Alval,[90] with bad hospitality. Rising on the thirtieth day before sunrise, riding briskly for ten leagues, we reached the city of Benevente. The way from Santiago to Benevente is fifty-six very long leagues, and mountainous and ill-maintained. However, we left aside the most illustrious city of Astorga, ornamented with a bishop and very strong walls and ditches. For from this city Astorga and from Cantabris, which they call Biscay,[91] all Spain, which once fell away from the Catholic law to the Mohammedan filth, has recovered. For only the [A]Sturians and the Biscayans remained strong soldiers in the faith of Christ, as you will see widely reported in the history of the Spaniards.

Pamplona, City of Navarre[92]
Pamplona, the best city in the kingdom of Navarre, is situated on a beautiful plain, and below it is a beautiful river. And this plain is large, filled with villages and towns, and abounds in wine and grain, but has no oil, because the place is at the base of the Pyrenees Mountains and Roncesvalles. It has a very beautiful cathedral church, whose choir is not yet finished; but it will be done shortly.[93] There are beautiful tables in the choir, with silver images. O how beautiful is the apse, in almost all ways like the apse of Toledo. The bishop today is the son of Pope Alexander VI. For on the death of the bishop at Rome, the apostolic honor was granted to his son.[94] He [the bishop] has, indeed, other beautiful churches and many monasteries. And it is a city as large as Ulm.

On the Kingdom of Navarre
The kingdom of Navarre is large. For after going out of Zaragoza along the banks of the Ebro[95] for four leagues, Navarre begins. And going out of Pamplona towards France for thirty leagues, we rode into that kingdom. For indeed the king having died without a son, the kingdom passed to his daughter, who married a Frenchman, lord John of Labrit. He has now been declared king on behalf of his wife.[96] But he does not hold power peacefully. For he has been greatly molested by the Count of Irún, who is suspected of having the help of the king of Castile. And

in these days he is keeping himself away, in a good town called Olite, in which were all his arms.[97] However we met the king near Toledo, through the mediation of the lord bishop Coseran of Gascony. We saw him, we kissed his hand. He is a tall figure, long and devout. The queen however was passing lugubrious days, on account of the recent death of her mother, the Countess of Foix. Therefore we could not see her. She[98] was the sister of King Louis. She was married previously to King Ladislaw, killed by poison at Lerick, it is said. And afterwards she married the Count of Foix, who was the king of Navarre. The king himself offered to do for us whatever we might desire, and this was accomplished through the mediation of the bishop.

Leaving Pamplona after breakfast, on February 7, going for three leagues through a valley rich and fertile enough in wine and grain, we came to the highest mountain, Roncesvalles. There we found a monastery of canons, who have an adjoining hospice, where wine, bread, lodging and other things are lavished on the pilgrims. There in the church we saw, among other relics, the horn of Roland who died there, and outside the monastery a great chapel, in which are many thousands of Christians killed by the Saracens, in the time of Charles, as I have written more fully and diffusely in the history of Saint James—how the Christians, trapped in a narrow place without hope, were attacked and cut down by the Saracens, from before and behind. It is horrible to see. And in that mountain [the River] Ebro has its source. However, descending to the north thorough a horrible and wooded valley, we came nonethelesss to the gateway of the valley, at Saint-Jean-Pied-de-Port. And there Gascony begins (144).

NOTES

[1] The text of Münzer's travels through Spain was published, with a brief introduction, by Ludwig Pfandl ("Itinerarium Hispanicum Hieronymi Monetarii 1494-1495"). The description of Compostela is on pages 93-9. In that article, Pfandl omitted the excerpts Münzer made from the manuscript he saw at Compostela. He listed and discussed these excerpts, printing them in full in another article, "Eine unbekannte handschriftliche Version zum *Pseudo-Turpin*." Because of the war, he was unable to consult the still unprinted *Codex Calixtinus* to compare Münzer's version, but he noted where Turpin material came in Castets' 1880 edition of the *Pseudo-Turpin*. The parallel texts of the *Codex Calixtinus* and Münzer's excerpts from Book I were printed by Adalbert Hämel, along with some brief comparisons of Turpin material, in "Hieronymus Munzer und der *Pseudo-Turpin*." I have made use of all three articles in my translation below. Parenthetical page references to Münzer's journey in the text are to Pfandl "Itinerarium." A brief account of his route to Spain, and his earlier travels, is in Goldschmidt, who supplies the names of his companions on p. 59.

[2] For Behaim, the best account in English is still Ravenstein's 1908 volume. The actual amount of his knowledge has been re-assessed by some modern geographers; see the entry in the *Encyclopedia Britannica*, with references.

[3] Boorde was unimpressed; like Münzer, he did not believe in relics he could not see. "There is not one heare nor one bone of saint Iames in Spayne in Compostell, but only, as they say, his stafe" (as cited in Davies and Davies 221).

[4] All references to Münzer's account are from Pfandl's transcription in "Itinerarium," unless otherwise specified.

[5] "Rex est homo mediocris stature, hilari et jocundo vultu cum quadam gravitate mixta. . . Regina autem est de 48 annis, senior Rege, statura procul et aliquantulum corpulenta, facie multum decora." According to an anonymous American traveller quoted by Prescott: "By the comparative heights of the armor [in the museum of the armory at Madrid], Isabella would seem to be the bigger of the two, as she certainly was the better" (1: 495; cited from *A Year in Spain, by a Young American* (Boston, 1829): 116).

[6] See Goldschmidt. The surviving volumes were then in the Fürstlich Dietrichsteinische Fideikommiss-Bibliothek, in the Schloss Nikolsburg in Mähren. For a description of Clm 431, see Goldschmidt 112-3. He records the existence of another copy, now lost, in the posesion of the Nürnberg bibliographer G. W. Panzer; it was in his sale catalogue, January 1907.

[7] His manuscript of Terence probably dates from that period. He also owned a manuscript psalter; a few items, such as the excerpts from Galen (no. 78) and related medical texts, were copied in his student days in 1477.

Volumes such as a Herbal and Physiognomy (no. 92) were copied or glossed *manibus suis*. As late as 1494, he copied Aristotle, *De celo et mundi*, correcting it from an incorrect volume, and glossed his *Opera nonnulla* thoroughly, but when he could, he bought printed editions. There is a printed Galen in his collection (Venice, 1490; no. 77), suggesting a desire to supplement or replace the manuscript. See Goldschmidt.

[8] "Et credo in tota Europa fructus maritimos in tanta perfeccione vix esse."

[9] "Coquina item patrum superba est."

[10] "Chorus autem patrum in posteriori parte ecclesie in alto est et magnus cum pulcris sedilibus et maioribus libris cantus, sicut in vita mea unquam vidi" (Pfandl 108). "Habent item inter se peritissimos pictores, scriptores, illuministas, aurifabros, ornamentarios, quod non est dicendum. O quam preclaros libros missales, omnes splendide illuminatos vidimus! Est item mirabilis fabrica tocius monasterii omnia ad commoditatem et decorem facta" (Pfandl 115).

The *-as* ending on *illuministas* does not imply female illuminators (on which one would expect Münzer to comment), but uses the originally Greek agent suffix *-ista*, found also in *evangelista*. The usual word for illuminators of either sex is *illuminator*.

[11] "In ambitu eius sunt ultra 20 altaria nobilibus et deauratis tabulis, item nobilis libraria, item ortus ex aranciis, limonibus, cipresso" (Pfandl 6).

[12] "quod stupendum est dictu."

[13] ". . . una aula maximis libris plena, ut magnam bibliotecam crederes, ubi annalia in singulo libro pro anno sunt scripta, nedum in vectigalibus et regimine, sed in singulis aliis. Et si quis dubium habuerit in aliquo gesto ante multos annos et diem vel annum notaverit, tunc in singulis ex annalibus illis potest cernor effici" (Pfandl 12-3).

[14] "Item Bibliam in tribus voluminibus, et duo folia semper subtilissime bituminata de pergameno virgineo, ut in marginibus foliorum primo textus, et sub eo corpus misticus, et in medio ymagines ex auro et lasurio illuminate historiam representantes. Credo in mundo non esse similem Bibliam. O quam egregia erat coopertura ex samato cum gemmis, perliis et aliis decorata" (Pfandl 118).

The three volumes of the thirteenth-century *Bible Moralisée* presented by Saint Louis IX of France to King Alfonso X are still in the Cathedral library (Robertson 313). For study of their decoration, see Branner and Laborde.

[15] The ceiling, painted by Fernando Gallego not long before Münzer saw it, was in the University Library until the eighteenth century, when the library became a chapel. Part of the ceiling was removed to the Sala Calderón de la Barca, in the Escuelas Menores, where it may still be seen. See the Michelin *Tour Guide Spain.*

[16] "Est item in libraria ecclesie maioris liber astronomicus cum celi ymaginibus punctis, numeris et caracteribus, quem false credunt librum magicum esse" (Pfandl 104). Salamanca was noted in the fifteenth century for teaching the still-controversial Copernican theories. Münzer's remark sounds as though he accepted them too. They were gaining ground; Columbus consulted Salamancan astronomers before sailing.

[17] "Item librariam optimam habent de antiquissimis libris, omnibus in pergamento. Inter cetera vidi unum banckum, in quo 8 volumina optima, littera ytalica scripta. Et erant opera Beati Jeronimi super prophetas, ewangelia, bibliam et alia eius opera" (Pfandl 139).

[18] Münzer: Patron, Yria. The Roman name for Yria was Iria Flavia. Münzer spells it Patron, no doubt accepting the etymology which derives it from St. James the patron of Spain, or from the rock (*padron*) of which his stone sarcophagus was made, which is still in the parish church of Santiago at Padrón. See Otero Pedrayo, *Guía de Galicia* (496, 498), who says it is a Roman stone, with an inscription to Neptune on it. Yria Flavia was the early bishopric before Compostela, and the first 28 bishops of Iria Flavia are buried in the old cathedral there, several kilometers north of modern Padrón.

[19] The stone is still there, and measures 6.5 feet in height (*Spain: The Nagel Travel Guide Series*, 316).

[20] There are three rivers at Padrón. The Sar flows south to Padrón, the Ulla flows across the south part of the city to merge with the Arousa.The church of Santiago is on the east bank of the Sar. Earlier in the fifteenth century, the Barca, or boat-stone, was removed from the church and put into the river to keep it from pilgrims, who cut pieces off it. William Wey mentions that, nevertheless, in the dry season, pilgrims could climb down and shave fragments off it. See Hogarth, 18. Some certainly succeeded in getting fragments, for the 1346 inventory of the goods in the Chapelle du Marché of St-Omer included a reliquary given by the Lord Dean Bocheux: "In a certain crystal vessel, portions of the stone tables whereon God wrote the law for Moses with his finger. Item, in the same vessel, of the stone whereupon St. James crossed the sea" (Coulton 1: 169). The stone is now behind the altar front, which is opened to pilgrims by a custodian. Photography is not allowed, but postcards are available.

[21] The mountain is called Mount Padrón by Wey, but neither the stone, nor the fountain are named (Hogarth 18). A baroque Carmelite church now crowns the mountain.

[22] Compostela lies approximately 22 kilometers northeast of Padrón. Münzer's league is about three miles. Münzer consistently spells the city *Compostella*, as did most medieval authors, who interpreted its name as *campus stellae*, the plain of the star.

[23] Santo Domingo de Bonval, which is still one of the biggest churches in Compostela (Otero Pedrayo, *Guía de Santiago*, 101).

[24] Both San Martin Pinario, adjacent to the Cathedral, and San Pelayo were Benedictine houses. As part of the reform program, the two had been joined in 1487 by the bull *Meditatis cordis nostra* of Pope Innocent VIII. The abbot had been ejected in 1487, but by a bull of Ferdinand, *In apostolice dignitatis*, issued on January 31, 1493, the monastery was allowed to organize its own reform (García Oro 87).

[25] The monastery of St. Clare is on the Calle S. Roque, but the present buildings are eighteenth century.

[26] There is no Carmelite foundation Münzer could have seen still in Santiago de Compostela; the community of Carmelite nuns there was founded in 1760 (Otero Pedrayo, *Guía de Santiago*, 112).

[27] The Convento de S. Francisco de Valdedios is on the Calle de Jerusalem, north of the Cathedral. The fourteenth-century chapter house is still standing (Otero Pedrayo, *Guía de Santiago*, 112).

[28] All these features are marked on Münzer's accompanying diagram, reproduced in Pfandl 92.

[29] Münzer frequently compares churches to the thirteenth-century cathedral of St. Sebald in his native Nürnberg. For a plan and detailed description of the cathedral as it was in 1912 see Hoffmann. There is a scale plan between pages 42 and 43 (Tafel V), according to which St. Sebald measures 85 m long, 30 m wide, with a center aisle and two side aisles. There are two small transepts, about 8 m long and 5 m wide. The plan is reproduced, with no scale, in Nussbaum 160. It is the church where Münzer was buried (Goldschmidt appendix) and, in the seventeenth century, his descendants put up a panel painting, by Georg Gärtner the Younger, with his arms and those of his daughter's husband and their descendants. It was still in the church in 1912 (Hoffmann 162).

[30] On December 14, Münzer apparently saw either the *Codex Calixtinus* or perhaps a copy of it. His notes on the book follow. The abbreviation CC is used for the *Codex Calixtinus* in these notes.

1494: Hieronymus Münzer, Compostela, and the *Codex Calixtinus* 89

For a discussion of Münzer's *Pseudo-Turpin* summary compared with the *Pseudo-Turpin* in the *Codex Calixtinus* and the texts from Book I, see Hämel (92-8). For the complete texts from the *Pseudo-Turpin* and Book I, see Pfandl, "Eine unbekannte" (600-5). The question of whether Münzer saw the *Codex Calixtinus* itself, or a copy, has been discussed by Hämel, who concluded that he had another manuscript, probably one from version 2, and not, like CC, from version 1. He suggested a text more like the Pollinger codex, Munich Clm 11319, and comparing, for the order of Münzer's excerpts (*Pseudo-Turpin*, Book I, introduction) three manuscripts in Rouen: O. 34 (12c); U 134 (13c) and Y 198 (12/13c), all of which also lack Book V, the *Pilgrim's Guide*, from which Münzer does not quote. From the fact that Münzer refers to a four-book compilation, Hämel assumes that the version of the Calixtine compilation which Münzer read was not CC itself. This view is endorsed by Short.

The matter is further discussed by Stones and Krochalis in *The Pilgrim's Guide, Vol. II: Manuscripts and Texts*, under "Lost Manuscripts." Our conclusion is that, as Münzer's notes are all adaptations, rather than scrupulous copies, of the material in front of him, the evidence is inconclusive. Short makes much of his failure to include any information from the fifth book of CC, the *Pilgrim's Guide*, but as it is a short text perhaps he failed to notice that it formed a separate fifth book. He included nothing from the Calixtine chapter 26 of the *Pseudo-Turpin* (but see note 56). If Ramus had a second copy at Compostela, it has not survived. The matter is futher complicated by the fact that the Munich manuscript is Schedel's copy, in Schedel's hand, not Münzer's autograph.

[31] Pfandl includes the chapter numbers for the *Pseudo-Turpin* excerpts in Castets' 33-chapter edition of 1881. I have included them at the start of each passage. They are the same as those in the *Codex Calixtinus* and the related Vatican and British Museum manuscripts, until chapter 21. In the *Codex Calixtinus*, chapter 21 is very long, with subdivisions. Castets used several Montpellier manuscripts, which gave chapter numbers to the sections of chapter 21. His text had 33 chapters and four appendices. The first three correspond to CC chapters 24-26; the fourth is an excerpt about Julius Caesar found in CC as part of the *Pilgrim's Guide*, but separately in manuscripts in the *Libellus* tradition. Chapter numbers in CC, which has 26 chapters in all, precede Castet's chapters in parentheses when they begin to differ. Münzer's five excerpts from Book I follow the *Pseudo-Turpin*. The Latin texts are found in Pfandl, "Eine unbekannte" (568-608). The excerpts not from *Pseudo-Turpin* are also in Hämel (89-98), who supplies CC folio numbers for them. His foliation differs from that currently in the manuscript, so his folio numbers are given after the CC numbers. Differences in readings are recorded in the notes to the passages.

[32] The repetition of St. James of Toulouse is not found in CC.

[33] The word used is *affer*, which in Classical Latin meant African. Here it implies pagan, but the *Pseudo-Turpin* does not tell us whether Agolandus originally came from Africa or not.

[34] Münzer: *De Campis; Ceya.*

[35] The Latin form of the more familiar French *Joyeuse.*

[36] Münzer changes the spelling of the Saracen king's name here, perhaps misreading the more usual *Aigolandus,* which is found in CC, and the Vatican and British Museum manuscripts.

[37] Münzer: *Regionensibus.* CC: *Legionensibus*; the information that it is next to Betin is added by Münzer.

[38] The list in *Pseudo-Turpin* is: "Sarracenos. Mauros. Moabitas. Ethiopes. Sarrannos. Pardos. Affricanos. Persos." Münzer omits the *Moabitos* and the *Sarrannos.* CC also includes a long list of kings by name.

[39] In *Pseudo-Turpin,* Milo is mentioned here only as the father of Roland; he did not himself go on the Spanish campaign, though he was present in the earlier fighting against Agolandus.

[40] That is, Oliver.

[41] Named *Estultus* in *Pseudo-Turpin.*

[42] *Gandebodus* in *Pseudo-Turpin.*

[43] In fact, the primacy of Compostela was obtained from Pope Calixtus II by Archbishop Diego Gelmírez in a bull of 26 February 1120. Calixtus had earlier granted it to Toledo. See the discussion of his correspondence and the bull ascribed to Calixtus at the end of *Pseudo-Turpin* in Stones and Krochalis. See Shaver-Crandell, et al.

[44] The reference, as the longer passage in the *Pseudo-Turpin* makes clear, is to the Bible, where the secret things shall be made plain; so the importance of the three apostles who were with Christ in the garden of Gethsemane is made plain in these three churches of Peter, John, and James.

[45] If this phrase means that Charles was eight feet long when lying flat with his feet extended, then he would have been about seven feet tall when standing.

[46] Pfandl prints this sentence in a footnote, assuming it is Münzer's comment. It is certainly his phrasing, but reflects the content of the concluding sentences of chapter XX: "Magis deficit manus et penna quam eius hystoria. Quemadmodum tamen post deliberationem telluris Gallecie ab Yspania rediit ad Galliam, nobis breuiter est dicendum."

[47] In the full text of *Pseudo-Turpin*, some of the warriors take both.

[48] Münzer: *Portus Cisera*. The modern village nearest this pass is St-Jean Pied-de-Port. See the note in Melczer (280) about the various paths across it.

[49] Münzer: *carissimis ut*; Pfandl emends to *carissimis suis*, with a footnote assuming the influence of *ut* in the line below (603); CC: *carissimis suis*. Given Münzer's numerous other changes, the repetition of *ut* is quite possible, but the plural *carissimis* assumes that Oliver—or someone—was joined with Roland in this command; see note below.

[50] Münzer: *et Blauiensi comiti et Olivero* omitted; Roland was not count of Gembloux, and Oliver's presence is necessary both historically and syntactically, as both *carissimis* and *facerent* are plural.

[51] Münzer: *Faciensque*, but the syntax requires a main verb. CC reads: "Deinde proprio cornu cepit altis sonis tonitruare."

[52] Among the extra material which Münzer dismisses with *et cetera* are Charlemagne's comparisons of Roland to the Biblical heroes Samson and Judas Macchabeus, and himself and Roland to Saul and Jonathan, and to David and Absalom.

[53] Münzer: *Ebro*.

[54] Münzer: *Burdegalis*. According to the CC, Roland was buried at *Blavium* (Blaye), of which he was count. Münzer must have been reading in haste; several lines later, Roland's horn was unworthily moved to the basilica of St. Severinus at *Burdegallum*, or Bordeaux. Aristargus king of Brittany was buried, according to the CC, at *Belinum,* that is, Belin, where he died; it is 50 kilometers SW of Bordeaux.

[55] Münzer: *omnibus*, which could mean he despoiled the church in all ways or destroyed all the things in it. In CC, the phrase reads: "Similiter basilicam apostolicam indigne totam deuastavit, codices et mensas argenteas et tintinnabula et cetera ornamenta ab ea abstulit."

[56] Pfandl noted that this last sentence is pure Münzer (605). It may, however, pick up on a phrase near the beginning of the bull ascribed to Pope Calixtus with which the text concludes in CC: ". . . quanta mala quantasque calamitates et angustias Sarraceni in Yspania fratribus nostris Christianis inferre usi sunt audistis." Among Münzer's books was the *Fortalicium Fidei*, the first book printed on witchcraft, which included acccounts of wars against heretics, Jews, and Saracens, including Spanish campaigns. It was written by a converted Spanish Jew, Alphonsus de Spina (Hain 8316; Goldschmidt, no. 15. 117). There is an article on Alphonsus and a plate of the first edition in Robbins 26. Alphonsus died in 1491,

having been a professor at the University of Salamanca whose scholars impressed Münzer five years later.

[57] Now follow five excerpts from the CC Book I. The first passage is from the "Magna Passio" (ff. 52v-53), or the long version of the sufferings and martyrdom of James read on his major feast, July 25.

[58] The opening folio of the *Codex Calixtinus*, as well as of a number of later copies of it, refer to the volume as *Liber Sancti Jacobi* or *Jacobus*. For a full discussion of the titles in all twelve extant manuscripts, see Stones and Krochalis, "Qui a lu," and Stones and Krochalis' information in the forthcoming second volume of Shaver-Crandell and Gerson.

[59] This sentence is not printed by Hämel.

[60] Apocryphal, in this context, need not be pejorative; the word can simply mean that the tales are not in the Bible, and so lack that final authority. But, of course, lacking Biblical authority, they need not be believed, and Münzer's skepticism about elements in the legend is apparent elsewhere.

[61] "Calixtus illam historiam, que Jacobus dicitur, tamquam autenticam assumpsit." As Hämel noted, the *Codex Calixtinus* begins with the phrase: "Ex re signatur, Jacobus liber iste vocatur."

[62] Pfandl, *suis*; Hämel: *secis*. The parallel phrases in CC do nothing to clarify Münzer's text. They are *in brachiis suis* and *caput tenens in ulnis, donec veniret*.

[63] Münzer has omitted a sentence which in CC explains that James raised his arms to heaven, and knelt, holding his head in his arms, until nightfall.

[64] *Lacius leges* is Münzer's usual phrase when he is condensing or omitting a long narrative. In this case, the long version of the translation of St. James is in Book III of CC.

[65] Here is a second excerpt from Book I from a sermon ascribed to Pope Leo.

[66] Pfandl and Hämel: *dolis*; CC: *ydolis*, which makes a better contrast between idols and the true God.

[67] This and the following extracts from CC ff. 80v and 81r are from the sermon "Veneranda dies," ascribed to Pope Calixtus. This sermon and the entire LSJ Book II Miracles have been translated into English by Coffey, Davidson, and Dunn.

[68] This is the third excerpt. The heading was omitted by Hämel.

[69] That is, little nests.

[70] This is the fourth excerpt.

[71] CC: *alme*; Pfandl and Hämel, *olive*. Münzer copies this prayer almost word for word.

[72] This is the fifth excerpt.

[73] This sentence is omitted by Hämel.

[74] Here the excerpts from the *Codex Calixtinus* end, and Münzer resumes his discussion of the church (Pfandl 95).

[75] Alfonso III de Fonseca, Archbishop of Santiago from 1486 to 1508. He also became patriarch of Alexandria (Gams, 26). His disagreements with the crown were frequent, the most recent at the time of Münzer's visit being in 1493. See Garcia Oro (70-1).

[76] This must reflect the fifteenth-century pay scale. The system described in the twelfth-century *Pilgrim's Guide* is different. For information on practice at Compostela in various periods, and in other places such as St. Leonard of Noblat, see *The Pilgrim's Guide*, vol. 3, notes to chapter X.

[77] Ferdinand seems to have had a personal devotion to St. James. Münzer records that three banners floated over the Alhambra: one with an image of the crucified Lord, another with St. James, and the third the banner of the King of Castile (Pfandl 58). Münzer's word is *vexilla*, which means battle-standard. According to Prescott, at Cordoba in 1486 three standards were raised "on the summit of the principal fortress": one banner with the royal arms, one pennon of St. James, and the third a cross "of massive silver" given to Ferdinand by Pope Sixtus IV, which travelled with Ferdinand. Ferdinand and Isabella had been on pilgrimage to Compostela in 1486 (Prescott 1: 496).

[78] St. Fructuosus was bishop of Braga in the seventh century, and was originally entombed there; his feast day was April 16. But in 1102, when Diego Gelmírez visited Braga, he persuaded the bishop Giraldus that, since Braga had many bodies of saints, some particular saints could be more widely known and venerated at Compostela. So Gelmírez had the bodies of Sts. Fructuosus, Cucuphatus, and Silvester moved from Braga to Compostela. The feast celebrated at Compostela on December 16 is the translation. See *Acta Sanctorum II Aprilis*, 436-7 for Hugo of Compostela's

contemporary account of the translation, and *The Book of Saints* under *Fructuosus*.

79 Münzer has reversed the third and fifth days before the feast of the apostle Thomas, which is December 20. He is counting Roman fashion, including the day from which he is counting and the day of the feast. This makes December 16 the fifth day before the feast and December 18 the third day.

80 Pfandl prints *inquietem querendo*. One could translate *in quietem*, implying that the procession was silent, without music or chant. Given Münzer's description of later services, however, it might be preferable to assume that the procession was moving while chanting a command to the congregation to be silent.

81 Münzer's copy has not survived, but doubtless it was similar to the list given to William Wey, who quotes it extensively, and cited by Purchas and other pilgrims. See Hogarth 18, for a translation of Wey's account.

82 Münzer: *Lugardum de Melit.*

83 Münzer: *Melit.*

84 The remains of the castle can still be seen at Sarria (Robertson).

85 Münzer: *Sebroros.*

86 This is *Mons Februarii* in the twelfth-century *Pilgrim's Guide*. According to Melczer, *Februarii* is *Zebrarii* in the *Historia Silense*, giving *Cebreiro* in modern Galician (279).

87 Münzer: *truttis*. The usual meaning of this word is trout *(tructa)*, and this is the sense in which Münzer used it in praising the fish of Portugal, but derivation from *trunca*, a ditch or moat, is also possible, and seems more likely in the context. Münzer usually separates his discussion of food from that of natural features of landscape.

88 Unidentified; perhaps Riego de Ambros, Map 24, square 93 te.

89 The modern Monte Guiana (6070 feet) is in about the right place to be identified with Münzer's *Mons Rasanellus*.

90 Perhaps Altobar de la Encomienda, on what is now a minor road between the NVI and the Orbigo River about halfway between Astorga and Benevente. It is not far north of the modern Léon/Zamora provincial border.

91 Münzer: *Piscayos*; he also spells the inhabitants with a P.

[92] Here Münzer departed from the pilgrim route, which did lie through Astorga, and headed south for Salamanca. He rejoined the pilgrim route at Pamplona. At Roncesvalles, on 7 February 1495, Münzer recalled what he had read at Compostela (Pfandl 143-4).

[93] It was completed about 1525 (Robertson 110).

[94] Pope Alexander VI was Rodrigo Borgia. His son, the notorious Cesare Borgia, became bishop of Pamplona in 1491, at the age of eighteen (Gams 63). He replaced Bishop Alfonso Carrillo, who became bishop in 1477, and died at Rome in 1491. Cesare Borgia became a cardinal in 1492.

[95] Münzer: *Yber.*

[96] In 1434 Lenor, daughter of John II of Aragon (1425-79) and Blanche of Navarre, married Gaston Phoebus IV de Foix. Lenor inherited Navarre from her mother. Thus the counts of Foix became Kings of Navarre. Their son Gaston Phoebus died before his father in 1470; on the death of the elder Gaston in 1472, Navarre went to his grandson François, son of the dead Gaston. When François died in 1483, his sister Catalina (1493-1512) inherited the kingdom. She married Jean d'Albret (Münzer's *Lambroto*) in 1484. Ferdinand of Aragon's father was Catalina's great-grandfather, John II of Aragon; Ferdinand was the product of his much later second marriage, to Joan Henriquez. He is the king of Castile of Münzer's reference. This relationship did not stop Ferdinand from deposing Catalina in 1512. See O'Callaghan 675; Bisson, genealogical tables; and Prescott, *passim.*

[97] The castle of Olite was built between 1400 and 1419, and is now an impressive Spanish parador.

[98] That is, Catalina's mother, widow of the younger Gaston Phebus who died in 1470. She was Madeleine (Magdalena), daughter of Charles VII of France, and thus sister of Louis XI (1423-83). According to the entry on Ladislaw V of Bohemia (1440-57) in the *Encyclopedia Britannica*, she was betrothed but not yet married to him when he died mysteriously at Prague.

CHAPTER 5

The Pilgrimage to Santiago de Compostela in the *Cantigas de Santa Maria*

Connie L. Scarborough

Alfonso X, the Learned, compiled the *Cantigas de Santa Maria*[1] between 1257 and 1279. Of the 427 songs contained in this work, the majority are narrative in nature and relate miracles performed by the Virgin Mary. In his collection Alfonso includes the common stock of Marian miracles known throughout Western Europe, many of whose settings are found outside the kingdoms under Alfonso's governance. The King also includes, especially in the later sections of the book, many miracles of local interest dealing with sites in Spain and even miracles from which he had personally benefited. Considering that Alfonso's other literary enterprises—the *Estoria de España*, the *Gran y general estoria*, the *Siete partidas*, for example—were encyclopedic in scope, it should not be surprising that he planned his Marian collection to be all-encompassing, a compilation of all the miracle narratives and lyric songs which came into his purview.

While we would not dispute that one of the primary motivations for miracle collections in the Middle Ages was to foster devotion to shrines dedicated to a saint[2]—in the case of Alfonso, shrines dedicated to the Holy Mother—the Learned King's compilation was not specifically designed to attract pilgrims to any one specific shrine. While the pilgrimage route to Compostela figures as an important element in a number of miracles related in the *CSM*, the collection is unlike others devised for promotion of the cult of a particular saint. Alfonso's text is usually considered to be a highly personal work, as much a manifestation of the King's personal devotion to the Virgin as an offering to her in hope of his own salvation (Snow, "Central Rôle," 305-16). In Prologue B to his collection, Alfonso states his desire to sing Mary's praises:

> . . .eu
> quero seer oy mais seu trobador,
> e rogo-lle que me queira por seu
> Trobador e que queira meu trobar

reçeber, ca per el quer' eu mostrar
dos miragres que ela fez. . . .[3] (1: 55, vv. 18-23)

[. . .I wish from this day forth to be Her troubadour, and I pray that She
will have me for Her Troubadour and accept my songs, for through
them I seek to reveal the miracles She performed. . . .][4]

Horton and Marie-Hélène Davies define pilgrimage simply as "a
quest for the soul's well-being" (22). This same phrase could be applied
to Alfonso's motivation for composing the *CSM*.[5] The King's
metaphorical quest for salvation through literary composition, along
with the pilgrim's physical quest through journey and trials, became
intertwined in the great Marian collection to produce a literary religious
reality in which pilgrimage served not only as a realistic motivation of
plot, but also as a powerful metaphorical undercurrent.

For the Virgin Mary, as for her Son, there could be no tradition of
veneration of a body in a tomb due to belief in Christ's resurrection and
Mary's assumption into heaven. In this way, the Heavenly Mother
differed from all other saints and her shrines marked sites of her
appearance or perhaps housed a relic such as an item of her clothing or
vials of her milk. The Cathedral at Santiago de Compostela, of course,
housed the bodily remains of St. James and the object of the pilgrimage
was the veneration of his tomb. Despite the obvious difference between
devotion to Marian sites and devotion to shrines such as that of St.
James, certain overriding hagiographic patterns and traditions allowed
for the insinuation of the pilgrimage to Santiago de Compostela into
Marian legend.

One of the central messages of the *Cantigas* which deal with
pilgrims is that pilgrimage is fraught with peril. Undertaking a
pilgrimage involved risk and might entail the need for divine
intervention to bring the pilgrim safely to his/her destination. If such
was the accepted reality of making a pilgrimage, it is not at all
unexpected that miracle accounts should grow up along the principal
roads. These narratives often involve intervention by the saint to whose
shrine one is *en route,* but they often also deal with the divine
assistance of other saints and the Virgin Mary. Since one of the primary
aspects of Mary's divine power was her role as mediatrix, an
intermediary between humankind and the Godhead, it is not surprising
that she should come to the aid of pilgrims on the Road to Santiago.
Mary is the sinner's ultimate refuge and even serves as advocate for the
petitions made by other saints, before her Son in His position as Judge
and King of heaven. Even though sinners by definition, pilgrims are
intent upon an act of Christian devotion and the Virgin was seen as ever
vigilant of them. While, of course, the motives for undertaking a
pilgrimage were not always strict religious devotion or acts of penance

and contrition,[6] the motif nevertheless deftly lends itself to scenes of distress and danger. Beyond the obvious use of pilgrimage as a setting in which weary travelers, far away from home, exposed to the perils of the road would, in all likelihood, find themselves in need of miraculous delivery, it is precisely such divine intervention in one's life that the pilgrim seeks when setting forth on a journey. Often the pilgrimage was made in order to fulfill a vow: "Such a vow could be made in the case of recovery from a severe illness [or] one might have been in severe physical danger and promised to visit a shrine if one should be delivered from the peril" (Davies 27). Likewise, while *en route* many pilgrims became ill or fell into hazards, situations in which they would appeal to the saint to whose shrine they were traveling or to the Holy Mother herself, mediatrix between not only humankind and Christ but also between the other saints and her Son.

Additionally, there are several parallels between the cult of the Virgin Mary and that of St. James. Just as almost all the information we have about Mary's life comes from apocrypha and popular legend so, too, the information surrounding St. James is largely the product of subsequent legend and invention. Stories concerning the childhood of the Virgin, her power to perform miracles during her lifetime, as well as her death and assumption into heaven are all based on non-Biblical materials. Similarly, the stories about St. James preaching the gospel in Spain and the belief that his body was brought to Spain by his followers and buried in Galicia are not based on historical record. There is no reference before the sixth or seventh century of St. James' having preached in Spain[7] and the first written evidence of the *Translatio* of his remains from Judea to Galicia is from the ninth century.[8] "It was under Alphonso II, king of Asturias and Galicia (792-842), and under Bishop Theodemir of Iria Flavia that the long-forgotten tomb of James was claimed to have been rediscovered" (Melczer 13). In the *CSM* we see a sharing of certain miracle accounts. Miracles attributed to Saint James are attributed to the Virgin and vice-versa. As Benedicta Ward observes, "[a]s devotion to the Virgin grew, so miracles were transferred from other saints to her" (210). This interchangeability appears especially marked with regard to the hagiographic protagonists of miracles associated with pilgrims on the Road to Santiago de Compostela.

Beyond this appropriation by the cult of the Holy Mother of miracles attributed to other saints, it is well to bear in mind that

> [i]n addition to being subject to the changes inevitable for any literary work in transmission, miracle stories were altered in detail in any number of ways. They record the intervention of God in human affairs, but how, where, when, and to what effect could vary. Miracles were not copyright; they were part

of a general world view and belonged to an essentially subjective kind of truth (Ward 211).

However, even though the nature of Marian miracles was different from those associated with a particular shrine or relics, they were often associated with particular churches dedicated to her. Many of these churches were found along the pilgrimage route to Compostela. Naturally, for the pilgrim motivated to undertake a journey as an act of penance, contrition, or spiritual need, his/her reliance on the *mater misericordiae* while *en route* (Ward 149), is indeed a plausible narrative element.

Let us look at some specific instances. *Cantiga* 175 deals with a German pilgrim on the Road to Santiago. Most intriguing for our purposes here is that the miracle related in this *cantiga* is attributed to Santiago himself, rather than the Virgin Mary, in the twelfth-century *Liber Sancti Jacobi*.[9] In *Cantiga* 175, Holy Mary saves a young man who is unjustly hanged. A father and son from Germany on route to Santiago de Compostela stop at the city of Toulouse[10] to ask for Holy Mary's protection on their journey. After lodging that night at an inn, the wicked innkeeper slips a silver cup into the boy's knapsack before he and his father depart to continue their pilgrimage. Accompanied by the bailiff and armed men, the innkeeper runs after them shouting that they have stolen his property. When the pair are searched, the silver cup is found among the boy's things. He is ordered to be hanged at once and the father witnesses his execution. Despite his distress, the father continues on his pilgrimage to Santiago[11] but, on his way home, visits the site where his son was betrayed. Upon arriving at the gallows, the son, very much alive, cries out to his father explaining that Holy Mary had held him aloft since he had been unjustly hanged. The father goes immediately to Toulouse to inform the authorities of his son's miraculous survival. They come without delay and cut the young man down. The boy then relates how he had been falsely accused and how the Virgin had sustained him for three months. The people then go after the boy's accuser and subject him to death by fire. The poem ends with an exhortation to place one's trust in the Virgin Mary.

Some of the practical problems of pilgrimage are encountered in the details of this miracle narrative. The protagonists are faced with finding lodging along the route and, in so doing, fall prey to an unscrupulous innkeeper. Melczer, in his discussion of lodging along the Road to Compostela reminds us of the fact "[t]hat not all innkeepers were honest, some only marginally so. . . . Some took assuredly more advantage of foreign pilgrims than others. . ." (56).[12] The fact that the miracle of sustaining the boy on the gallows for three months is attributed to the Virgin Mary and not to St. James does not, in anyway, undermine the importance of the protagonists' journey. In fact, even after the tragedy of his son's unjust execution, the father feels bound by his promise of pilgrimage to complete the journey to Santiago de Compostela. His return to Toulouse three months later is a realistic time frame and suggests the extent of the father's conviction, both in terms of time and expense, to undertake the pilgrimage. His determination to not abandon the trip upon meeting with disaster in France intimates the seriousness of intent and the willingness to expose both himself and his son to the danger inherent on the Road.

Perhaps the best known of the Marian miracles associated with the Road to Compostela is number 26 of the *CSM*.[13] This miracle appears in the *Liber Sancti Jacobi* as well as in the works of Guaiterio de Benevento (eleventh century) where, as is the case with *Cantiga* 175, it is attributed to Santiago and the Virgin's role is reduced to that of presiding at the Heavenly court (Dutton 86). The protagonist of *Cantiga* 26 makes a yearly pilgrimage to Santiago. The text tells us that his motivation is sincere: "Este romeu con bõa voontade / ya a Santiago de verdade" (1: 123, vv. 20-21) [This pilgrim used to go to Santiago in all good faith]. However, before he departs on the journey related in the poem, he spends the night with an immoral woman to whom he is not married. The next day he starts on his pilgrimage without confessing this sin. The devil, who takes the form of St. James, appears to the pilgrim on the road telling him of his displeasure at his sin and instructing him to cut off his offending member and then to cut his throat. The man truly believes that Santiago has appeared to him and so does as instructed. When a group of his companions catches up with him and finds the body, they immediately flee to avoid being accused of his murder. This minor detail of the plot illustrates the likelihood that one faces being killed or injured while on pilgrimage. The fact that the other men fear they will be accused of the crime attests to the fact that the Road was plagued by false pilgrims whose sole purpose was to prey on the devout travelers. Since the pilgrim had committed suicide and died in a state of mortal sin, demons come to take his soul to Hell, but St. James appears and tells the demons they cannot have the man's soul because he killed himself only after having been deceived by the devil masquerading as the Saint. The demons argue that the soul is rightfully theirs and St. James proposes that they submit the case to the judgment of Holy Mary. After presenting their respective arguments, the Virgin rules that the pilgrim's soul be returned at once to his body so that he might be saved but, in so doing, she fails to restore his missing member. The actual intervention of the Virgin in the series of events related is very late. Up until the judicial proceedings to determine the ultimate fate of the pilgrim's soul, the miracle is centered on the Road to Compostela and St. James. The fact that the pilgrim credulously accepts the appearance of the Saint while he is *en route* to Santiago illustrates the medieval mind set that believed that miraculous appearance was associated with pilgrimage and was seen as a type of heavenly recognition of one's journey. Also, the fact that he is so ready not only to castrate himself but even commit suicide at the Saint's behest indicate the absolute seriousness of the pilgrim's intent. Furthermore, since he knowingly began his pilgrimage in a state of sin, without having received absolution, his subsequent feelings of guilt make him all the more ready to obey whatever the Saint to whose shrine he is traveling might direct him to do. And while Santiago does not impose such a harsh penance as self-mutilation, once the act has been committed, Holy Mary does not see fit to reattach the severed organ. While the rightness of her decision is not explicitly extolled, one should note that the *cantiga* opens with several lines which refer to the Virgin's power of sound judgment and discretion:

> Mui gran razon é que sábia dereito
> que Deus troux' en seu corp' e de seu peito
> mamentou, e del despeito
> nunca foi fillar;
> poren de sen me sospeito
> que a quis avondar. (1: 123, vv. 6-11)

[It is only fitting that the one who bore God in Her body and nursed Him at Her breast and never had displeasure from Him should be able to judge fairly, for I trust that He endowed Her richly with discretion.]
Even the refrain of this *cantiga* repeatedly alludes to the good judgment exercised by Holy Mary: "Non é gran cousa se sabe bon joyzo dar / a Madre do que o mundo tod' á de joigar" (1: 123, vv. 4-5, and also repeated between strophes) ["It is not surprising that the Mother of Him who will judge the whole world should demonstrate good judgment"]. When Santiago proposes that he and the devils submit the case to the Virgin for her decision he states:

> pois nos e vos est' assi rezõamos,
> ao joyzo vaamos
> da que non á par,
> e o que julgar façamos
> logo sen alongar. (1: 125, vv. 84-88)

[We shall resolve this question by going before the judgment of Her who has no peer, and we shall abide by Her decision.]
Santiago appears as an advocate for his devotee before the Virgin. While his role is certainly subordinate to Holy Mary's and he vows to abide by her decision, the pilgrimage to his shrine is the catalyst that sets the chain of events in motion (Connolly 45). Also, the devil chose the guise of St. James for his deception rather than any other saint.

Another version of the miracle of the pilgrim who castrates himself is found in Gonzalo de Berceo's *Milagros de Nuestra Señora*. Berceo gives his source as "Sant Ugo . . . de Grunniego" (81, v. 182c) [Saint Hugo of Cluny].[14] In Berceo's version, the pilgrim is a monk who has led a less than stellar life. One day he feels inspired to undertake a pilgrimage to Santiago de Compostela. Berceo's text gives some interesting details of the arrangements the friar makes before departing on his journey: "aguisó su facienda, buscó su compannía, / destajaron el término como fuessen su vía" (81, vv. 184cd) [He arranged his affairs, sought out companions. They determined the duration [of the trip] as they went on their way[15]]. Instead of spending the night before departure in prayerful vigil, as was the practice before undertaking any arduous task, the friar elects to spend it with his girlfriend and does not confess his sin before embarking. On the third day of the trip, Berceo's version recounts that the devil appears to the friar in the guise of an angel. And, even though he does not immediately identify himself as Santiago, this can be easily inferred when the devil tells the man that he (the pilgrim) has left his own house to come to mine (i.e., the house or shrine of the Saint): "Essisti de tu casa por venir a la mía" (82, v. 189a). Furthermore, the angel/demon tells him that beginning the pilgrimage without having confessed his sin is offensive to the Virgin, but does not overtly contend that it is offensive to Santiago, to whose church the pilgrim is bound. In the following strophe, the visage finally identifies himself as Santiago with the phrase "Yo so Jácobo, fijo de Zebedeo" (82, v. 190b) [I am James, the son of Zebedee]. Just as in Alfonso's version, the false-Santiago instructs the pilgrim to cut off the members "qe facen el fornicio" (82, v. 192b) [which performed the fornication] and to then cut his throat. When his companions find him thus disfigured, Berceo's account adds some details which give more hints about the nature of pilgrimage. After recovering from the initial shock of discovering the maimed body, his fellow travelers dismiss the possibility that he was killed by robbers because his possessions are not missing. They also assert that their companion had no sworn enemies who might have committed the atrocity. Here we learn that indeed robbery and even murder were very real consequences of undertaking the pilgrim road. Also, the allusion to the dead man's lack of enemies could infer that a person on pilgrimage presented a golden opportunity to anyone who might wish to do him/her harm. Despite their shock and puzzlement, the pilgrim's companions, as in Alfonso's version, beat a hasty retreat so as not to be implicated in the murder. When the devils come to take away the pilgrim's soul, Santiago appears and stops them in their path accusing them of deceiving his pilgrim. As in the Alfonsine version, the parties in dispute take their case before Holy Mary. She orders the soul returned to the body so that the pilgrim may do penance. Berceo's version has a vivid description of how his decapitated body is restored with the exception of his "natura" which does not grow back.[16] In spite of his loss, the pilgrim is happy to be alive and gives thanks to the Virgin. He also resumes his pilgrimage to Santiago de Compostela and, along the way, he and his companions take comfort in the miracle wrought on the road: "cueitóse de andar, trobó la compannía, / Avién esti miraclo por solaz cada día" (85, v. 214cd) [He decided to walk on, he found his companions, they had this miracle for comfort every day]. When he arrives in Compostela and news of the miracle spreads, the citizens decide to write it down in order to make it known to other pilgrims. Thus, the people of Santiago de Compostela appropriate the pilgrim's miraculous encounter with the Virgin into the folklore of the Road and as additional proof of the sanctity of undertaking the perilous journey. The pilgrim's ordeal inspires him to enter a Cluniac monastery where, according to Berceo, the abbot wrote down the miracle for posterity. The pilgrim-monk lives out his days in faithful Christian service and dies repentant.

While Berceo's tale gives more details than Alfonso's version, the basic elements of plot are the same. Berceo's version does, however, give us additional hints about the perception of the Road and the audience's expectations for a narrative involving a pilgrimage journey. Since Berceo himself adopts the guise of pilgrim for his collection of Marian miracles, it has been concluded that he composed the collection for the entertainment of pilgrims who stopped at San Millán de la Cogolla.[17] The Road as backdrop for an appearance by Santiago, albeit in this example the devil in the guise of the saint, was perceived as feasible by the audience. Moreover, the intervention by the Virgin to resurrect the dead pilgrim was of course reminiscent of the greater mystery of Christ's resurrection, the cornerstone of the faith.[18] On a more practical level, the people of Santiago de Compostela immediately seized on the publicity possibilities of this juicy tale. The narrative combined all the elements necessary for success—an illicit sexual encounter together with the curiously alluring yet repulsive nature of the act of castration were guaranteed to attract pilgrims. If the Road was the scene of such miraculous happenings surely the journey itself was an opportunity for direct divine intervention in the lives of the holy travelers.

The Road to Compostela is also the setting for Alfonso's *Cantiga* 218. As John Keller points out, this poem seems to somewhat belittle the shrine to St. James while promoting the Virgin's church at Villasirga (62). Nonetheless, the recipient of the Virgin's grace in number 218 is on route to Compostela and undertakes the journey in search of a cure. The pilgrim-protagonist, as in *Cantiga* 175, is from Germany. He suffers from a paralysis in which his hands and feet are badly twisted. Having observed that many people from his country travel to Santiago de Compostela, he begs some pilgrims to take him with them. And, the text informs us, despite the great poverty into which the formerly wealthy man had been forced due to his debilitating illness, out of pity, the other pilgrims agree to, quite literally, carry him in a litter to the Apostle's shrine. The poem tells us that the journey was a long and painful one: "a mui grandes pêas alá con el chegavan" (2: 280, v. 32) [with great difficulties, they arrived there with him]. And, despite his and his companions' efforts to complete the trip to Santiago, the man is not cured, according to the text, because of his sins (2: 280, v. 38). On the return trip, moreover, near Carrión de los Condes the crippled man goes blind. His group feels they can no longer care for him on the long trek ahead so they decide to leave him at the Virgin's church at Villasirga. When his companions have departed the pilgrim cries out in desperation to Holy Mary. She cures him of all his disabilities and he returns to Germany where he tells about the miracle the Virgin performed for him. He also bestows gifts on her church at Villasirga.

According to Keller, "*Cántiga* [sic] 218, then, shows that an afflicted man went to Compostela, prayed, and was not heard: in the Virgin's shrine at Villa-Sirga his prayers were answered" (78). While Keller does not give a definitive reason for Alfonso's seeming disparagement of the shrine of St. James in favor of the Virgin's shrine at Villasirga, he does offer some intriguing speculations. One suggestion is that Alfonso wanted "to curb the political influence of the Francophile monks of Cluny who had become entrenched along the Way of St. James. . . . Cluny owed allegiance to the royal house of France, and King Alfonso may have feared the widespread influence of this Benedictine brotherhood" (76). It must be acknowledged, then, that the composition of the *CSM* was not without political motive. While the book, undeniably, echoes the Learned King's personal devotion to the Virgin, the inclusion of narratives which stress her role and aid in victories over the Moors, the promotion of newly-formed Christian strongholds such as Puerto de Santa María, and the accounts of Mary's divine intervention in the lives of Alfonso and his immediate family certainly contributed to the king's personal political agenda and the strengthening of his divine right as sovereign. A ruler so keenly aware of the politics of concentration of personal power and promotion of Castilian hegemony was undeniably aware that a primary contributing factor to his kingdom's international renown was the shrine of St. James and the pilgrims' Road which converged from all points of Western Europe to traverse northern Spain on route to Compostela. That a shrine of the Virgin along the road of St. James, i.e. Villasirga near Carrión de los Condes, should figure prominently in a collection dedicated to Holy Mary's miracles is most plausible. The fact that the pilgrim protagonist of *Cantiga* 218 is not cured of his paralysis at the shrine of Santiago is, according to the Alfonsine text, attributed to the man's sins. That he should later throw himself on the mercy of the Virgin Mary after having been refused relief by another saint (St. James) is certainly in keeping with the characterization of the Virgin in the *CSM* as the ultimate source of mercy when all others have been exhausted, the ever-forgiving Mother to whom any sinner can turn and expect to receive relief. Mary's multi-faceted representation as judge, advocate, physician, etc., includes, and is perhaps predicated upon, her portrayal as the feminine face of God, as the Mother who stands forever ready to pardon. Although the text is silent about what sins the pilgrim of *Cantiga* 218 has committed, his journey to Santiago de Compostela does not seem to constitute adequate penance. That the Virgin's mercy is granted to such a person, together with his pitiable condition of paralysis and blindness, only enhances her capacity for benevolence. And while this poem certainly promotes pilgrimage to Villasirga, its author is obviously aware that this Marian shrine is on the pilgrims' Road to Compostela and that most offerings to the church there will come from travelers to and from Galicia.

Cantiga 253 also appears to promote the Virgin's shrine at Villasirga to the detriment of Santiago de Compostela. The protagonist of number 253 is a man from Toulouse who, as penance for his sins, is instructed by an abbot to make the pilgrimage to Compostela.[19] Penitential pilgrimages had been imposed since the sixth century and were most often given as a type of public penance for private sins that had come to public knowledge or for some particularly scandalous behavior (Davies 30). While the text does not specify the man's sin, he is instructed to carry an iron staff weighing 24 pounds and place it before the altar of St. James in sight of all present.[20] When he arrives at Villasirga he learns that its church is the site of many miracles performed by the Holy Mother. As he is a great devotee of the Virgin, he detours to her church and there asks pardon for his sins. At that moment the bar falls and breaks in two but no one is able to pick up the pieces of iron. He tells those present why he was carrying the staff and it is understood that no one can lift the iron bars because the pilgrim has been freed of his penance. Nonetheless, he continues on his pilgrimage to Compostela, but without the heavy discomfort of the iron bar. He returns home and is thereafter very devoted to the Virgin. While Holy Mary alone is credited with the miracle of the breaking of the iron bar staff, the central thrust in this poem, as in *Cantiga* 218, is the Virgin's mercy in the face of human suffering. Even the repeated refrain of *Cantiga* 253 emphasizes the Virgin's mercy to all who humbly ask her pardon: "De grad' á Santa Maria mercee e piadade / aos que de seus peccados lla pede[n] con omildade" (2: 355, vv. 4-5) [Holy Mary gladly sheds Her mercy and compassion on those who humbly ask Her for forgiveness of their sins]. The pilgrim in this poem is perfectly willing to undertake the exacting pilgrimage imposed on him but, upon arriving at Villasirga weary from the weight, throws himself on the Virgin's mercy. His prayer accentuates his own unworthiness and Mary's boundless goodness.[21] Furthermore, it must be noted that the pilgrim completes his journey even after experiencing the Virgin's divine intervention at Villasirga. While promoting the church at Villasirga, Alfonso again is undoubtedly aware that the Frenchman's goal is Santiago de Compostela, a destination which he will be allowed to reach in relative comfort after his encounter with Holy Mary at Villasirga. Since other poems have drawn attention to the natural perils and difficulties of the trip to Santiago, the reader's sympathies are certainly with the pilgrim who must not only confront these hazards but do so while carrying a hefty load of iron. Relieving him of the iron staff does not excuse the pilgrim from completing his journey, an act of contrition which the poem emphasizes that the man has undertaken willingly as atonement for his sins.

In *Cantiga* 278, a blind woman from France makes a pilgrimage to Santiago de Compostela but she is not cured. On the way home, near Carrión de los Condes, it begins to rain heavily and the woman, accompanied by her daughter, seeks refuge in the church at Villasirga. While there the blind woman prays before the Virgin's altar and her sight is restored. Upon resuming their journey the next day, the woman happens upon a blind man who is on his way to Compostela. She advises him to go to Villasirga if he wishes to regain his sight. Keller points out that "[t]he woman is definite in her criticism of Santiago as a miracle-working shrine" (80) and cites the following strophe to support his contention:

> E contou todo seu feito, como fora con romeus
> muitos pera Santiago, mas pero nunca dos seus
> ollos o lum' y cobrara, mas pois a Madre de Deus
> llo dera en Vila-Sirga pelo seu mui gran poder. (3: 52, vv. 43-46)

[She recounted all her story, how she had gone with many pilgrims to Santiago, but had never recovered the light of her eyes. However, then the Mother of God had given it to her in Villa-Sirga through Her great power.] The blind man does as the woman directs and also has his vision restored at the church in Villasirga. The woman's words do seem to promote the Virgin's church at Villasirga over the shrine of the Apostle and this *cantiga*, as almost all others in the Alfonsine collection, stresses Mary's capacity for pity. This poem also implies that not all who suffer physical disability or illness will be cured at St. James' shrine—a stance which can not be considered the best of publicity for Compostela. In the case of *Cantiga* 278 the Learned King's propaganda for the Virgin's church at Villasirga seems to overshadow any negative effect the narrative might have had on pilgrims' decision to undertake the pilgrimage to Compostela. However, it is critical to keep in mind that the major import of this *cantiga* is to highlight the Virgin's capacity for mercy on those who suffer. The narrative gives us no information about the motivations for these blind pilgrims to embark on the Road to Compostela other than their desire to be cured. We must assume that their faith is indeed genuine in order to have undertaken the dangers inherent on the Road in spite of their disability. While these pilgrims do not undertake the trip alone, we must still assume that their blindness contributed significantly to the difficulty of the journey. The motif of pilgrimage becomes a symbol of their willingness to undergo hardship in faithful pursuit of a cure.

The pilgrimage to Santiago de Compostela serves as a powerful *leitmotif* in all the miracle narratives discussed. It is an outward sign of inner devotion and/or contrition. That Holy Mary intervenes in the lives of pilgrims is also a sign of God's benevolence toward the faithful on the pilgrimage Road. Her grace and mercy are inexhaustible toward all regardless of the sins one has committed. Even the pilgrims who find themselves on the Road as the result of their own feelings of guilt or as an imposed penance from a confessor are candidates for her compassion. Alfonso continuously stresses the inability to adequately praise Mary's goodness, and one of the primary themes of the collection is to inspire others to her devotion. The Road to Compostela as a concrete setting as well as its metaphorical interpretation as the pilgrimage of life were obvious and clear motifs for Alfonso's thirteenth-century audience. That the pilgrimage could be used to foster all manner of Christian dedication, including but not limited to dedication to the Virgin, attests to the psychic power of the pilgrimage journey as manifestation of the medieval Christian consciousness.

NOTES

1 Hereafter, *CSM*.

2 "Churches with the patronage of a great saint were always enriched by offerings. . . . The miracles of the saint and the acquisitions of his monastery were initimately connected" (Sumption 62).

3 This and all subsequent quotes are taken from the edition of Walter Mettmann.

4 This and all subsequent translations from the *CSM* are courtesy of Kathleen Kulp-Hill who will soon publish a complete English translation of the collection.

5 In his article, "Self-Conscious Awareness. . . ," Snow contends that the King's "own search for the reward of eternal salvation is the central story" (62).

6 Among the possible motives for pilgrimage were one's geographic proximity to a particular shrine, the enthusiastic reports of returning pilgrims or one's relatives, good advertising by officials of a shrine, and indulgences offered by the Church (Davies 19-20). The Davies also mention that many who traveled the pilgrimage routes were "parasites who battened on the pilgrims, such as robbers, buccaneers, cheating innkeepers, unscrupulous shopkeepers, pardoners and the like" (20). Some of these latter types appear as important characters in the *cantigas* we shall discuss.

7 For example, the *Breviarum apostolorum* of the sixth or seventh century speaks of the preaching of St. James in Spain (Melczer 10). Also, the *Carmen in duodecim apostolorum aris* by Aldhelm of Malmesbury, who died in 709, alludes to James converting the Spaniards as does the eighth century text *De ortu et obitu Patrum*, attributed to Isidore of Seville (Melczer 11).

8 "Ado of Vienne, in his revision of the *Martyrologium* of Florus of Lyons, as well as in the *Libellus de festivitatibus SS Apostolorum*, both mid-[ninth-]century texts, speaks of the *Translatio* of the remains of James to Spain, their burial close to the British sea—this cannot be anywhere but in Galicia—and their subsequent veneration. . . . The famous *Martyrologium of Usuard*, of the third quarter of the century, and Notker Balbulus of St. Gall, a little later, report the *translatio* in terms similar to those of Ado" (Melczer 12-13).

9 Also known as the *Codex Calixtinus*, this latter term "is now commonly used only to refer to the manuscript housed in the cathedral library in Compostela" (Davidson and Dunn-Wood 152). The second part of

the five part *Liber Sancti Jacobi* relates 22 miracles performed by St. James, including the story related as *CSM* 175.

The *Speculum historiale* of Vincentius Bellovacensis (d. 1264) and the *Dialogus miraculorum* of Caesarius Heisterbacensis (late twelfth-early thirteenth century) also attribute this miracle to Santiago (Mettmann 2: 183).

10 Desto direi un miragre de gran maravill' estranna
que mostrou Santa Maria por un romeu d' Alemanna
que a Santiago ya, que éste padron d' Espanna,
e per Rocamador vêo a Tolosa a cidade. (2: 183, vv. 5-8)

[Concerning this, I shall tell a great and remarkable miracle which Holy Mary performed for a pilgrim from Germany who was going to the shrine of Santiago, who is patron saint of Spain. He passed through Rocamadour and came to the city of Toulouse.]

11 E el foi-ss' a Santiago, u avia prometudo . . . (2: 184, v. 45) [He went on to Santiago, where he had promised to go . . .].

12 In this discussion of unscrupulous innkeepers, Melczer specifically cites the version of the miracle of the unjustly accused man sustained on the gallows as it appears in the *Liber Sancti Jacobi* (56). In this version a pilgrim and his son are double-crossed by the innkeeper who plots to take their money once the pilgrims are convicted of theft.

13 This miracle also appears in Gautier de Coinci's *Les Miracles de Nostre Dame* and in Gonzalo de Berceo's *Milagros de Nuestra Señora* (no. 8) (Mettmann 1: 123). Additionally, versions of it are found in Gil de Zamora's Latin legends and the Catalan *Recull de eximplis* (Connolly 38). On the miracle's popularity, Connolly states that "[i]t should not be surprising that this miracle, whose roots date from the eleventh century, received special attention in Spain. Indeed, as José Filgueira Valverde indicates, the tale was referred to in the twelfth century as the 'gran milagro' and was celebrated in the cathedral at Compostela" (38).

14 All references from the *Milagros de Nuestra Señora* are from the edition of Brian Dutton and are referred to in the text by page and verse number or, for references to editorial comments, as "Dutton" with corresponding page number(s).

15 The translations from the *Milagros de Nuestra Señora* are my own.

16 La plaga qe oviera de la degolladura
abés parecié d'ella la sobresanadura;
perdió él la dolor, e toda la cochura,
todos dizién: "Est omne fue de buena ventura."

Era de lo ál todo sano e mejorado,
fuera de un filiello que tenié travesado;
mas lo de la natura quanto qe fo cortado,
no li creció un punto, fincó en su estado.
De todo era sano, todo bien encorado,
pora verter su agua fincóli el forado. . . . (84-5, vv. 211a - 213b)

[The wound that he had from cutting his throat
One could barely perceive the scar;
He was relieved of suffering, and all stinging pain,
Everyone said: "This man had good fortune."
From everything he was well and recovered,
Except for a thin line where he had been cut;
But regarding his organ which he had cut off,
It did not grow back a bit, it remained as it was.
From everything he was cured, all was well scarred over,
In order to make water, he had only a hole. . . .]

[17] On this point, see Dutton, especially page 12: ". . . parece lógico suponer que las obras marianas de Berceo formaban parte del culto de la Virgen, sobre todo para el entretenimiento e instruccíon de los peregrinos que llegaban al monasterio" [. . . it seems logical to assume that Berceo's Marian works formed part of the cult of the Virgin, above all for the entertainment and instruction of pilgrims who arrived at the monastery].

E. Michael Gerli agrees with Dutton's conclusion: "they [the *Milagros*] were probably composed to be read aloud for pilgrims on their way to Compostela, and . . . they are in all likelihood intimately connected to the existence of a shrine to the Virgin dating from the eleventh century at the monastery of San Millán de la Cogolla, just seventeen kilometers off the heavily traveled main route to Santiago. Created in order to inspire piety and contrition, the *Milagros* were also designed to stimulate a reverence— and badly needed donations—for the shrine of the Virgin at the economically depressed monastery" (141).

[18] In Berceo's text, the pilgrim is compared to Lazarus:

Quando fo en su tierra, la carrera complida,
E udieron la cosa que avie contecida,
Tenien grandes clamores, era la gent movida
Por veer esti Lázaro dado de muert a vida. (216)

[When he was again in his homeland, his journey completed,
And they heard about what had happened to him,
The people were moved and loudly clamored
To see this Lazarus who dead had been given life.]

[19] "One of the most powerful motives for going on pilgrimage was simply to get rid of an overwhelming sense of guilt, and penances often

took the form of a pilgrimage prescribed by a priest. This is the chief motive recognized by the author of the "Veneranda dies" sermon [*Liber Sancti Jacobi*, Book 1]. . . . The sermon includes the promise to sinners that if they are truly penitent, they will obtain through the influence and merits of Saint James the remission of their sins at his altar, for Santiago retains the privilege granted by Jesus to his apostles that whosoever's sins are remitted the Lord will also remit" (Davies 29).

20 Going on pilgrimage barefoot, in minimum clothing, or in chains were not unusual requirements. Pilgrims undergoing such ordeals were seen as public examples to other pilgrims on the road. Such arduous conditions of pilgrimage were often imposed on clergymen or members of religious orders who had committed crimes which dishonored their religious calling (Davies 30-1).

21 Ay, Madre de Deus, catade
. . .
A vossa mui gran mercee e on a mia desmesura
grand' e sobeja e fera, que me fez fazer locura
d' eu querer o bordon vosso levar; mais vos, Virgen pura,
valla-mi a bondade vossa, e esto me perdõade.
(2: 357, vv. 64-69)

[Oh, Mother of God, consider. . . your great mercy and not my bold, overweening indiscretion which caused me so stupidly to try to take away your staff. However, Pure Virgin, may your goodness avail me, and pardon me this trespass.]

CHAPTER 6

The Iconography of St. James in the Indianapolis Museum's Fifteenth-Century Altarpiece

David M. Gitlitz

The Indianapolis Museum of Art houses a beautifully comprehensive, but not widely-known nor thoroughly-understood, example of late fifteenth-century pilgrimage art.[1] The twelve-panel triptych is by an anonymous painter, presumably Flemish and of the school of Dirk Bouts, c. 1510 (Van Herwaarden 358-60). Janson and Frasier (np), who attribute it to The Master of the Legend of St. Ursula, active in Bruges toward the end of the fifteenth century, also perceive influences of Memlinc, David, and van der Weyden.[2] A painting somewhat similar in subject and style, and almost certainly by the same painter, is found in the private Argüelles collection in Madrid (Lavalleye 2).

The twelve individual oak panels of this one-story, oil-painted triptych[3] are set into a frame on which various items of standard pilgrim equipment—pilgrim staves (*bordones*), the pilgrim wallet or scrip hanging from the staff on a twisted belt, scallop shells—are repeated symmetrically. The panels depict events from nine episodes from the life and death of St. James, and various miracles attributed to him. While several of the Santiago episodes on the panels are well known, others are relatively obscure. The purpose of this paper is to identify and suggest probable sources for the principal episodes depicted on the panels.

A number of stylistic and narrative conventions link the twelve panels. With the exception of the first panel, which depicts a single scene, all the rest contain multiple scenes from a single story: one scene—not always the most important event in the story—appears in the foreground and occupies the bulk of the painting; another often appears in middle ground, while a third, and sometimes a fourth and fifth, episode is relegated to tiny figures acting on the background landscape. The protagonists of these multiple scenes are linked by replications of clothing, and in fact throughout the twelve panels the images of St. James are clothed consistently in a red robe over a blue undergarment. Five stories are narrated on single panels, two are told on paired panels: 9 and 10 (the hanged innocent), and 3 and 4 (the demon pilgrim assassin), while one is told on three panels: 8, 11, and 12 (the sick pilgrim miraculously transported to Compostela).

The iconography of the twelve panels deals with the Saint's life and martyrdom, his miraculous journey to Galicia, and miracles worked through his intercession both during his life and after his death. It incorporates the Saint's two major guises, pilgrim and Moor-slayer, with an emphasis on Compostela and on the pilgrimage experience, as is only to be expected on a triptych associated with the pilgrimage route. I will discuss the iconography of each of the twelve panels in turn, first identifying the principal and secondary incidents and their probable sources, and then discussing their individual depictions, following an order on each panel which goes from top to bottom (i.e., from background to foreground figures); when two or more episodes are on the same level I will proceed from left to right.

PANEL 1. ST. JAMES TRANSPORTED TO GALICIA (*TRANSLATIO*)

The twelfth-century *Liber Sancti Jacobi* [LSJ] includes three versions of the *Translatio*, all indicating that the body of the martyred Saint was transported miraculously by boat.[4] The boat later appears in countless southern European retellings of the legends surrounding St. James' death. In the LSJ (f. 75v) the author of the "Veneranda dies" sermon makes passing mention of two other versions of the story, in which the body, seated on a rock (half of which remained in Jaffa) was brought by the ocean's waves to Galicia; or that the rock itself was transported in the miraculous boat. However, the author explicitly rejects these two versions as fables and lies, saying that he personally has examined the rock (presumably the one venerated in Padrón), and that it is Galician in origin.[5] Nonetheless, the journey by floating island seems to have lodged in the folklore of northern Europe in late Middle Ages, with one variant even recorded in modern times in a Scandinavian folk song popular on the Faroe Islands (Almazán 189-90).

1a. The floating island appears to be the version of the *Translatio* depicted on the Indianapolis panel. In the single episode narrated on this panel, St. James (identified by his halo, his staff from which hangs his scrip, attached by the same twisted belt as in the scrips on the triptych's frame, and his pilgrim hat marked with insignia of scallop shell), sits on an island, bent over as if asleep with his head resting on his right hand. Under his elbow is a leather-bound book, presumably the Gospel of Christ that St. James is to preach in Iberia. To one side stands a vision of Jesus, his right hand raised in blessing. This may depict Jesus giving St. James his mission to proselytize Galicia, and if so the panel conflates the two events. The prominence given to the rock leads Moralejo to identify the locus of this scene as Padrón, the Galician port city to which St. James' body was miraculously transported (238-41); the city or castle walls in the background landscape reinforce this view.

PANEL 2. ST. JAMES THE MOOR-SLAYER

The warrior Saint's miraculous intervention on behalf of the Christians in the battle of Clavijo (c. 840) and many subsequent battles is not chronicled in the LSJ, although he is termed Soldier of Christ in Book II chapter 19 (f. 154r). Yet by the twelfth century St. James' reputation as the Moor-slayer was widely known, as portal sculptures in the Compostela Cathedral and Abbey of Conques attest. The Saint is invariably depicted with the iconography of the pilgrimage (scallop shells on his hat, cloak, or pennant, or other insignia on his hat) or with a red cross that recalls the insignia of the military order of Santiago; brandishing a sword; astride a white horse that crushes the heretic Muslims underfoot.

2a. Background: Above Santiago floats God the Father in a cloud, holding a globe marked with a cross. The similarities between his dress (red cloak, dark undergarment) and St. James' clothes may suggest divine endorsement of James' mission.

2b. Foreground: Faithfully reproducing the popular iconography, St. James, mounted on white charger, tramples infidels under his horse's feet. From the Saint's lance floats a pennant bearing a cross and scallop shells, and these motifs are repeated on his horse's cloak. Curiously, in this panel and in every other panel where one can see the Saint's feet, he is barefoot. The Saint's hat bears the shell insignia. The horse's cloak is the same red color as the Saint's, suggesting that they are united as agents of the Christian deity against the infidel. Anachronistically reflecting Western Europe's Islamic enemies of the late fifteenth century, the Moors are turbaned like Turks.

PANELS 3 AND 4. THE DEMON PILGRIM ASSASSIN

The 1924 Indianapolis Museum "Ten Primitives" catalog suggests, without citing the source, that this relates the story of "a palmer who received a pair of shoes from a demon in the guise of St. James. Asked by the disguised demon to take his life he does so, supposing that in this way he would honor the Saint. He cuts his throat with a sickle. The true James implores the aid of Christ and Mary and then appears with an angel before the palmer, to whom life has been restored" (44). The LSJ Book II, Miracle 17 (attributed to St. Anselm) is similar in many respects, although the details differ significantly. It relates how a pilgrim, who fornicated with a woman the night before beginning his pilgrimage and failed to confess his sin, was persuaded by a demon St. James to castrate himself, and was later restored to life, if not virility. Voragine, citing Hugh of Saint Victor, tells two stories of pilgrims who were persuaded by a false St. James to slay themselves and who were later miraculously restored to life (2: 7-8). None of these appears to be the direct source of the legend depicted on the Indianapolis panels. In these panels the sinful pilgrim's throat is cut by the demon, eliminating both the castration and the suicide motifs. The pilgrim depicted on these panels is old, poor, and sickly, not the young man of the LSJ and Voragine versions. And the demon, while disguised as a human being, does not wear anything which would associate him directly with St. James or with the pilgrimage. The intercession of the Virgin Mary in restoring life to the dead pilgrim is a common enough miracle motif that it does not argue for any specific source.

The narrative order of the incidents on these panels is 4a, 4c, 4b, 3b, 3a.

4a. Background: The tiny disguised demon and his pilgrim victim encounter each other on a hilly road.

4b. Middle-ground: The devil cuts the throat of the poor pilgrim.

4c. Foreground: The poorly dressed and shod pilgrim, with a staff and pilgrim hat bearing three pilgrim insignia, listens to a yellow-cloaked demon with bird feet, whose blue cowl barely masks his three horns. Under his right arm the demon carries a pair of elegant boots; with his left hand he points to them as if to tempt the poor pilgrim.

3a. Background (see Fig. 6.3): In heaven St. James appears before God the Father, an angel, and the Virgin Mary, presumably to beseech the resuscitation of the dead, deceived pilgrim.

3b. Foreground: A red-cloaked pilgrim St. James, with hat and staff, flanked by an angel in white, succors a scaggy elderly pilgrim, whose callused knees and torn shoes mark him as a poor man.

PANEL 5. THE HERMOGENES LEGEND
The museum has labeled this "St. James visiting a rich man's house," but the scene is indisputably the miracle of the magician Hermogenes,[6] told in the LSJ Book I chapter 9 (ff. 49v-50r), the *Actes apocryphes* and Voragine's thirteenth-century *Legenda aurea*.[7] In this story the evil Hermogenes, who as a magician is in league with the Devil, sends his agent Philetus to confound Santiago, but Philetus instead witnesses several miracles and finds himself converted and one of the Saint's disciples. Hermogenes, furious, immobilizes Philetus, but Santiago sets him free. Hermogenes sends demons to bring James and Philetus to him, but God's angel confounds the demons, who instead bring the magician to the Saint who tells Hermogenes that God commands that good be returned for ill, and sets him free. Hermogenes then asks Santiago for help against the demons, and the Saint gives him his staff

as a protective talisman. Hermogenes, convinced of James' Christian sanctity, burns his magic books and converts to Christianity. Panel 5 relates several episodes from this story, jumbled together without regard to their narrative sequence.

5a. Background: Hermogenes, identified by his yellow cowl in this and subsequent scenes, peeks through a doorway.[8]

5b. Background: Inside the house Hermogenes sits in a chair asleep, surrounded by demons. Georges believes this to be the scene in which they inspire the magician to attempt to corrupt the Saint (219). It may also be a reference to Philetus' claim that he accepted Christianity after seeing Santiago drive demons from the bodies of the possessed.

5c. Background: In another room a man, staff in hand, sleeps peacefully. According to Georges, this too is Hermogenes, protected from demons by Santiago's staff (219). It might also represent Philetus, bound in his bed by the magician until he was freed by the staff's touch.

5d. Background: At the door to Hermogenes' house Santiago hands him the talismanic staff. Three demons scatter in defeat.

5e. Foreground: Four men are burning books. To the right Hermogenes, still clothed in rich brocade, stands before the fire, while a nobleman, undoubtedly Philetus, and a haloed Santiago look on. A servant dressed in red tights carries four books to the fire.[9] In this scene the Saint's hat bears no insignia at all.

PANEL 6. THE ARREST AND CONDEMNATION OF ST. JAMES (See Fig. 6.4.)

Georges links this panel to the previous, pointing out that according to the legend as related in the *Actes apocryphes*, it was the conversion of Hermogenes and Philetus which so enraged the Pharisees in Jerusalem that they denounced James to Herod Agrippa for inciting rebellion (220). The LSJ Book I chapter 9 (f. 49) gives additional details: how after Hermogenes' conversion his disciples flocked to hear Santiago preach; how the Jews sent two centurions, Lisias and Theocritus, to put him in prison; how the high priest Abiathar, jealous of Santiago's successful sermonizing, had him taken to Herod, who condemned him to be beheaded; how Santiago baptized the converted soldier Josiah before their execution; and how the Saint's decapitated head did not fall to the ground but was cradled in Santiago's arms; and how the earth opened to swallow the evil executioners.

6a. Background: Through a window St. James (with halo and hat) can be seen preaching to a crowd of men and women. Georges speculates that the black-clad figure and the two men with pointed hats symbolize the agents of the Pharisees sent to rouse the crowd against St. James (220). The black-clad figure is most likely Abiathar; the agents could be the two centurions, Lisias and Theocritus.

6b. Background: Through another window we see St. James (halo, no hat) being pushed into a tower prison with barred windows, probably by one of the two centurions Lisias and Theocritus.

6c. Foreground: A soldier, probably Josiah,[10] brings St. James (halo, hat bare of insignia) before Herod, richly attired in red brocaded robe, sitting on a brocaded throne. His beard trails off in two points, much like those medieval Jews were frequently forced to wear. To the right are two dandies, one with a walking stick, again most probably Lisias and Theocritus.[11]

PANEL 7. THE MARTYRDOM AND BURIAL OF ST. JAMES

This panel depicts St. James' martyrdom, which could derive from almost any medieval source relevant to the Saint and the events leading to his burial in Galicia, as discussed below. Thus, temporally it brackets the *Translatio* depicted in Panel 1.

7a. Background: Above a wall a kneeling St. James is being beheaded as two people watch.[12] Behind him is a towered city, perhaps Jerusalem, where the martyrdom is traditionally said to have occurred.

7b. Background: Through the city gate come two tiny bulls, hitched to a cart on which is barely glimpsed the haloed body of St. James.

7c. Middle-ground: The cart, in which St. James' head and halo still are barely seen, pulls up to a building, which is under construction. Although the edifice bears no resemblance to constructions in Compostela, it may signify the building of James' chapel over the site of his tomb.[13] This scene is probably meant to suggest the well-known story of the widow[14] Lupa's reluctance to allow James' burial in Galicia until the miraculous power of his body could be demonstrated by harnessing wild bulls to pull his funeral cart. According to the LSJ Book III chapter 1 (ff. 157v-159r) Lupa was a rich noble widow who lived five miles from Iria Flavia, and who maintained a pagan temple in which she worshipped an idol. Lupa passed the Christians' request along to the king, who tried to have the disciples killed, but the soldiers he sent to chase them fell into a river and drowned. When they asked Lupa for sanctuary, she required them to bring her the Saint's body on a cart pulled by some gentle oxen—in truth wild bulls—grazing in her mountain pasture. The bulls grew tame, the body was brought, and Lupa converted with all her household, destroyed her pagan idols, and buried the Saint in the former pagan temple, which she reconstructed as a fine church.

7d. Foreground: The cart's arrival is watched by a servant who stands behind the contrite Queen Lupa, richly dressed in red brocade. Facing Lupa is the king (wearing what appears to be a crown, and holding a scepter and some sort of bag in his left hand) who appears to reproach her (Georges 224). The king is depicted in precisely the same fashion as Herod in panel 6, perhaps linking the two men as agents of similar anti-Christian forces arrayed against the Saint. On the ground between the king and queen grows a flower.[15]

PANELS 8, 11, AND 12. MIRACLE OF THE SICK (DEAD?) PILGRIM TRANSPORTED TO COMPOSTELA
The Indianapolis Museum merely labels panel 8 the interior of a chapel dedicated to St. James. In fact panels 8, 11 and 12 relate one of many stories of a dead pilgrim miraculously transported to Compostela. Perhaps the earliest version of this legend—later much imitated—appears in LSJ Book II chapter 4 (ff. 143v-144r).[16] In this rendition one member of a group of thirty Laurentian pilgrims who have vowed to help each other reach Compostela takes sick and with great difficulty is carried into the Pyrenees. Despite their vow, his companions leave him behind in the company of the one pilgrim who had not sworn the oath of constancy. The next night on the mountain top the sick pilgrim dies and, when his frightened companion prays to St. James for help, the Saint takes them on horseback to Compostela, where the corpse is buried with honor on the Monte de Gozo. The Indianapolis panels 8, 11, and 12 depict some elements of this story, omit others, and add still others not found in the LSJ version of the legend. Several of the figures are portrayed with identical facial features and/or clothing in the three panels, which argues that the three panels depict episodes in a single story. The fact that they are separated in the current disposition of the panels suggests that the original order of the panels may have been disturbed.

The Indianapolis Museum identifies panel 12 as the "witnessing of sacred vessels."[17] Yet Moralejo's (239) theory that it is an unidentified episode of the miracle of the dead pilgrim, narrated in panels 8 and 11, is plausible, for the clothing of the pilgrim taking leave of his family in 12a indicates clearly that he is the same pilgrim Samaritan who aids the dead pilgrim in panels 8 and 11; the face and hair of the saintly nobleman in 12c also replicates that of panels 8 and 11.

In addition to the episode of the dead pilgrim, these panels seem to have a secondary plot line, most of whose details and source still remain unclear to me. But the story may go something like this. A pilgrim takes leave of his wealthy family (12c). On the road to Compostela he meets and assists a dying pilgrim (11b and 11a), and is rewarded both spiritually (the halo) and materially (the crown hanging from his right wrist). After the miraculous translation to Compostela, the dead pilgrim is resuscitated (8c). The saintly pilgrim returns home where he rewards first his mother (crowned in 12b and 12c) and his father (crowned only in 12c). The family prospers, as the increasingly rich attire of the pilgrim and servant (?) girl indicates. Yet for some reason his family is skeptical of the supernatural events of his journey until their authenticity is confirmed when some church vessels miraculously float to the top of a local fountain (12c). None of the LSJ miracles contains a scene reminiscent of this one, but there is a vague similarity with a legend associated with St. Francis of Assisi's founding of a monastery near Compostela, funded by a "treasure" miraculously discovered in a fountain (Vázquez de Parga 1: 77).

11a. Background: The saintly pilgrim good Samaritan carries the dead man over his shoulder through a high mountain pass, presumably the Port of Cize. Moreover, the saintly pilgrim carries both pilgrim staves. In the distance is a city—perhaps Compostela—and behind it a bay with two ships under sail.

11b. Foreground: The poor dead pilgrim lies on the ground, his head resting on his scrip, his shoes and staff on one side, his begging bowl on the other. Over him kneels the richly-dressed, haloed pilgrim good Samaritan.

8a. Background: On a church altar sits a crowned figure of St. James, his head resting on his right hand, his elbow resting on a book, in a pose that duplicates the meditating or visionary St. James in panel 1, and dressed in red and blue similar to St. James in the other panels. Three unidentified figures stand behind him; one, who carries a black scrip, reaches forward to touch the crown or to place it on the Saint's head. Another figure on the right climbs a ladder to reach the altar.

8b. Middle-ground: The altar is depicted in great detail, with a rich brocaded frontal cloth; a retablo in the center of which Christ, his hand raised in blessing, is flanked by the twelve apostles; on the altar stand two gold candle sticks; over it hangs a cloth baldacchino, and over that thirteen hanging oil lamps; the four corners of the altar are marked with columns topped by sculpted angels. Stokstad believes that the architectural details and the altar of this panel are fairly accurate depictions of the Compostela Cathedral sanctuary toward the end of the fifteenth century (528-31). To the right of the altar stands a man in black carrying a sickle; another sickle rests on the altar itself. Presumably these are two representations of the same sickle, touted by the sanctuary as that used to behead St. James. Stokstad (528) demonstrates that the sickle, crown, and ladder are documented by fifteenth- and sixteenth-century visitors to the Cathedral. The crown is probably one reputedly donated to the Cathedral in the mid-fifteenth century by Castilian king Enrique IV; pilgrim tales for the next two hundred years cite instances of visitors to the Cathedral removing the crown from the image of the Saint and placing it on their own heads.[18] Behind the man with the sickle is another James-like figure dressed in red over blue. Yet none of these figures carry any pilgrim insignia or wear haloes. Unlike the other eleven panels, which show considerable thematic unity, in panel 8 the background and middle-ground have nothing to do with the miracle narrated by the panel, but rather evoke the ambiance of the Cathedral of Compostela.

8c. Foreground: In front of the altar the dead pilgrim is laid out on a tile floor, his hands folded as if in prayer. Kneeling on the left side are two men dressed in black and one in red. On the right are another four; one carries a pilgrim staff and has another staff embroidered on his cloak. These seven presumably represent the contrite companions of the dead pilgrim, while the careful detail work of their faces suggests that they may be portraits of donors. Another kneeling figure, richly dressed, a crown hanging from one wrist, is the haloed saintly pilgrim from panel 11 who had carried the dead man to Compostela.[19]

12a. Background: In a porch doorway a haloed pilgrim, his scrip over his shoulder, takes leave of a man and a woman to set out on pilgrimage.[20] None of the three have crowns. The leave-taker has the same hair, hat, scrip, clothes, hose, and shoes as the pilgrim Samaritan of panels 8 and 11. The woman reappears with a crown in 12b and 12c; the gold-brocaded man reappears in 12b, and in 12c wears a crown. Another pilgrim, identified as such by his staff, leans against the porch balustrade; his clothing suggests that he may be the pilgrim companion who sickens and dies in panels 8 and 11.

12b. Middle-ground on left: The haloed man, now richly attired in a red cloak over blue with a black velvet hat, stands in front of two women (one with a crown, the other presumably a servant) and a man clothed in gold brocade. The face of this man, painted full on, does not quite so closely resemble the face of the pilgrim Samaritan in the other scenes which are in the three quarter or profile, views at which this painter seems particularly adept.

12c. Foreground: The haloed man in the red cloak, now with brocaded sleeves and with a purse hanging from his belt, points at three golden vessels floating in water down a flight of stairs. The top vessel is a hunting or drinking horn; the middle vessel appears to be an orb or an ecclesiastical pyx; the third is a spouted pitcher. Behind the Saint are the same two women and the brocaded older man, now wearing a crown. The Saint's face is turned toward the crowned man, with whom he appears to be engaged in earnest conversation.

PANELS 9 AND 10. MIRACLE OF THE HANGED INNOCENT

The well-known story of the hanged innocent is sketched in the LSJ Book II, Miracle 5. It tells how in Toulouse a greedy innkeeper framed some German pilgrims by concealing a silver cup in one of their bags. The father and son were convicted, and the judge hung the son and let the father continue to Compostela. When he returned thirty-six days later he found his son still alive, held up by St. James. In the latter Middle Ages the miracle is often associated with the town of Santo Domingo de la Calzada.[21] In many later versions of this story a village girl, often an inn-keeper's daughter, tries to seduce the handsome son of a passing German pilgrim family. Angry that he rebuffs her, she places some stolen church silver in his scrip, and when the family leaves she denounces him to the authorities. The boy is condemned and hanged. His parents continue to Compostela, and when they return find their son still alive on the gibbet, where he has been sustained by St. James himself. They relate the miracle to the incredulous judge, who looks up from his chicken dinner[22] to say that their son must be as alive as the roast chicken, whereupon the chicken reincorporates itself and flies away.

The story is told on two panels, whose narrative sequence is 10a, 10b, 10d, 10c, 10e, 9e, 9a, 9b, 9d. I so far have been unable to relate 9c to the sequence.

10a. Background: The pilgrim father, mother and son, who is being arrested by the bailiff, are seen on a road which passes between buildings. They are watched by a man peering out of a door.

10b. Middle-ground: An unidentified woman watches from a window the pilgrims' arrival.[23]

10c. Middle-ground: In an upstairs room of an adjacent building the pilgrim family—the son in the middle—sleep in a single bed. The innkeeper's daughter, identified by her yellow hair or cowl, stands in the doorway of the room, planting a metal cup in the young man's scrip.

10d. Middle-ground: Downstairs, in the interior of the house, the young man and his parents are eating—ironically—a chicken dinner. The innkeeper's daughter waves with one hand as she exits through the door. The other hand holds the cup which she is either stealing or showing to them.

10e. Foreground: A bailiff presents the young man to the judge as in 9e. Behind his back he holds the pilgrim boy's scrip in which the stolen cup can be glimpsed. The boy's parents plead on their knees.

9a. Background: Two tiny figures represent the hanged innocent's parents returning along the road from Compostela.

9b. Background: To the right of the two travelers, and nearer the town, is the gibbet where St. James supports the hanged innocent, whose parents, with arms outstretched, express astonishment.

9c. Middle-ground: On the left side of the panel an unidentified elegant man in white enters a porch where he is greeted by a man in yellow, carrying a pilgrim staff.[24]

9d. Middle-ground: In the interior of another building an astonished servant boy still turns the spit from which the resuscitated chicken has flown. The miracle is broken into mini-episodes that are shown in sequence from left to right, and then from top to bottom: first the fowl on the spit, then the resuscitated bird flying through the air, then two additional birds walking in the street in front of the house. Strangely, for a painter who is able to render clothing and architecture with such precision, two of this panel's three depictions of the legendary bird appear to be doves with chicken feet.

9e. Foreground: The hanged innocent's parents plead before the judge. The pilgrim father carries a staff and wears the typical pilgrim hat, though without insignia, even though the pilgrims are returning from Compostela. The mother wears a pilgrim hat over a wimple, and rests her staff in the crook of her arm. The judge carries a staff which represents his judicial authority ("vara de la justicia"). Between the foreground figures grows a flower resembling a columbine.

The Indianapolis triptych, then, might well have served a pilgrimage church on the route to Compostela as a comprehensive indicator of the principal aspects of the St. James legends. It narrates the key events of the Saint's life that relate to the pilgrimage: his preaching, his election by Jesus, his martyrdom and miraculous journey to Galicia, and his burial in Compostela. It recalls the Saint-Warrior who defends Christendom, and the road, from the infidel. It recounts the miraculous powers of the Saint, in miracles accomplished during the Saint's life and after his death, and concentrates on miracles which aided sick, dead, deceived, and unjustly accused pilgrims. It displays these stories in a frame festooned with the insignia of the Compostela pilgrim: scallop shells, staff, and scrip.

The painter, or his patron, knew the stories and sources and—if we believe that panel 8 accurately depicts the sanctuary at Compostela—had probably himself made the pilgrimage to Compostela. While the stories depicted on the panels undoubtedly come from a variety of sources, the LSJ is the ultimate fount for most of them.

Fig. 6.1 *Indianapolis Museum's Altarpiece: Triptych Closed, Panels 1-4*

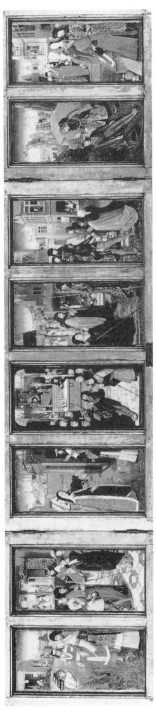

Fig. 6.2 *Indianapolis Museum's Altarpiece: Triptych Open, Panels 5-12*

Fig. 6.3 *Indianapolis Museum's Altarpiece: Panel 3,
St. James Succors a Dying Pilgrim*

Fig. 6.4 *Indianapolis Museum's Altarpiece: Panel 6,*
The Arrest and Condemnation of St. James

NOTES

[1] IMA Art. 24.3-6, James E. Roberts Collection; purchased in 1924 from Ehrich Galleries, NY, who acquired it from a private German collection in 1905 (Stokstad 527).

[2] For Stokstad, who promises a study of the triptych's iconography, style, and date, the attribution remains a mystery; it has been associated variously with Germanic, Catalán, and French traditions, as well as the workshop of the Master of the Reyes Católicos (527-8). Madou believes it to be from a south Netherlands workshop (49). On stylistic, structural, and technical grounds, Ronda Kasl, the Associate Curator of Painting and Sculpture before 1800 at the Indianapolis Museum of Art, believes the triptych to come from Bruges (letter of July 25, 1994).

[3] Each panel is approximately 68 x 31 cm. For the purposes of this paper the panels will be referred to with sequential numbering, left to right: 1-4 are the outside panels, visible when the triptych is closed; 5-12 are the interior panels. See Illustrations 6.1 and 6.2. The motifs on the surrounding frame appear both when the triptych is open and closed. Panels 1, 5, 6, 7, and 8 are reproduced in black and white in Van Herwaarden (359-61); 6 is in Stokstad (529); 1-12 are in Jansen (np) and in "Ten Primitives" (36, 38, 40); color reproductions of panels 1, 6, 9, 10, and 12 are in Moralejo (1993, 236, 238-9). I would like to thank my daughters Deborah and Abigail Gitlitz, whose close reading of the triptych in the Indianapolis Museum was essential to the preparation of the final draft of this paper, and Linda Davidson, who helped me track the sources and whose discussions helped clarify points of its iconography.

[4] In Calixtus' Prologue to the Passion of St. James (LSJ 190); in Book III, chapter 1 (387); and in the Letter of Pope Leon (3:2, 393-4). These stories are reduced to a brief paragraph by Voragine (2:5). Medieval Spanish versions of *Translatio*, which appear in a variety of Spanish sources from as early as the ninth century, all feature the boat (Melero Moneo 72-3).

[5] *Pedrón* [large rock] may relate to the toponym Padrón. Moralejo (240-1) speculates that this version of the legend, iconographically popular in Northern France and in Flanders, abetted the efforts of the bishopric of Compostela to rival Rome by asserting that if Christ founded the Roman church on a rock (Peter), he did likewise in Galicia.

[6] Roberts (37-9) correctly identified this episode. See also Coffey, et al.

[7] Calixtus, in his prologue and Passion of Santiago in the LSJ, cites as his source the *Historia eclesiastica* (Moralejo 122-6). The story is retold without significant variant in Voragine (2:4).

[8] Scenes 5a-d appear almost identically through two arched windows in the Argüelles triptych, as—through another window—do scenes 6a-b (Lavalleye Pl. XXV).

[9] The foreground scene is reproduced almost without change on the left side of the central panel of the Argüelles triptych (Lavalleye Pl. 25).

[10] Identified in the LSJ Book I chapter 9 (f. 48v) as Josías, who, seeing how Santiago cured a sick man, avowed his own Christianity and was martyred along with the Saint.

[11] The soldier, St. James, Herod, and the two dandies are reproduced with some few insignificant changes in the center of the principal panel of the Argüelles triptych (Lavalleye Pl. 25).

[12] It appears that half of the Saint's body has been smudged or painted out. Moreover, his head is missing.

[13] For Georges it represents the transformation of Lupa's palace into a church (224). This scene appears as early as the Sant Jaume de Frotanya reredo (late 13th or early 14th centuries) now in the Solsona museum.

[14] In the *Legenda aurea* she is Queen Lupa (2:5).

[15] The significance of this unidentified flower, whose blooms (but not leaves) resemble those of a violet or pansy, and that which appears in the foregound of panel 9 (which appears to be a columbine), remains unexplained.

[16] Moralejo 344-6; a condensed version appears in the *Legenda aurea*, chapter 99 (2:6-7).

[17] The scene is reproduced almost without change as the right interior panel of the Argüelles triptych (Lavalleye Pl. 25).

[18] The itinerary of the British pilgrim William Wey, written about 1460, states that Enrique IV captured Malaga in 1456 (not true) and "in token of victory the king of Castile and León sent the king of Granada's crown, which was of gold or gilded, to St. James in Compostela; and the crown was placed on the head of the seated image of St. James on the high altar" (Hogarth 17). A German pilgrim in 1499 noted that "pilgrims ascend behind the altar and place the crown on their heads" (Stokstad 528). This custom was still followed as late as 1765, as comments in Morales indicate.

[19] Georges' identification of the protagonist of this panel as St. Jodocus, based on the crown embroidered on the Saint's wrist, which is an occasional attribute of this Saint in Flemish and Burgundian art, is disputed

by Stokstad on the reasonable grounds that St. Jodocus is generally depicted as elderly, that he never went to Compostela, and that there are no resuscitations recorded among his miracles (527).

[20] "Ten Primitives" asserts that he greets the woman upon returning home (43).

[21] A condensed version, which appears in the *Legenda aurea*, chapter 99 (2:7), is cited in Toulouse.

[22] This detail does not appear in the LSJ or the *Legenda aurea*; in the LSJ the only reference to fowl is temporal: the German pilgrims set off for Compostela in the morning after the cock crowed.

[23] The whole of panel 10 is reproduced almost without change on the left interior panel of the Argüelles triptych (Lavalleye Pl. 25).

[24] Georges describes this as "un petit porche, s'entretiennent deux personnages assez mystérieux, vêtus de blanc" (232).

CHAPTER 7

The Pilgrim-Shell in Denmark

Vicente Almazán

Studies about the pilgrimage to Santiago de Compostela in the Middle
Ages comprise a tremendous number of aspects: religious, historical,
artistic, literary, geographical, archaeological, sociological, economic,
etc., which, in the last twenty years, has produced an avalanche of
publications. Particularly abundant are, of course, those dealing with
themes related to Spain. Works concerning St. James in France,
Germany, Switzerland, and Italy have also increased considerably.
However, the part that the Scandinavian countries, particularly the
Kingdom of Denmark, play in this matter is far from negligible.[1] In
this presentation, I will limit myself to only one aspect of the traces of
these medieval pilgrimages: the Santiago shell in Denmark.

The frequent pilgrimages to Santiago from within the boundaries of
what was in the Middle Ages the Kingdom of Denmark (i.e., present
Denmark plus the southernmost provinces of present Sweden, and the
northern part of the present "Bundesland" Schleswig-Holstein in today's
Germany) left many traces in the cultural history of Denmark. Not only
do we possess evidence of historical pilgrimages, but we also find
twenty-three churches and chapels, and five fountains bearing the name
of St. James[2] as well as paintings, sculptures, poems, and song which
point unmistakably to a very widespread cult of St. James in medieval
Denmark (see Fig. 7.1). Among the tangible artifacts of this cult of St.
James and the pilgrimages to his distant tomb in Compostela, we are
struck by the frequent appearance of the pilgrim-shell.

The pilgrim-shell is called *Ibskal* in the Danish language. *Ib* is one
of the ninety-one forms that James has in Danish (Hornby I: cols., 587-
99) and *skal* is the Danish equivalent of the English "shell." Thus
Ibskal means "St. James' shell." This shell appears in:
1) its natural form;
2) as a symbol;
3) in calendars;

4)   in the coat (See Figs. 7.2, 7.3); and,
5)   in sigillography.
I will look at each one in turn.

1. THE SHELL IN ITS NATURAL FORM

When the well-known Swedish naturalist Carl von Linné (1708-1778) classified the vegetal and animal kingdoms, he created for the scallop shell some names that have resulted in a certain ambiguity for the expression "pilgrim-shell." The German scholar Kurt Köster, in his study on the pilgrim-shell (*Pilgerzeichen* 121), observes the confusion existing, which results from the labels "scallop shell" or "pilgrim-shell." The scientific name *Pecten jacobæus* (St. James' shell) was given by Linné to a shell living in the Mediterranean, while the true shell, i.e., the one we associate with the Santiago pilgrim, belongs to the one that Linné named *Pecten maximus,* which is found on the Atlantic coast, particularly numerous along Galician coasts. The latter differentiates from the former by its rounded edge, while the Mediterranean shell has angular edges.

Two scholars have written recent studies on the authentic pilgrim-shell in Europe: the German Kurt Köster[3] and the Swedish Lars Anderson.[4] From their works we learn that the first Santiago shells were already sold in Santiago de Compostela at the beginning of the twelfth century (Vielliard 96). Evidence of pilgrim shells having been found earlier is rare. From the 180 authentic shells studied by Köster, 140 came from tombs. Anderson makes a list of 122 shells discovered in the Scandinavian countries Denmark, Norway, and Sweden. Since this Swedish scholar indicates the exact place of origin of every shell, it is easy to determine those originating in the old Kingdom of Denmark. There are at present 46 in Denmark. We have to add 54 in the province of Scania, one in Småland, and 11 in Schleswig, for a total of 112 authentic Santiago shells found in the medieval Kingdom of Denmark. Ten more have been found recently in Holbæk (Koch 11-26), bringing the total to 122. This total places Denmark at the head of all European countries in number of pilgrim-shells found in tombs.

2. THE SHELL AS A SYMBOL

The scallop shell as a symbol is, of course, much older than the cult of the Apostle St. James. In antiquity it was a symbol for love, or also an amulet against all kinds of magic spells. It appeared in Christian iconography in the cult of St. James (Köster 142). The reasons for its expanding popularity vary according to the authors we consult (Hohler 56-61). In the Scandinavian countries the oldest record dates from the middle of the eleventh century.[5]

3. THE SHELL IN CALENDARS

Calendars have always been typical examples of the use of symbols. Today only a glance is required to know if a certain day falls on a Sunday, or what day of the week is February 3, or what day of the month is the first Monday. During the Middle Ages such knowledge was a mystery respected and envied by everyone.[6] Olaus Magnus, in his famous *Historia de gentibus septentrionalibus,* dedicates chapter 34 to the theme "De baculis," sticks which served as calendars: "The fathers teach their inexperienced sons [the usage of sticks or tablets] and the mothers teach their daughters which days are working days and which are festival days when they go to church." In the first edition of this work of 1555 we see an illustration of this homey activity.

Almanacs, as we know today, appeared around 1500, and their main characteristic was the fact that they were only valid for one year, while in the Middle Ages calendars were known to be valid for up to 532 years (Lithberg 77). Scandinavian calendars were known by several names, according to their shape and aspect. First it was the *runstav* (Runic sticks) which consisted of a stick on which special days were marked. These calendars were made of wood or leather. These sticks were marked with small strokes, others with geometrical figures or symbols. The calendars from 1531, kept at the National Museum of Copenhagen, measures 78 cm. long, 4 cm. wide, and 2 cm. thick. On one side we see the days between the 25th of December and the 24th of June. The different symbols indicate the saint of the particular day. The tablet reads from right to left (see Fig. 7.2, showing the period between June 24 and December 24). Beginning at the right we find that the first symbols corresponds to St. Knud Lavard (June 25). After the key of St. Peter and the sword of St. Paul (June 29) comes the Visitation of the Virgin Mary (July 2) which, as in all festivities of the Virgin, is indicated by a crown. We then see the lance of St. Knud, the king (July 10), an unknown symbol (St. Margaret?) for July 20, a vase of perfumes for Mary Magdalene (July 22), and the shell of St. James for July 25. After this the ax of St. Olaf (July 29), another key of St. Peter (August 1), the grill of St. Lawrence (August 10) and Mary's Assumption (August 15). This is only one example among many showing that the shell and the Apostle St. James were already inseparably associated.

4. THE SHELL IN THE COAT OF ARMS OF FAMILIES AND CITIES

Danish heraldry owes its foundation to the works of Anders Thiset (1850-1917), Henry Petersen (1849-1896), Louis Bobé (1867-1951), and Sven Tito Achen (1922-1986). Thanks to these scholars, Danish students have acquired sources of great value, giving abundant material for research. In Europe there are approximately 20,000 coats of arms with one or more shells (Achen 69). From 25 November 1983 through 15 January 1984 an exhibition was held in the Museum of Industry in

Copenhagen in which the importance of the Santiago shell in heraldry and along the pilgrimage roads was emphasized.[7]

Poul Bredo Grandjean mentioned as early as 1919 that the Santiago shell was "very frequent in Danish heraldry" (140). Obviously not all of these shells necessarily indicate a pilgrimage to Compostela. The presence of the shells may be due to other factors: the person was named James, his family name was Jakobsen or Ibsen, he was born on July 25, he had a special devotion to St. James, or he wanted to indicate that his life was a continuous pilgrimage, not necessarily to Compostela.

Many families exhibit one or several shells on their coats of arms. in 1904 a New Dictionary of Danish Nobility (*Nyt Dansk Adelslexikon*) was published by Anders Thiset and Ludvig Peter Wittrup. Since this work had no illustrations, Henry Storck published in 1910 a voluminous book containing all armorials studied by Thiset and Wittrup.[8] Among these we see eighteen which include one or more shells on their armorials (see Fig. 7.3). These appear again in a more recent work by Sven Tito Achen (*Danske Adelsvåbener*). It should be pointed out that the oldest armorial in Denmark originated in the city of Roskilde (1277) and exhibits a Santiago shell.

As in the case for families, the presence of one or more shells on the armorials of a city or province (*Amt*) does not mean that this particular city has a connection with Santiago de Compostela. At times the shell signifies merely the maritime character of the city. The Danish cities or provinces having one or several shells on their armorials are, in alphabetical order, Ballerup, Blåvandshuk, Brovst, Herlufsholm, Otterup, Randers, Rougsø, and Skælskør. Among these armorials there are at least three that do have a connection with Santiago de Compostela.

The town of Brovst, located in northern Jutland, adopted its armorial in 1969, based on an old seal from the middle of the sixteenth century belonging to the family Rotfeldt.

With similar procedure the town of Herlufsholm, today incorporated into the city of Næstved, depicted on its armorial two figures: a monster for the family whose name was Trolle (in Danish it means elf, hobgoblin, ghost or monster), and the three scallop shells from the family Gøye.

The closest armorial to Jacobean tradition is the armorial of the city of Ballerup, adopted in 1935. At that time, Grandjean, the expert on heraldry from the Royal Archives in Copenhagen, was charged to create a coat of arms for this city, only a few miles northwest from the

Danish capital. It was inaugurated, together with a new city hall. In the upper part we see two Santiago shells, representing the two churches dedicated to St. James in this city during the twelfth and thirteenth centuries, still existing in the present. The lower part of the shield shows three streams of water representing the fountain of St. James, which today no longer exists, but, according to Siegfred Svane, was considered sacred in the medieval period and "many sick people used to come there for betterment" (76).

The old province (*Amt*) of Randers, in the north of Jutland, has today an armorial representing the city wall and a tower, taken from an old seal from 1524. However, before this the province of Randers, located on the old road to Santiago, its name recorded in so many sources, had another coat of arms taken also from an old medieval seal from the thirteenth century which exhibited two deer in the upper part and a big Santiago shell in the lower. Because of the strong pilgrimage tradition in this province, it can be assumed that the presence of the shell has something to do with Santiago de Compostela.

5. THE SHELL IN DANISH SIGILLOGRAPHY

Several churches dedicated to St. James exhibit a shell in their seals. Some of them are kept in various museums. For instance the seal of the Church of St. James of Søderbrårup (c. 1250) is displayed today in the National Museum of Copenhagen. This seal, made of lead, bears the inscription S. P(A)ROHIAL IE. SVD BRAR [Seal of the Parish of Søderbrårup]. It contains a pilgrim's staff and on it a shell, symbol of the pilgrimage to Santiago.[9] Another example comes from the no-longer-existing Church of St. James of Ham on the Frisian island of Nordstrand. The seal is from 1570, and it belongs at present to the State Archives of Kiel, Germany.[10]

The medieval Danish confraternities also possessed a seal. Thanks to the works by Poul Bredo Grandjean[11] and Camillus Nyrop[12] we possess today many seals reproduced in these studies. In some of them, the Apostle St. James appears with the trappings of a pilgrim, including the shell. We will mention four of these seals.

The seal of the confraternity of Svendborg displays a big shell in the center with a rose on each side surrounded by the inscription CONVIVII SUTORUM IN SWINEBORG [Seal of the Confraternity of Shoemakers of Svendborg].

In the Historical Museum of Stockholm, Sweden, there is a seal of the confraternity of St. James from the city of Trelleborg, which belonged to Denmark in the Middle Ages. On it we distinguish the Apostle Santiago with a pilgrim staff, a bag, and a Bible. The inscription reads SANCTI IACOBS GILDES INSIGLEI I TTRELEBORG [Seal of the Confraternity of St. James of Trelleborg].

Another interesting seal, this one belonging to a member of a confraternity, represents St. James walking, dressed as a pilgrim, wearing a strange hat and carrying a sword in his left hand. It is rather difficult to determine the object he has in his right hand. Since the seal belonged to a member of a confraternity of shoemakers, we suppose that it is a working instrument of this trade. The inscription reads S. FRATRIS IOHANNIS SCI IACOBI [Seal of John, member of the Confraternity of St. James].

The last example, now lost, belonged to the Confraternity of Ystad, Scania, from 1450. We know, however, that it had three shells with an eagle surrounded by the inscription SANCTUS IACOBUS MAIOR (Danmarks 1:199).

More important and quite numerous are the seals of families belonging to the nobility or to members of the clergy. A survey of Danish sigillography from the fifteenth to the seventeenth centuries[13] reveals 116 seals in which the shell appears as an essential part. In the seals of noble families, it is obvious that not all of the shells indicate a pilgrimage to Compostela. The reason for this presence can be attributed to other factors, as we have previously discussed. In Denmark the use of seals among families belonging to the nobility began during the thirteenth century, reaching its widest usage in the fifteenth century. Many families included one or several shells in the armorials; Storck shows eighteen.

Among the seals listed by Henry Petersen in his work on the seals of members of the clergy, there are sixteen with shells corresponding to bishops, canons, deans, a vicar, priors, a "prepositus," and priests. We also find the seal of an abbess from 1466. The seals date from 1310 to 1501. Some are repeated because the clergymen appear first as canons and later as bishops (see Fig. 7.4).

The most striking appearance of the Santiago shell in Danish heraldry occurred, of course, on the first national flag of Denmark in 1427. The Danish scholar Erik Christian Werlauff, in a book published in 1872 (*Danebrog og Danebrogsordenen* 18), called the attention of the Danish public to the existence of a Danish flag which the Hanseatic armies snatched in 1427 from the forces of the Scandinavian Union[14] during a naval battle. This flag was displayed in the Church of St. Mary in the city of Lübeck. A few years later, another Danish historian, Henry Petersen, somehow skeptical, visited that church in 1879 and became convinced that the exhibited flag was indeed authentic. He then initiated the necessary steps to have a copy of the flag made. After this was done, the flag became a permanent part of the exhibits of the Museum in the Castle of Frederiksborg, a few miles northeast of downtown Copenhagen[15] where up to the present time it still can be seen by everyone. With the destructions of the last World War, the real flag disappeared among the ruins of Lübeck, but the authentic reproduction is still part of the Frederiksborg Museum.

This flag was captured by the armies of the Hanseatic League. The colors of the flag were still very bright in the last century, but its most striking feature is the presence of St. James bearing a huge shell in his left hand. The size of the figure of the Saint is even larger than the coat of arms of Denmark, Norway, and Sweden, and of Erik of Pomerania. These, together with a figure of the Virgin Mary, share the whole flag.

Why is the Apostle St. James holding the shell in this flag? According to Petersen, there is no doubt that the flag is an authentic copy, and dates from 1427 (1:56). Petersen proposed several theories in his articles: maybe St. James was the protector of King Erik of Pomerania, or the boat was built by someone named James, or St. James was the Patron Saint of the city where the boat was built, or it could even be that the boat was named *Saint James*. As yet no one has satisfactorily explained the presence of the Saint or the Virgin in this flag. However, it is a fact that the Apostle Santiago with the shell in hand waved on the German-Scandinavian seas in the month of July of 1427, together with the colors of the three Scandinavian countries.

Fig. 7.1 *Danish Churches, Chapels, and Fountains Dedicated to the Apostle St. James*

Replica of original flag captured by the Germans during Baltic sea battle in 1427, presently on display in the castle of Frederiksborg

Segment of notched stick calendar for the month of July from the fifteenth century (National Museum of Copenhagen)

Sixteenth century seal of shoemakers' guild from the city of Svendborg

Sixteenth century seal of shoemakers' guild from the city of Trelleborg

Sixteenth century personal seal of Danish guild member

Fig. 7.2 *The Shell Motif in Danish Iconography*

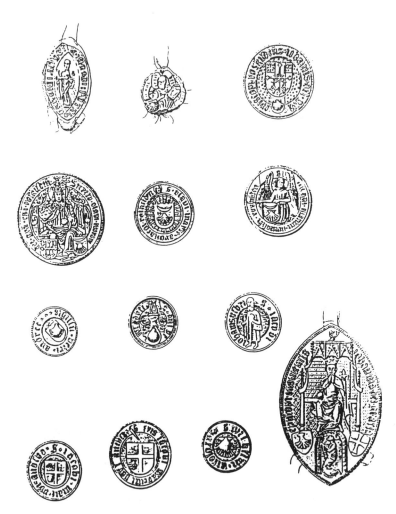

Fig. 7.3 *The Shell Motif in Seals of Danish Clergy, 14th-16th Centuries*

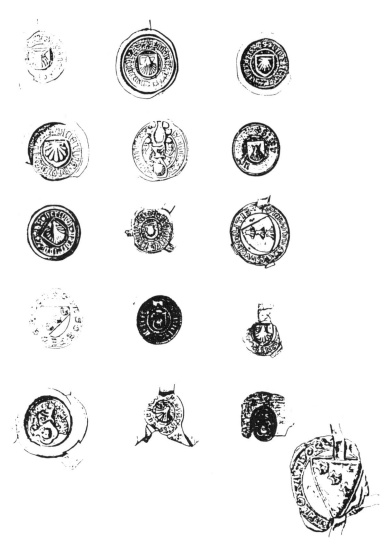

Fig. 7.4 *The Shell Motif in Seals of Danish Nobility, 14th-16th Centuries*

NOTES

[1] I have been studying the subject for several years, and have come to surprising conclusions which are shown in *Dinamarca jacobea: Historia, Arte y Literatura.*

[2] See map in Almazán, "Historie," 106-7.

[3] Although I refer specifically to *Pilgerzeichen*, Köster has published over thirty-five works on pilgrims' badges.

[4] *Pilgrimsmarken och vallfart. Medeltida pilgrimskultur I Skandinavien.* He is also the author of other works concerning pilgrims' badges, in particular those related to Saint Birgitta.

[5] For Denmark see the article by Søgaard, *Kulturhistorisk.*

[6] For the study of Scandinavian calendars, see Liebgott, *Kalendere.*

[7] See the articles of Achen (69-74) and Haastrup (61-8) published in *Konklien og Mennesket.*

[8] *Dansk Vaabenbog.*

[9] National Museum of Copenhagen. Inv. N° D1445/1977, plate 33 b 34.

[10] Karl Boie, *Die mittelalterlichen Siegel Nordfrieslands*, plate IV, N° 31.

[11] Especially *Danske Gilders Segel fra Middelalderen* and *Dansk Sigillografi.*

[12] *Danske Haandværkerlavs Segl.*

[13] Thiset, *Danske adelige Sigiller fra det XV, XVI og XVII Aarhundrede.*

[14] Called "Kalmar Union," grouping Denmark, Norway and Sweden from 1397 to 1521.

[15] See "Et dansk flag fra Unionstiden I Maria-Kirken I Lübeck."

CHAPTER 8

A Medieval Pilgrimage
to Santiago de Compostela
on the Information Highway

John Dagenais

One of the biggest challenges facing those of us who teach the literature of the Middle Ages in the late twentieth century is to find a way to make the human life experiences of that period more accessible for students who have never even known a time when there was no TV. Unless students have some feel for the background to the literature and the values of the civilizations which created it, the gap between their own experiences and those portrayed in the literature of Medieval Europe is almost unbridgeable for all but a few highly motivated students. And if we make the literature even more remote by placing it not only in a foreign language, but also in an archaic form of that language, a survey course in medieval Spanish literature for third-year Spanish students can be a frustrating experience for students and teachers alike.

It was in trying to overcome some of these obstacles that I decided to try to organize my course around a medieval pilgrimage to Santiago de Compostela in Galicia, the place where the body of the martyred apostle, St. James the Greater, was believed to rest, and an extremely popular goal for pilgrims from all over Europe in the Middle Ages and today. I restructured the course in order to present the readings and their cultural context, not chronologically or in terms of an established canon of "medieval classics," but rather as medieval people might have experienced them as they moved through geographical space and seasonal/liturgical time on a pilgrimage to Santiago in January-March of the year 1300.

Thus, students read and perform an Old Spanish play about the Three Wise Men on Epiphany, January 6. Students hear an epic fragment on Roland and Charlemagne as we pass through Roncesvalles. In the monastery of San Millán de la Cogolla, we read the *Vida de Santo Domingo de Silos* and the *Milagros de Nuestra Señora* by Gonzalo de Berceo, a thirteenth-century resident of the monastery, just as these texts were probably presented to pilgrims who happened to

143

stop there in the year 1300. We take a lengthy rest stop to read the epic *Poema del Cid* in Burgos, the center of the Cid cult. At the end of the journey, like the thousands of pilgrims before us, we tour the Cathedral of Santiago de Compostela. I use slides to illustrate the landscape and artistic monuments we visit and recordings to introduce music, both sacred and secular, which medieval pilgrims may have heard along their way. If they wish, students can choose a profession, a home town, and a pilgrim name for the duration of the journey (the name of their rather dubious guide is Jehan D'Agenet, a Gascon by birth). By providing concrete, if imaginary, geographical, temporal, and even subjective anchors like these, I hope to overcome, at least in part, the disorientation late twentieth-century students inevitably feel when they are asked to transport themselves back 700 years to a rather alien place, culture, and language.

As a second stage in the development of the course I began to use an electronic discussion list or "listserver" mounted on a local server and connected to the Internet.[1] Students subscribe to the list and thereafter receive copies of everything I or their fellow students post to it. Students can use the list to ask questions of me or of other students, to continue discussions begun in class, and to arrange group study or film-viewing sessions. I can use the list to post answers to student questions, supplemental reading materials (the life of St. Valentine on February 14, for example), topics for on-line discussion, and any changes in assignments.

One feature of the on-line discussion list has been especially valuable: because the list is open to off-campus subscribers as well as Northwestern students, experts on the medieval pilgrimages to Santiago de Compostela from the U.S., Canada, England, and Spain have joined the list. Thus, when students have a question about the readings and lectures, they are as likely to get an answer from a leading authority on their problem as from me. Eventually, I hope to have residents of the major cities along the Camino on-line, ready to give us virtual tours of their cities as we pass through. I have been impressed at how willing the students have been to engage these experts in discussion and how enthusiastically the experts have responded. We have had some especially interesting conversations this year on the nature of pilgrimage itself as a perennial human activity: are trips to Graceland, or to the lake where Susan Smith drowned her children, or to The Mall of America examples of modern pilgrimages?

The immediate goal of the on-line discussion list is to expand the physical and temporal boundaries of the classroom experience, to create a sense of group cohesion, and to foster cooperative, group learning, as opposed to competitive, individual learning. The ultimate goal is a democratization of the learning process in which teacher, students, and outside specialists participate in a common intellectual enterprise.

In December 1994, I began the latest phase in the development of the course. I attended a workshop on "Technology in Learning and Teaching" sponsored by Northwestern University's Academic Computing and Networking Services. Using what I learned in the workshop, I have developed a World Wide Web site (http://www.humnet.ucla.edu/iagohome.html) for students in the Camino de Santiago course. The Web offers some unique features which make it especially valuable as a way of merging medieval culture and modern technology in the university setting. It works across platforms, so it doesn't matter if the student has a Mac or a PC. It allows the easy integration of text, graphics, sound, and even video media, including easy hyperlinking of text and media. Through the Web, students can proceed with their "virtual pilgrimage" at their own pace, on the computer, and more class time can be devoted to discussions in the target language of the cultural background and the texts themselves.

The Web site helps to make these discussions far more lively and informed: students can click on a map to learn about a particular medieval Spanish city. They can tour parts of the Cathedral of Santiago de Compostela, see pictures of monuments, and hear music or readings of poetry associated with each place (the monks of Silos are a particular attraction these days).[2] They can also pull up the latest course syllabus and, via the syllabus, many of the assigned readings (see Appendix). Eventually all the "course pack" readings will be available for downloading here. Students can go to Northwestern's Multi-Media Learning Center or to any of the computer labs on the campus to visit the Camino de Santiago Web site if they do not have access to the Internet from their own or a roommate's computer.

I have gradually figured out ways to use the features of HTML (Hyper Text Markup Language, the codes used to design hypermedia Web pages and links) and Web browsers such as Netscape to make the site into a place for active, and interactive, learning. The first thing I tried was to use the linking feature to link unfamiliar spellings and words in an Old Spanish text to a glossary (see, for example, http://www.humnet.ucla.edu/roncpoem.html). Enhancements under development to speed delivery of audio files over the World Wide Web will soon allow fast links to sample pronunciations of these words and sounds as well.

The "clickable map" of the Camino forms the heart of the Web site and certainly has a pedagogical value of its own for students in these geographically innocent times. But the clickable map feature can also be used to create an interactive instructional environment. Clickable "maps" can, in fact, be any graphics file. Each clickable image must have a "default" file which appears if the user fails to click on one of the hot spots the designer has identified. I have used these features to give mini-lessons in architectural terminology or to get students to examine a given image more closely than they might otherwise do. Thus, beside an image of the Portada das Praterías of the Cathedral of Santiago de Compostela, students are asked to "click on the left tympanum" to see a more detailed image (a text link gives them a definition of "tympanum"). If they click on the correct spot, they are taken to a more detailed image; if they miss, the default file appears and they are told to try again (see http://www.humnet.ucla.edu/comptour.html).

Even something as simple as icons can be used to convey important distinctions. The standard way of identifying sound files on Web pages is to use an icon showing an audio speaker. This would clearly be an anachronism in a medieval Web page, and so I stumbled onto the idea of using icons of monks in a choir to identify samples of Christian sacred song and icons of troubadours to identify secular song samples. This choice itself conveys the idea that medievalists tend to divide medieval music into sacred and secular categories and suggests, as well, that there may have been more than one sort of religious song in medieval Spain. (I would welcome suggestions as to how one sets up an appropriately medieval icon to identify video files.)

Special features of the Netscape browser 1.1N and above allow for additional decorative and pedagogical elements, elements which may not be visible for a while to students using other browsers. A cloned portion of a page from the *Codex Calixtinus* has been used to create a parchment "background" for some of the Web pages. One can also specify the colors of on-screen fonts. One thing I may do is use this feature to incorporate liturgical colors into the on-line syllabus: purple background or fonts for Lent, black for Good Friday, and so on. In the Middle Ages *everything* was symbolic and the HTML Extensions in Netscape allow one to create a similarly symbolic virtual world.

By far the greatest pedagogical benefit of the Web, however, is that students can be involved, not just in passively receiving materials produced by their instructor, but in actively *creating* multimedia and hypertext materials. With some trepidation at first, I decided to offer students the option of doing a Web page in lieu of the time-honored oral report. The result was one of the most rewarding experiences of my teaching career. I learned that the challenge of producing a Web page on a given place, saint, or other topic related to medieval Spain allows students to be creative, a thing they like a great deal. It gets them to go to the library far more spontaneously than the prospect of churning out yet another written or oral report ever did. And while they are at the library they look, not just at texts, but at pictures as well. The creation of a hyperlinked Web page forces (allows) them to think in very concrete ways about how to organize and hierarchize information. These are all things we humanists say we want our students to do, the very things we would defend as one of the general benefits of a humanistic education.

Students work on their mini Web sites in small groups (three to four students) and, since their names will be on the Web Pages for all the world to see, they have added incentive to do a good job. There is cooperation within the groups and a healthy and productive competition between groups. In addition, when they are home over break, students can crank up their Web Browsers from home and give their parents what I hope will be a positive view of what their children have been doing with the money they are spending to send them to college. At least it will show that they have been doing *something*.

You can learn the basics of HTML in a few minutes, even faster if you have a good HTML editor. For technoclutz students I gave a two-hour workshop along with a colleague, Harlan Wallach, in our Multi-Media Learning Center lab at Northwestern. At the end of the two hours, students had overcome residual phobias, learned all the basics of creating multimedia Web pages, and, most importantly, were having fun working on and thinking about their projects. The results were of a superior quality and the students in the class this year learned more about medieval Spanish culture than any group I've taught in recent years, probably because they taught themselves (see the sample student projects at http://www.humnet.ucla.edu/santiago-proj.html). A further unexpected benefit of the "Web Page Option" was that even students who stuck with the more traditional oral reports worked harder on them and included more multimedia materials than students in previous years had done.

I hope eventually to have enough images and sound files stored on the site so that we can run virtual pilgrimages on a regular basis using guest tour guides. Experienced guides at other institutions in the U.S. or abroad can lead groups of virtual pilgrims through their favorite places along the Camino.[3]

Berceo, the medieval poet from the monastery of San Millán used pilgrimage as a metaphor for human life in his *Milagros de Nuestra Señora*: we are all pilgrims on the road of life. In a similar way, I have come to understand that the medieval Camino de Santiago and the Internet mirror each other in numerous ways. We must first get rid of the notion that the Internet is a *super*highway, with limited on and off ramps and food that tastes exactly the same in Mobile as it does in San Francisco. The Internet resembles much more closely the old two-lanes like, say, Route 66, where cross-country journeys had a certain epic quality about them and each stop had its own home-cooking (for better or worse), its curiosities and sights, its souvenir shops and speed traps. Both the Internet and the Camino de Santiago are places where travelers from every walk of life and from all over the known world come together to share common interests as well as to learn about each others' differences and to poke around together in interesting places along the way. And these similarities allow for the creation of yet another link, another road: from the Middle Ages to today.

APPENDIX

A reproduction of portions of the syllabus as it appears in the Camino de Santiago Web site. Underlined words or phrases represent links to other documents: texts, course information, graphics, campus facilities, and so on.

Northwestern University, Department of Hispanic Studies

HISPANIC STUDIES B01-3:
INTRODUCTION TO SPANISH LITERATURE (MEDIEVAL)

John Dagenais
Francisco Castro

El Camino de Santiago
Winter '95
Revision of 1/18/95

ITINERARIO

A.D. 1300, Julian
—Hispanic Era: 1338 —Jewish Era: 5060 —Hijra: 699—

There are several shareware and freeware DOS/WINDOWS utilities available for downloading to help you explore medieval ways of keeping track of time and to see how the heavens looked to pilgrims in the year 1300.

NAVARRA
4 enero
Valcarlos (entrada en España)
    Introducción; Leyenda de Santiago y el Camino de Santiago
6 enero [January]
Roncesvalles (Epifanía)
    Auto de los reyes magos (xerox)
    Celebrate a Medieval Spanish Christmas
9 enero
Roncesvalles
    "Leyenda de Roldán" (xerox, Codex Calixtinus, pp. 462-476)
11 enero
Pamplona
    "Leyenda de Roldán" (xerox, Codex Calixtinus, pp. 462-476)
13 enero
Pamplona (S. Hilario)
    "Cantar de Roncesvalles" (xerox)
16 enero
Medieval Pilgrimage to Compostela on the Information Highway 149

Puente la Reina (S. Marcelo; SS. Berardo, Oto, Acursio y Adjuto)
"Romances del Conde Julián" (xerox)
18 enero
Puente la Reina (S. Leobardo)
"Romances del Conde Julián" (xerox)

LA RIOJA
20 enero
Nájera (S.Sebastián)
"Los navarros" (CC, pp. 516-523)
Película: "And They Sang a New Song" (in the Library
    Marjorie I. Mitchell Media Center; see the film on your own
        before class)
23 enero
San Millán de la Cogolla (S. Ildefonso de Toledo; S. Ramon de
Penyafort)
    "Ferragut" (CC, 447-53)
    "Como los peregrinos hayan de ser recibidos" (CC 575-576)

. . . .
. . . .

3 marzo
Compostela (S. Marino)
    La Catedral de Santiago (diapositivas)
(Cuaresma—a. 1995)
6 marzo
REPASO [review]
7 marzo
READING PERIOD BEGINS
    Taller sobre la preparación de las Web Pages, Multi-Media
                Learning Center Lab, 2-4 PM, 46 Kresge (See the
Web Page   Guide for Students in B01-3)
10 de marzo
Sessión de Repaso: 11:00 AM, 245 Kresge
Entrega de los proyectos de Web Page: 1 PM

FINAL EXAM: Thursday, March 16, 9-11 AM

Return to Camino de Santiago Home Page

NOTES

[1] Readers of this volume are invited to join the SANTIAGO listserv. To join, send a regular e-mail message to the following address:
listserv@listserv.acns.nwu.edu
The message should read:
subscribe santiago Your_First_Name Your_Last_Name
You will receive a confirmation of your subscription. Thereafter, you can post messages to the SANTIAGO listserv at the following address:
santiago@listserv.acns.nwu.edu

[2] I use a recording of the monks of Silos made before their *Chant* album went platinum: *Canto Gregoriano en el Monasterio de Silos* (EMI Classics: CDZ 7 62735 2).

[3] Readers of this article are invited to contribute pages or even "expansion sites" to the Camino de Santiago. One of the beauties of the Web is that it does not matter where files are located physically as long as links can be established. See now the new Camino de Santiago site created by Prof. Raulston at the University of Texas at Austin: http://www.utexas.edu/depts/spn/sbr/home.html

Notes on the Contributors

VICENTE ALMAZÁN, Emeritus Professor of Spanish at University of Wisconsin-Oshkosh, is the author of several books which treat the Pilgrimage to Santiago and its relationship to Scandinavia and France: *Gallaecia Scandinavica* (1986), *Alsacia Jacobea* (1994), and *Dinamarca Jacobea* (1995). He is editor of a collection of essays, *Seis Ensaios sobre o Camiño de Santiago* (1993). In addition, he has published articles on Scandinavia-Spain relationships in the thirteenth century in a variety of journals. Currently, Professor Almazán is part of the Xunta de Galicia committee preparing for the year 2000 when Santiago de Compostela will be the Council of Europe's Cultural City.

VINCENT CORRIGAN, Associate Professor of Music History at Bowling Green State University, has interests in twelfth-century polyphony, conductus repertory, modal transmutation, rhythmic modes and the *Codex Calixtinus*. His publications include various articles for the *International Music Journal* and transcriptions for *The Medieval Lyric. Anthology III: Guillaume de Machaut, Remede de Fortune*. He has delivered papers about the music of the *Codex Calixtinus* at the Thirteenth and Fifteenth Medieval Forums at Plymouth State College, and at the Twenty-fourth through the Twenty-ninth International Congresses on Medieval Studies at Western Michigan University.

JOHN DAGENAIS, Associate Professor Spanish at UCLA, connects the Middle Ages to the twentieth century not only through the virtual reality of pilgrimage, but also by maintaining two listservs (Mediber and Santiago); an FTP site; two WWW sites; and also by serving as a founding member of the editorial board of *Ciberia: A* [electronic] *Journal for Early Iberian Studies*. His other interests are Catalán studies (especially Ramón Llull), the *Libro de buen amor*, and rhetoric. He has recently published the *Ethics of Reading in Manuscript Culture. Glossing the* Libro de buen amor (Princeton UP, 1994).

LINDA KAY DAVIDSON, Spanish Instructor at the University of Rhode Island, first walked the Road to Santiago in 1974. She has repeated that trek three other times (1979, 1987, Holy Year 1993), and is planning the fifth for Summer 1996, as co-director with David Gitlitz in a university program that studies the Iberian Middle Ages along the Route. Her three previous books, all co-authored with Maryjane Dunn, have concentrated on the pilgrimage and its output, both literary and sociological.

MARYJANE DUNN, Spanish Instructor at Metropolitan Community College in Omaha, NE, has been interested in the pilgrimage to Compostela since taking Spanish in high school. She has walked the Camino twice, in 1979 and in 1986. In 1989 she founded the Friends of the Road to Santiago in the U.S., and became editor of its annual newsletter. The last four years have been busy, with the publication of two bibliographies dealing with pilgrimage (co-written with Linda Davidson), and the first English translation of the Miracles of St. James and the "Veneranda dies" sermon from the *Codex Calixtinus* (with Linda Davidson and Tom Coffey). Her other interests and publications have dealt with allegorical pilgrimage as represented in the Spanish translation of Guillaume de Deguileville's *Le Pélérinage de la Vie Humaine*, an edition and study of which served as her dissertation at the University of Pennsylvania.

ALBERTO FERREIRO, Professor of History at Seattle Pacific University, received a Fulbright Dissertation Fellowship, which led to the publication of his first book, *The Visigoths in Gaul and Spain A.D. 418-711: A Bibliography* (1988). In addition, he has published more than a dozen articles about aspects of his various interests: Priscillianism, Caesarius of Arles, and St. Martin of Braga, among others. Currently Professor Ferreiro is editing a casebook for Garland Publishing, entitled, *The Goths: A Book of Essays*; and is writing another entitled *Simon Magus in the Early Christian and Medieval Tradition*.

DAVID M. GITLITZ, Professor of Hispanic Studies at the University of Rhode Island, first walked to Compostela with a student group in 1974. His publications, ranging from archaeology to popular culture and from quantitative stylistic analysis to theater criticism, include translation/ editions of works by Lope de Vega, Quevedo, and Calderón; as well as *La estructura lírica del teatro de Lope de Vega;* a history of a late-medieval converso clan, *Los Arias Dávila de Segovia, entre la iglesia y la sinagoga;* and an ethnography entitled *Secrecy and Deceit: The Religion of the Crypto-Jews*. In 1996 he and Linda Davidson will make their fifth academic-pilgrimage trek to the shrine of St. James.

JEANNE E. KROCHALIS, Associate Professor of English at Pennsylvania State University, New Kensington, is currently focused on the pilgrimage to Compostela with the publication of *The Pilgrim's Guide to Santiago* (2 vols., with Paula Gerson, Annie Shaver-Crandell, and Alison Stones). In addition, she has also seen the publication of an article, "Qui a lu le *Guide de Pélérin de Saint-Jacques de Compostelle*? (with Alison Stones) in *Pélérinage et Croisade* (Ed. Léon Pressouyre, 1995). In addition to her interests in the *Codex Calixtinus*, she has many other research interests—in medieval books and libraries, paleography, Chaucer, and Langland. Currently she is serving as Associate Editor of *The Chaucer Review*.

CONNIE L. SCARBOROUGH, Associate Professor of Spanish at the University of Cincinnati, co-edits the *Bulletin of the Cantigueiros de Santa María* (with John E. Keller). Her interests encompass nearly all aspects of the writings of Alfonso X, el Sabio, and she has published several articles based on his *Cantigas*. Her books, *Women in Thirteenth-Century Spain as Portrayed by Alfonso X's 'Cantigas de Santa Maria'* (1993), and *Text and Concordance of* Castigos y dotrinas que un sabio daba a sus hijas: *Escorial MS. a.IV.5* (1994) offer views of women's lives in medieval Spain. Her latest book (in press) is a critical edition of the *Libro de los exenplos por a.b.c.* (with John E. Keller).

COLIN SMITH, Emeritus Professor of Spanish at the University of Cambridge, has the distinction of being the Honorary Vice-consul for Spain in Cambridge and a Corresponding Member of the Real Academia Española (for his language and dictionary work). His teaching and research interests include the history of the Spanish language, aspects of linguistics applied to modern Spanish, medieval and Renaissance literature and history, and aspects of modern Galician writing. As a medievalist, he is best known for several books, including an edition of the *Poema de mio Cid* (1972, revised 1985), *Spanish Ballads* (1964), *The Making of the "Poema de mio Cid"* (1983), and *Christians and Moors in* Spain (2 vols., 1988-9).

Works Cited

Acta Sanctorum Aprilis II. Ed. G. Henschen, and Daniel Papenbroch. Antwerp: Michael Cnoben, 1685.

Adams, Percy. *Travel Literature and the Evolution of the Novel.* Lexington, Kentucky: UP of Kentucky, 1983.

Albani, Nicola. *Viaje de Nápoles a Santiago de Galicia.* Ed. Isabel González. Biblioteca facsimilar compostelana 1. Madrid: Edilán for the Consorcio de Santiago, 1993.

Alfonso X, el Sabio. *Cantigas de Santa Maria.* Ed. Walter Mettmann. 3 vols. Madrid: Clásicos Castalia, 1986-89.

Almazán, Vicente. *Alsacia Jacobea.* Vigo: Nigra Arte, 1993.

—. *Dinamarca jacobea: Historia, Arte y Literatura.* [Vigo]: Consellería de Cultura, Dirección Xeral de Promoción do Camiño de Santiago, 1995.

—. "Historie." *Byhornet* 22 (1993): 106-7.

—. "Huellas jacobeas en la cultura escandinava." *Santiago, Camino de Europa: Culto y cultura en la peregrinación a Compostela.* Compostela: Fundación Caja de Madrid, Xunta de Galicia, Arzobispado de Santiago de Compostela, 1993. 181-93.

Alphonsus de Spina. *Fortalicium Fidei.* Nürnberg: A Koberger, 1485.

Anderson, Lars. *Pilgrimsmärken och vallfart. Medeltida pilgrimskultur I Skandinavien.* Stockholm: Almqvist & Wiksell, 1989.

Annales Regni Francorum. Monumenta Germaniae Historica, Scriptores I. Hanover: n.p., 1826.

Antiphonale monasticum. Tournai: Desclée, 1934.

Aymard, R. *Régard sur les Pyrénées de Saint-Jacques. Hagiotoponymie de l'ouest pyrénéen.* N.p.: n.p., n.d.

Baby, Françoise. "Toponomastique du pèlerinage en Languedoc." *Le pèlerinage.* Cahiers de Fanjeaux 15. Toulouse: Edouard Privat, 1980. 57-78.

Badía Margarit, Antonio. "Más sobre la aportación de la toponimia al 'Camino de Santiago' y su justificación histórica." *Revista de filología española* 38 (1954): 212-23.

—. "Toponymie et histoire dans le 'Chemin de Saint Jacques' en Espagne." *Quatrième Congrès international de sciences onomastiques. 2. Actes et Mémoires.* Uppsala, 1952. Eds. J. Sahlgren, et al. Uppsala: A.B. Lundequistska, 1954. 143-58.

Barlow, Claude W., ed. *Martini episcopi Bracarensis opera omnia.* New Haven, Ct.: Yale UP, 1950.

Bates, Katerine Lee. *Spanish Highways and Byways.* Chautauqua, NY: Chautauqua P, 1920.

Baudot, Marcel. "Influence du pèlerinage à St. Jacques de Compostelle sur la toponymie et l'anthroponymie française." *Actes et mémoires du Ve Congrès international de toponymie et d'anthroponymie.* Salamanca, 12-15 Apr. 1955. Filosofía y Letras 10.1. Madrid: Talleres Gráficos "Jura", 1958. 1: 343-55.

"Behaim, Martin." *Encyclopedia Britannica.* 14th ed. Ed. J.L. Garnin. London: Encyclopedia Britannica, 1929.

Beltrán Torreira, Federico-M. "La conversión de los suevos y el III Concilio de Toledo." *Mayurqa* 22.1 (1989): 69-83.

Bennett, Matthew. "First Crusaders' Images of Muslims: the Influence of Vernacular Poetry." *Forum for Modern Language Studies* 22 (1986): 101-22.

Berceo, Gonzalo de. See Gonzalo de Berceo.

Bisson, T. *The Medieval Crown of Aragon: A Short History.* Oxford: Clarendon, 1986.

Blomgren, Sven. "In Venantii Fortunati carmina adnotationes novae." *Eranos* 69 (1971): 104-50.

Blue Guide Spain: The Mainland. See Robertson.

Boie, Karl. *Die mittelalterlichen Siegel Nordfrieslands.* Neumünster: K. Wachholtz, 1931.

The Book of Saints. A Dictionary of Persons Canonized or Beatified by the Roman Catholic Church. 5th ed. The Benedictine Monks of St. Augustine's Abbey, Ramsgate. New York: Thomas Crowell, 1966.

Boorde, Andrew. *Andrew Boorde, Introduction of Knowledge, 1547, Dyetary of Helth, 1542, Barnes in Defense of the Berde, 1542-3.* Ed. F.J. Furnivall. EETS es 10. London: Kegan Paul, Trench, Trübner, 1870.

Braga, Alberto Veira. "Influência da S. Tiago de Galiza em Portugal." *Homenagem a Martins Sarmento.* Guimarães: Sociedade Martins Sarmento, 1933. 411-35.

Branner, Robert. *Manuscript Painting in Paris during the Reign of St. Louis.* Berkeley: U of California P, 1977.

Bredo Grandjean, Poul. *Dansk Heraldik.* Copenhagen: J.H. Schultz, 1919.

—. *Dansk Sigillografi.* Copenhagen: J.H. Schultz, 1944.

—. *Danske Gilders Segl fra Middelalderen.* Copenhagen: J.H. Schultz, 1948.

Brennan, Brian. "The Career of Venantius Fortunatus." *Traditio* 41 (1985): 49-78.

—. "The Image of the Frankish Kings in the Poetry of Venantius Fortunatus." *Journal of Medieval History* 10 (1984): 1-11.

Brown, Peter. *The Cult of the Saints: Its Rise and Function in Latin Christianity.* Chicago: U of Chicago P, 1981.

—. *Society and the Holy in Late Antiquity.* Berkeley: U of California P, 1982.

Cal Pardo, Enrique. "Dispersión del Santoral Hispano-Mozárabe en la Diócesis de Mondoñedo." *Memoria Ecclesiae II. Las raíces visigóticas de la iglesia en España: En torno al Concilio III de Toledo. Santoral Hispano-Mozárabe en España.* Acts of the Congress celebrated in Toledo, 21-2 Sept. 1989. Oviedo: n.p., 1991. 177-86.

Camino de Santiago. Ensemble Frühe Musik Augsburg. Christophorus, CD 74.530; SCGLX 74.032, 1986.

Camino de Santiago I. Studio der Frühen Musik. Dir. Thomas Binkley. Reflex, Stationen Europäischer Musik, EMI Electrola 1 C 063-30 107, 1973.

Camino de Santiago II. Studio der Frühen Musik. Dir. Thomas Binkley. Reflex, Stationen Europäischer Musik, EMI Electrola 1 C 063-30 108, 1973.

Camino de Santiago. CD-ROM. Madrid: Secretaria General de Turismo TURESPAÑA, [1993].

Campos, Julio. *Idacio. Obispo de Chaves, su* Cronicon. Salamanca: Ediciones Salamanca, 1984.

Cantera Orive, Julián. "Un ilustre peregrino francés en Albelda (Logroño), años 950-1." *Berceo* 3.9 (1948): 427-42; 4.10 (1949): 107-21; 4.11 (1949): 299-304; 4.12 (1949): 329-40.

Cardini, Francis. *Europe 1492.* New York: Facts on File, 1989.

Casariego, J. E. "Asturias proclamó el patronazgo de Santiago para España." *Boletín del Instituto de Estudios Asturianos* 33 (1979): 3-54.

Castets, Ferdinand. *Turpinus Historia Karoli Magni et Rotholandi.* Montpellier: Société des langues romanes, and Paris: Maisonneuve, 1880.

Chadwick, Henry. *Priscillian of Avila: The Occult and the Charismatic in the Early Church.* Oxford: Clarendon, 1976.

Chaves, Luis. "São Martinho de Tours." *Revista de etnografía* 1 (1963): 91-116.

Codex Calixtinus. Ensemble Venance Fortunat, Dir. Anne-Marie Deschamps. Solstice, SOL 45, 1986.

Codoñer Merino, Carmen, ed. *El 'De viris illustribus' de Isidoro de Sevilla.* Salamanca: U de Salamanca P, 1964.

Coffey, Thomas F., Linda Kay Davidson and Maryjane Dunn. *The "Miracles of Saint James" and the Pilgrimage to Compostela:*

Translations from the Liber Sancti Jacobi. New York: Italica, [1996].

Coleman, Shirley. Telephone interview. 14 Nov. 1995.

Collins, Roger. *The Arab Conquest of Spain 710-797.* London: Blackwell, 1989.

—. *Early Medieval Spain: Unity in Diversity, 400-1000.* London: MacMillan, 1983.

Connolly, Jane E. "Three Peninsular Versions of a Miracle of St. James." *Saints and their Authors: Studies in Medieval Hispanic Hagiography in Honor of John K. Walsh.* Eds. Jane E. Connolly, Alan Deyermond, and Brian Dutton. Madison: Hispanic Seminary of Medieval Studies, 1990. 37-46.

Corbett, John H. "Changing Perceptions in Late Antiquity: Martin of Tours." *Toronto Journal of Theology* 3.2 (1987): 236-51.

—. *"Praesentium signorum munera:* The Cult of the Saints in the World of Gregory of Tours." *Florilegium* 5 (1983): 44-61.

—. "The Saint as Patron in the Work of Gregory of Tours." *Journal of Medieval History* 7 (1981): 1-13.

Cordero Carrete, Felipe R. "Peregrinos mendicantes." *Cuaderno de estudios gallegos* 17.51 (1962): 83-9.

Costa, Avelino de Jesus da. "Quem trouxe a cabeça de Santiago, de Jerusalém para Braga-Compostela?" *Lusitania sacra* 5 (1960): 233-43.

Couffon, René. "Notes sur les cultes de Saint Jacques et de Saint Eutrope en Bretagne. Contribution à l'étude des chemins de Compostelle au moyen-âge." *Mémoires de la Société historique de Bretagne* 48 (1968): 31-75.

Coulton, G. G. *Life in the Middle Ages.* 4 vols. in 1. New York: Macmillan, 1930.

Dahlerup Koch, Hanne. "Jakobspilgrimme fra Holbaek." *Fra Holbaek Amt* (1990): 11-26.

Dalyrymple, William. "Pilgrimage to Galicia." *Conde Nast Traveler* (Aug. 1992): 11-26.

David, Pierre. "Études sur le livre de St. Jacques attribué au pape Callixte II." *Bulletin des Études Portugaises et de l'Institute Français au Portugal* ns 10 (1945): 1-41; 11 (1947): 113-185; 12 (1948): 70-223; 13 (1949): 52-104.

—. "Notes Compostellanes 1. La lettre du Pseudo-Léon sur la translation de Saint Jacques." *Bulletin de études portugaises et de l'Institut française au Portugal* 15 (1951): 180-93.

—. "Les Saints Patrons d'églises entre Minho et Mondego jusqu'à la fin du XIe siècle: Étude d'hagiotoponymie." *Revista portuguesa de historia* 2 (1943): 221-51.

Davidson, Linda Kay, and Maryjane Dunn-Wood. *Pilgrimage in the Middle Ages: A Research Guide.* Garland Medieval Bibliographies 16. New York: Garland, 1993.

Davies, Horton, and Marie-Hélène Davies. *Holy Days and Holidays: The Medieval Pilgrimage to Compostela*. Lewisburg: Bucknell UP, 1982.

Dennet, Laurie. *A Hug for the Apostle*.Toronto: Macmillan of Canada, 1987.

Díaz Martínez, Pablo de la C. "La monarquía sueva en el s. V. Aspectos políticos y prosopográficos." *Studia historica. Historia antigua* (Salamanca) 4-5 (1986-7): 205-26.

Díaz y Díaz, Manuel C., María Araceli García Piñeiro, and Pilar del Oro Trigo, eds. *El códice calixtino de la Catedral de Santiago*. Santiago de Compostela: Centro de Estudios Jacobeos, 1988.

Donini, Guido, and Gordon B. Ford, Jr. *Isidore of Seville's History of the Goths, Vandals, and Suevi*. Leiden: Brill, 1970.

Donnersöhne/Sons of Thunder: Gesänge für den Hl. Jakobus aus dem Codex Calixtinus. Sequentia, Dir. Benjamin Bagby. Deutsche Harmonia Mundi, 05472-77199-2, 1992.

Dreves, Guido Maria, ed. *Hymnodia Hiberica: Carmina Compostellana*. Vol. 17 of *Analecta Hymnica*. Leipzig: n.p., 1894.

Duchesne, Louis. "Saint Jacques en Galice." *Annales du Midi* 12 (1900): 145-79.

Dujardin, Richard. "R.I. pilgrims drawn to Pope." *Providence Journal-Bulletin* 4 Oct. 1995: B1, B4.

Dunn, Maryjane, and Linda Davidson. *The Pilgrimage to Santiago de Compostela: A Comprehensive, Annotated Bibliography*. Garland Medieval Bibliographies 18. New York: Garland, 1994.

Dutton, Brian. See Gonzalo de Berceo.

Einhard. *Vita Caroli Magni*. Ed. Louis Halphen. Paris: n.p., 1938.

Elorduy, Eleuterio. "De re Iacobea." *Boletín de la Real Academia de la Historia* 135 (1954): 323-60.

—. "La tradición Jacobea de Galicia en el siglo IX." *Hispania* 22 (1962): 323-56.

Engels, Odilo. "Die Anfänge des spanischen Jakobusgrabes in kirchenpolitischer Sicht. *Römische Quartalschrift für christliche Altertumskunde und Kirchengeschichte* 75 (1980): 146-70.

Erasmus, Desiderius. "A Pilgrimage for Religion's Sake." *The Colloquies of Erasmus*. Trans. Craig R. Thompson. Chicago: U of Chicago P, 1965. 285-312.

EuroAtlas Spain Portugal. New York: American Map, 1993.

Ewig, Eugen. "Der Martinskult im Frühmittelalter." *Archiv für mittelrheinische Kirchengeschichte* 14 (1962): 11-30.

Farmer, Sharon. *Communities of Saint Martin: Legend and Ritual in Medieval Tours*. Ithaca: Cornell UP, 1991.

Feinberg, Ellen O. *Following the Milky Way. A Pilgrimage Across Spain*. Ames: Iowa State UP, 1989.

Fernández Alonso, Justo. *La cura pastoral en la España romanovisigoda*. Rome: Iglesia Nacional Española, 1955.

Fernández Conde, F. Javier. *La Iglesia de Asturias en la baja edad media. Estructuras económico-administrativas*. Oviedo: Instituto Asturiano, 1987.

Fernández Sánchez, José María, and Francisco Freire Barreiro. *Guía de Santiago y sus alrededores*. Santiago: Seminario Conciliar, 1885.

Ferreiro, Alberto. "Braga and Tours. Some Observations on Gregory's *De virtutibus s. Martini* (1.11)." *Journal of Early Christian Studies* 3.2 (1995): 195-210.

——. "Early medieval missionary tactics: The example of Martin and Caesarius." *Studia historica. Historia antigua* (Salamanca) 6 (1988): 225-38.

——. "Jerome's Polemic Against Priscillian in his *Letter* to Ctesiphon (133,4)." *Revue des études augustiniennes* 39.2 (1993): 309-32.

——. "*Linguarum diversitate*: 'Babel and Pentecost' in Leander's Homily at the Third Council of Toledo." *Concilio III de Toledo XIV Centenario 589-1989*. Toledo, 10-14 May 1989. Ed. R. González. Toledo: n.p., 1991. 237-48.

——. "The Missionary labors of St. Martin of Braga in 6th Century Galicia." *Studia monastica* 23 (1981): 11-26.

——. "A Reconsideration of Celtic Tonsures and the *Ecclesia Britoniensis* in the Hispano-Roman Visigothic Councils." *Annuarium historiae conciliorum* 23 (1991): 1-10.

——. "St. Martin of Braga and Germanic Languages: An Addendum to Recent Research." *Peritia* 6-7 (1987-8): 298-306.

——. "St. Martin of Braga's Policy Toward Heretics and Pagan Practices." *American benedictine review* 34 (1983): 372-95.

——. *The Visigoths in Gaul and Spain. A.D. 418-711: A Bibliography*. Leiden: Brill, 1988.

Fontaine, Jacques. *Sulpice Sévère. Vie de S. Martin*. 3 vols. Sources chrétiennes 133-5. Paris: Editions du Cerf, 1967-9.

Ford, Richard. *A Hand-Book for Travellers in Spain*. 1845. 2nd ed. London: John Murray, 1847.

Fuentes Noya, Jesús. *Las peregrinaciones a Santiago de Compostela: Estudio histórico*. Santiago: Galaica, 1898.

Galicia: da romanidade á xermanización. Problemas históricos e culturais. Santiago de Compostela: n.p., 1992.

Gams, Pius Bonifatius. *Series Episcoporum Ecclesiae Catholicae*. Regensburg: Jos. Mainz, 1873-86. Rpt. Graz: Akademische Druck- und -Verlag, 1957.

García Campello, María Teresa. "Enfermos y peregrinos en el Hospital Real de Santiago durante el siglo XVII." *Compostellanum* 18.1-4 (Jan.-Dec. 1973): 5-40.

García Oro, José. *Cisneros y la Reforma del Clero español en tiempo de los Reyes Católicos*. Estudio 13. Madrid: C.S.I.C., Instituto Jerónimo Zurita, Biblioteca "Reyes Catolicos", 1971.

García Rodríguez, Carmen. *El culto de los santos en la España romana y visigoda*. Madrid: C.S.I.C., 1966.

George, Judith W. *Venantius Fortunatus. A Latin Poet in Merovingian Gaul.* Oxford: Clarendon, 1992.

Georges, André. *Le pèlerinage à Compostelle en Belgique et dans le Nord de la France, suivi d'une étude sur l'Iconographie de saint Jacques en Belgique.* Brussels: Académie Royale de Belgique, 1971.

Gerli, E. Michael. "Poet and Pilgrim: Discourse, Language, Imagery, and Audience in Berceo's *Milagros de Nuestra Señora.*" *Hispanic Medieval Studies in Honor of Samuel G. Armistead.* Eds. E. Michael Gerli and Harvey L. Sharrer. Madison: Hispanic Seminary of Medieval Studies, 1992. 139-51.

Gil, J.M. "Recuerdos de viaje por Galicia." *Revista de Galicia* (1850): 116-20.

Goffart, Walter. *The Narrators of Barbarian History (A.D. 550-800): Jordanes, Gregory of Tours, Bede, and Paul the Deacon.* Princeton: Princeton UP, 1988.

Goldschmidt, Ernest Philip, *Hieronymus Münzer und seine Bibliothek.* London: Warburg Institute, 1938.

González, José Manuel. "Martín genio mítico popular." *Archivum* 9 (1959): 154-78.

Gonzalo de Berceo. *Obras completas II: Los Milagros de Nuestra Señora.* Ed. Brian Dutton. London: Tamesis, 1980.

Graduale sacrosanctae Romanae ecclesiae. Tournai: Desclée, 1957.

Gregory of Tours. *De virtutibus s. Martini, Monumenta Germaniae Historica, Scriptorum rerum Merovingicarum, pars II, Miracula et Opera Minora.* Eds. W. Arndt and Br. Krusch. Hannover: n.p., 1885.

—. *Liber in gloria confessorum, Monumenta Germaniae Historica, Scriptorum rerum Merovingicarum, pars II, Miracula et Opera Minora.* Eds. W. Arndt and Br. Krusch. Hannover: n.p., 1885.

—. *Libri Historiarum, Monumenta Germaniae Historica, Scriptorum rerum Merovingicarum, 1, 1.* Eds. B. Krusch, and W. Levison. Hannover: n.p., 1951

Guerra Campos, José. "Orígenes del culto jacobeo en Compostela (1)." *Razón española* 13 (1985): 145-62.

Guide du pèlerin de Saint-Jacques de Compostelle. See Vieillard.

Haastrup, Ulla. Article in *Konkylien og Mennesket.* Copenhagen: Industrimuseum, 1983-4. N. pag.

Hamann, Stefanie. "Vorgeschichte und Geschichte der Sueben in Spanien." Unpublished diss. Regensburg, 1971.

Hämel, Adalbert. "Hieronymus Münzer und der Pseudo-Turpin" *Zeitschrift für romanische Philologie* 54 (1934): 89-98.

—. "Los manuscritos latinos del falso Turpino." *Estudios dedicados a Menéndez Pidal.* Madrid: C.S.I.C. Patronato Marcelino Menéndez y Pelayo, 1953. 4: 67-85.

—. *Uberlieferung und Bedeutung des Liber Sancti Jacobi und des Pseudo-Turpin.* Sitzungsberichte, Philosophisch-historische Klasse 2. Munich: Bayerischen Akademie der Wissenschaften, 1950.

Hamilton, Rita, and Janet Perry, eds. and trans. *The Poem of the Cid. A Bilingual Edition with Parallel Text*. London: Penguin, 1975.

Haselbach, Hans. *Senèque des IIII vertus la 'Formula Vitae Honestae' de Martin of Braga (pseudo-Senèque) traduite et glosée par Jean Courtecuisse (1403): étude et édition critique*. Berne: Herbert Lange, 1975.

Helmer, Paul. *The Mass of St. James: Solemn Mass for the Feast of the Passion of St. James of Compostela According to the Codex Calixtinus*. Musicological Studies 49. Ottawa: Institute of Medieval Music, 1988.

Henggeler, Rudolf. "S. Jacobus Major und die Innerschwiez." *Spanische Forschungen der Görresgesellschaft. Reihe 1: Gesammelte Aufsatze zur Kulturgeschichte Spaniens 20 (1966): 283-94.*

Herbers, Klaus. *Deutsche Jakobspilger und ihre Berichte*. Tübingen: Guntar Narr, 1988.

Hiley, David. "Two Unnoticed Pieces of Medieval Polyphony." *Plainsong and Medieval Music* 1. 2 (Oct. 1992): 167-73.

Hillgarth, Jocelyn N. "Ireland and Spain in the Seventh Century." *Peritia* 3 (1984): 1-16.

—. *The Spanish Kingdoms, 1250-1516*. 2 vols. Oxford: Clarendon, 1976-8.

—. "Visigothic Spain and Early Christian Ireland." *Proceedings of the Royal Irish Academy* 62, sect. C, no. 6 (1962): 167-94.

Historia Silense (or, *Seminensis*). See Pérez de Urbel.

History of Spanish Music, Volume IV. Musical Heritage Society, MHS 1584, [1973].

Hitt, Jack. *Off the Road: A Modern-Day Walk Down the Pilgrim's Route into Spain*. New York: Simon & Schuster, 1994.

Hoffmann, Friedrich Wilhelm. *Die Sebalduskirche in Nürnberg Ihre Baugeschichte und ihre Kunst-denkmale*. Eds. Th. Hempt, E. Mummenholt, and Jos. Schmitz. Vienna: Gerlach and Wiedling, 1912.

Hogarth, James. "An English Pilgrim to Compostela." See Wey.

Hohler, Christopher. "A Note on *Jacobus.*" *Journal of the Warburg and Courtauld Institutes* 35 (1972): 31-80.

Hoinacki, Lee. *El Camino: Walking to Santiago de Compostela*. University Park: Pennyslvania State UP, [1996].

Hornby, Rikard. *Danmarks Gamle Personnavne*. Copenhagen: Gad, 1936.

Hüffer, Hermann J. "La significación del culto de Santiago en España y sus irradiaciones en Alemania." *Revista de la Universidad de Buenos Aires* 5th epoch. 1.3 (1956): 375-93.

Huglo, Michel. "Les Débuts de la Polyphonie à Paris: Les Premiers *Organa* Parisiens." *Forum Musicologicum III. Basler Beiträge zur Musikgeschichte*. Winterthur, Schweiz: Amadeus, 1982. 93-163.

Hydatius. *Continvatio Chronicorvm Hieronymianorum*. *Monumenta Germaniae Historica*. *Auctorum Antiquissimorum 11*. Ed. T. Mommsen. Berlin: n.p., 1894.

Isidore of Seville. *De viris illustribus*. See Codoñer.

—. *Historia Gothorum Wandalorum Sueborum*. *Monumenta Germaniae Historica*. *Auctorum Antiquissimorum 11*. Ed. T. Mommsen. Berlin: n.p., 1894.

Jacobus de Voragine. *The Golden Legend*. Trans. William Granger Ryan. 2 vols. Princeton, NJ: Princeton UP, 1993. 2: 3-10.

Jacomet, Humbert. "Santiago: En busca del gran perdón." *Santiago, Camino de Europa: Culto y cultura en la Peregrinación a Compostela*. Catal. eds. Serafín Moralejo Alvarez, and Fernando López Alsina. Santiago de Compostela: Fundación Caja de Madrid; Xunta de Galicia, Consellería de Cultura e Xuventude, Dirección Xeral do Patrimonio Histórico e Documental; Arzobispado de Santiago de Compostela, 1993. 55-81

Janson, Anthony F., and A. Ian Fraser. *Handbook of European and American Paintings to 1945: Indianapolis Museum of Art*. Indianapolis: Indianapolis Museum of Art, n.d.

Jaspar, Edmond. *Relation d'un pèlerinage à St. Jacques de Compostelle*. Douai: n.p., 1883.

Jenkins, Ms. Telephone interview. 14 Nov. 1995.

John of Biclar. *Chronica, Monumenta Germaniae Historica*. *Auctorum Antiquissimorum 11*. Ed. T. Mommsen. Berlin: n.p., 1894.

Karp, Theodore. *The Polyphony of Saint Martial and Santiago de Compostela*. 2 vols. Berkeley and Los Angeles: U of California P, 1992.

—. "St. Martial and Santiago de Compostela: An Analytical Speculation." *Acta musicologica* 39 (1967): 144-160.

Kasl, Ronda. Letter to the author [David M. Gitlitz]. 25 July 1994.

Keller, Hans-Erich. "Changes in Old French Epic Poetry and Changes in the Taste of its Audience." *The Epic in Medieval Society*. Ed. Harald Schöller. Tübingen: Max Niemeyer, 1976. 150-73.

—. "The *Song of Roland*: a Mid Twelfth Century Song of Propaganda for the Capetian Kingdom." *Olifant* 3 (1976): 242-58.

Keller, John E. "King Alfonso's Virgin of Villa-Sirga, Rival of St. James of Compostela." *Collectanea Hispanica: Folklore and Brief Narrative Studies by John Esten Keller*. Eds. Dennis P. Seniff and María Isabel Montoya Ramírez. Newark: Juan de la Cuesta, 1987. 61-8.

King, Georgiana Goddard. *The Way of St. James*. 3 vols. Hispanic Notes and Monographs, Peninsular Ser. 1. 3 vols. New York: Putnam's, 1920. 2nd ed. 1930. Rpt. New York, 1980.

Köster, Kurt. *Pilgerzeichen und Pilgermuscheln von mittelalterlichen Santiago Strassen: Saint-Léonard-Rocamadour-Saint-Gilles-Santiago de Compostela. Schleswiger Funde und*

Gesamtüberlieferung. Ausgrabungen in Schleswig. Berichte und Studien 2. Neumünster: Karl Wachholtz, 1983.

Krötzl, Christian. "Del Mar Báltico a Santiago de Compostela. Peregrinajes e influencias culturales." *Santiago. La Europa del peregrinaje.* Ed. Paolo Caucci Von Saucken. Barcelona: Lunwerg, 1993. 385-91.

Kunstmann, Fr. "Hieronymus Münzers Bericht über die Entdeckung der Guinea, mit einleitender Erklärung." *Abhandlungen der koenigliche bayrische Akademie der Wissenschaft, historische Klasse* 7.2 (1854): 1-74.

Laborde, Alexandre de. *La Bible Moralisée illustrée conservée à Oxford, Paris et Londres. Reproduction intégrale du manuscrit du XIIIe siècle, accompagnée de planches tirés de Bibles similaires et d'une notice. Vols 1-4: Planches; vol. 5: Étude.* Paris: [By the author], 1911-27.

"Ladislaw V, of Bohemia." *Encyclopedia Britannica.* 14th ed. Ed. J.L. Garnin. London: Encyclopedia Britannica, 1929.

Lambert, Adalbert. "La fête de L'Ordinatio Sancti Martini: ses origines, sa doctrine, dans la liturgie wisigothique." *Revue Mabillon* 26 (1936): 1-27.

La-Orden Miracle, Ernesto. *Santiago en América y en Inglaterra y Escocia.* Claves de España 7. Madrid: Publicaciones españolas, 1970.

Lavalleye, J. "Les primitifs flamandes." *Répertoire des peintures flamandes des XVe et XVIe siècles.* Antwerp: Sikkel, 1958.

Lejeune, Rita, and Jacques Stiennon. *La Légende de Roland dans l'art du moyen âge.* 2 vols. Brussels: Arcade, 1967.

Lelong, Charles. "De l'importance du pèlerinage de Tours au VIe siècle." *Bulletin trimestriel de la Société archéologique de Touraine* 32 (1960): 232-7.

Lewis, Archibald R. "Le commerce maritime et les navires de la Gaule occidentale (550-750)." *Études Mérovingiennes. Actes des Journées de Poitiers.* 1-3 May 1952. Paris: A.J. Picard, 1953. 191-9.

Liber Sancti Jacobi, Codex Calixtinus. Eds. Walter Muir Whitehill, Germain Prado, and J. C. García. 3 vols. Santiago de Compostela: Seminario de Estudios Gallegos, 1944.

Liber Sancti Jacobi. Codex Calixtinus. Trans. A. Moralejo, C. Torres, and J. Feo. Santiago: C.S.I.C., Instituto Padre Sarmiento de Estudios Gallegos, 1951. Rpt. Ed. X. Carro Otero. Compostela: Xunta de Galicia, 1992.

Liber Sancti Jacobi. Codex Calixtinus de la Catedral de Santiago de Compostela. Barcelona: Kaydeda, 1993.

Liebgott. *Kalendere, Folkelig Tidregning I Norden.* Copenhagen: Nationalmuseum, 1973.

Lithberg, Nils. "Kalendariska Hjälpmedel" *Nordisk Kultur* 21 (1934): 77.

Logan, William Bryant. "Pilgrim on Wheels." *house beautiful* [sic] 137:2 (Dec. 1995): 40-4.

López-Caló, José. *La música medieval en Galicia*. La Coruña: Fundación "Pedro Barrie la Maza Conde de Fenosa", 1982.

Madou, Mireille. "Zittende Jacobus." *de Jacobsstaf* (Nederlands Genootschap Van Sint Jacob) 22 (1944): 44-54.

Martin of Braga. See Barlow.

Martins, Mario. "A 'Formula vitae honestae' em Jean Courtecuisse e Cristina de Pisano." *Revista portuguesa de filosofía* 12 (1956): 125-37.

McDermott, William C. *Monks, Bishops and Pagans: Christian Culture in Gaul and Italy, 500-700*. Pennsylvania: Pennsylvania UP, 1975.

McGrew, Herb. "The Massif Central: A Walk in the Mountains." *Gourmet* (Sept. 1990): 94, 110, 112, 114, 118.

—. "[Traveling the Route to Compostela.]" *Newsletter* of the Friends of the Road to Santiago [3.1] (Jan 10, 1991): 4-8; 4.1 (July 25, 1992): 3-6; 5.1 (Apr. 1994): 3-7; 7.2 (Oct. 1995): 1-5.

—. "A Walk in the French Countryside." *Gourmet* (May 1991): 100, 189-94.

Medieval France: An Encyclopedia. Eds. William Kibler and Grover Zinn. New York: Garland, 1995.

Melczer, William, ed., trans. *The Pilgrim's Guide to Santiago de Compostela*. New York: Italica, 1993.

Melero Moneo, Marisa. "Traslatio Santi Jacobi: Contribución al estudio de su iconografía." *Los caminos y el arte: Actas. VI Congreso español de historia del arte*. Santiago de Compostela: U de Santiago de Compostela, 1989. 71-89.

Meredith-Jones, *Historia Karoli Magni et Rotholandi ou Chronique du Pseudo-Turpin*. Paris: Droz, 1936. Rpt. Geneva, 1972.

Mettman, Walter. See Alfonso X, el Sabio.

Missa sancti iacobi. Reconstructed by Paul Helmer. McGill Records, McGill 750037-2, 1992.

Moralejo, Serafín. "Idea de una exposición." *Santiago, Camino de Europa: Culto y cultura en la peregrinación a Compostela*. Compostela: Fundación Caja de Madrid, Xunta de Galicia, Arzobispado de Santiago de Compostela, 1993. 235-42.

Moralejo Laso, Abelardo. "Sobre el sentido de unos versos de Venancio Fortunato a San Martín Dumiense en relación con la tradición Jacobea." *Bracara augusta* 9-10 (1958-9): 18-24.

Morales, Ambrosio de. *Viage de —— por orden del rey D. Phelipe II, a los reynos de León y Galicia, y principiado de Asturias. Para reconocer las Reliquias de Santos, Sepulcros Reales, y Libros manuscritos de las Catedrales y Monasterios*. Madrid: Antonio Marin, 1765. Rpt., Ed. José María Ortiz Juárez. Oviedo: Biblioteca Popular Asturiana, 1977.

Moreno Astray, Félix. *El viajero en la ciudad de Santiago. Reseña histórica, descriptiva, monumental, artística y literaria de la antigua capital del Reino de Galicia.* Santiago: n.p., 1865.

Mozarabic Chant and the Calixtine Codex. Choir of the Abbey of Santo Domingo de Silos. Dir. Dom Ismael Fernández de la Cuesta. Hispavox, HHS 4, 1973. Reissued by Musical Heritage Society, MHS 1584.

Myers, Joan, photog. *Santiago: Saint of Two Worlds.* Essays by Joan Myers, Mark Simmons, and Donna Pierce. Albuquerque: U of New Mexico P, 1991.

Neira de Mosquera, Antonio. *Manual del viajero en la Catedral de Santiago.* Madrid: Imprenta y establecimiento de Grabado de D. Baltasar González, 1847.

Nussbaum, Norbert. *Deutsche Kirchenbaukunst der Gotik: Entwicklung und Bauform.* Cologne: Dumont, 1985.

Nykiel, Dennis. "Paso a paso." Unpublished manuscript, [1995].

Nyrop, Camillus. *Danske Haandvoerkerlavs Segl.* Copenhagen: Gad, 1899.

O'Callaghan, Joseph. *A History of Medieval Spain.* Ithaca: Cornell UP, 1975.

Oliveira, Ernesto Veiga de. "Le culte de Saint Martin en Portugal. Saint Martin de Tours et Saint Martin de Dume." *Revista de etnografía* 10.2 (1968): 313-28.

Oliveira, Miguel de. "Lendas apostólicas peninsulares." *Lusitania sacra* 4 (1959): 7-27.

Orlandis, José. "Comunicaciones y comercio entre la España visigótica y la Francia merovingia." *Hispania y Zaragoza. Estudios varios.* Zaragoza: n.p., 1985. 171-80.

Otero Pedrayo, Ramón. *Guía de Galicia,* 4th ed. Vigo: Editorial Galixia, 1965.

—. *Guía de Santiago de Compostela.* Santiago: Editorial Compostela, 1945.

Ozanan, A.F. "Un pèlerinage du Pays du Cid, 1852." *Mélanges* (1872): n. pag.

"Las peregrinaciones: Datos estadísticos." *Compostela. Revista de la Archicofradía del Glorios Apóstol Santiago.* 2nd epoch. 2 (Jan. 1994): 25-35.

Pérez de Urbel, Justo. "Orígenes del culto de Santiago en España." *Hispania sacra* 5 (1952): 1-31.

—. "Primeros contactos del Islam con el reino asturiano." *Arbor* 24 (1953): 501-25.

—, and A.G. Ruiz-Zorrilla, eds. *Historia Silense.* Madrid: C.S.I.C., 1959.

Petersen, Henry. "Et dansk flag fra Unionstiden I Maria-Kirken I Lübeck." *Aarboger for Nordisk Oldkyndighed og Historie* 17 (1882): 1-52.

—. *Gejstlige Sigiller fra Middelalderen*. Copenhagen: C.A. Reitzel, 1886.

Pfandl, Ludwig, ed. "Itinerarium Hispanicum Hieronymi Monetarii 1494-1495." *Revue hispanique* 48 (1920): 1-179.

—. "Eine unbekannte handschriftliche Version zum Pseudo-Turpin." *Zeitschrift für romanische Philologie* 38 (1918): 586-608.

Piel, Joseph M. "Coteifes Orpelados, Panos D'arrazes e Martinhos." *Revista portuguesa de filología* 14 (1966-8): 1-12.

—. "Nomes de 'possessores' latino-cristãos na toponímia asturo-galego-portuguesa." *Biblos* 23 (1947): 143-202; 283-407.

Pietri, Luce. "Le pèlerinage martinien de Tours a l'époque de l'évêque Grégoire." *Gregorio di Tours*. Convegni del Centro di Studi sulla spiritualità medievale, 12. 10-13 Oct. 1971. Todi: Accademia Tudertina, 1977. 95-139.

—. *La ville de Tours du IVe au VI siècle: Naissance d'une cité chrétienne*. Collection de L'école française de Rome 69. Rome: École Française de Rome, 1983.

"Pilgrim of the Week." *Time* (9 Oct. 1995): 17.

The Pilgrim's Guide to Santiago de Compostela. See Melczer; Shaver-Crandell.

The Pilgrimage to Santiago. New London Consort. Dir. Philip Pickett. Editions de L'Oiseau-Lyre, 433 148-2, 1991.

Prescott, William H. *History of the Reign of Ferdinand and Isabella the Catholic*. Vol. 1. Ed. John Foster Kirk. Philadelphia: Lippincott, 1837. Rpt. 1872.

Ravenstein, Ernest George. *Martin Behaim, His Life and His Globe*. London: G. Philip, 1908.

Reilly, Bernard F. *The Contest of Christian and Muslim Spain, 1031-1157*. Cambridge, Mass., and Oxford: Blackwell, 1992.

Reinhart, Wilhelm. *Historia general del reino hispánico de los suevos*. Madrid: Publicaciones del Seminario, 1952.

Robbins, Russell Hope. *The Encyclopedia of Witchcraft and Demonology*. New York: Crown, 1959.

Robertson, Ian. *Blue Guide Spain: The Mainland*. 4th ed. London: Benn, 1980.

Rouche, Michel. *L'Aquitaine des Wisigoths aux Arabes (418-781) Naissance d'une région*. Paris: Editions Jean Touzot, 1979.

—. "Les relations transpyrénéennes du Ve au VIIIe siècle." Actes de *Colloque de les communications dans la Peninsule Iberique au Moyen Âge*. 28-9 Mar. 1980. Paris: C.N.R.S., 1981. 13-20.

Saitta, Biagio. "I visigoti negli 'Historiarum libri' di Gregorio di Tours." *Los visigodos. Historia y civilización*. Antigüedad y Cristianismo 3. Murcia: Murcia UP, 1986. 75-101.

Salmon, Pierre. "Le lectionnaire de Luxeuil. Ses origines et l'église de Langres." *Revue bénédictine* 53 (1941): 89-107.

Sánchez Albornoz, Claudio. "En los albores del culto Jacobeo." *Compostellanum* 16 (1971): 37-71.

——. *Galicia histórica: Estudios sobre Galicia en la temprana Edad Media.* La Coruña: Fundación Barrie de la Maza, 1981.

——. *Orígenes de la nación española. Estudios críticos sobre la historia del reino de Asturias.* 3 vols. Oviedo: Instituto Asturiano. 1972-5.

Santiago e América. Exposition. Compostela, 1993. Compostela: Xunta de Galicia, Consellería de Cultura e Xuventude, Arcebispado de Santiago de Compostela, 1993.

"Santiago na toponímia portuguesa." *Revista de Portugal* 30.231-40 (Jan.-Dec. 1965): 286-92.

Scudieri Ruggieri, Jole. "Il pellegrinaggio compostellano e l'Italia." *Cultura neolatina* 30.1-2 (1970): 185-98.

Selby, Bettina. *Pilgrim's Road.* London: Little, Brown, 1994.

Shaver-Crandell, Annie, and Paula Gerson. *The Pilgrim's Guide to Santiago de Compostela. A Gazetteer with 580 Illustrations.* London: Harvey Miller, 1995.

——, Jeanne Krochalis, and Alison Stones. *The Pilgrim's Guide to Santiago de Compostela: A Critical Edition.* 2 vols. Vol. 2: *Manuscripts and Texts.* London: Harvey Miller, [in press].

Short, Ian. "A Study in Carolingian Legend and its Persistence in Latin Historiography (XII-XVI Centuries)." *Mittellateinisches Jahrbuch* 7 (1972): 127-52.

Sidonius Apollinaris. *Carmina Carm, V, Monumenta Germaniae Historica. Auctorum Antiquissimorum* 8. Ed. C. Luetjohann. Berlin: n.p., 1887.

Smith, Colin. *Christian and Moors in Spain.* 2 vols. Warminster: Aris & Phillips, 1988.

Snow, Joseph T. "The Central Rôle of the Troubadour *Persona* of Alfonso X in the *Cantigas de Santa Maria.*" *Bulletin of Hispanic Studies* 56 (1979): 305-16.

——. "Self-Conscious References and the Organic Narrative Pattern of the *Cantigas de Santa Maria* of Alfonso X." *Studies in Honor of John Esten Keller.* Ed. Joseph R. Jones. Newark: Juan de la Cuesta, 1980. 53-66.

Søgaard. Article in *Kulturhistorisk lexikon for Nordisk Middelalder.* 13 (1968): 314-20.

Spain: The Nagel Travel Guide Series. Ed. Gilbert Martineau. Paris: Nagel, 1953.

Stäblein, Bruno. "Modale Rhythmen im Saint-Martial Repertoire?" *Festschrift Friedrich Blume zum 70. Geburtstag.* Kassel and Basel: Bärenreiter, 1963. 340-62.

Stancliffe, Clare. *St. Martin and His Hagiographer: History and Miracle in Sulpicius Severus.* Oxford: Clarendon, 1983.

Stanton, Edward. *Road of Stars to Santiago.* Lexington: UP of Kentucky, 1994.

Starkie, Walter. *The Road to Santiago. Pilgrims of St. James.* London: John Murray, 1957.

Stewart, George R. *American Place-Names.* New York: Oxford UP, 1970

Stokstad, Marilyn. "The Sanctuary of St. James at the end of the 15th Century." *Compostelanum* 32.3-4 (July-Dec. 1987): 527-31.

Stones, Alison, and Jeanne Krochalis. "Qui a lu le *Guide de Pèlerin de Saint-Jacques de Compostele*?" *Pèlerinages et Croisades (118e Congrès du Comitié de Recherches et d'histoire de textes, 1993).* Ed. Léon Pressouyre. Paris: CRHT, 1995.

Storck, Herman. *Dansk Vaabenbog.* Copenhagen: V. Tryde, 1910.

Storrs, Constance. *Jacobean Pilgrims from England from the Early Twelfth to the Late Fifteenth Century.* Santiago de Compostela: Xunta de Galicia, 1994.

—, and F.R. Cordero Carrete. "Peregrinos ingleses a Santiago en el siglo XIV." *Cuadernos de estudios gallegos* 20.60 (1965): 193-224.

Sulpicius Severus. *Chronicle. Corpus Scriptorum ecclesiasticorum latinorum, 1.* Vienna: n.p., 1866.

Sumption, Jonathan. *Pilgrimage: An Image of Mediaeval Religion.* Totowa, New Jersey: Rowman and Littlefield, 1975.

Svane, Siegfred. *Danske Helligkilder og Laegedomskilder.* Copenhagen: F. Jacobsens, 1984.

Taliani de Marchio, Marqués. "Peregrinos de Italia a Santiago." *Santiago en la historia, la literatura y el arte.* [Ed. Francisco Iñiguez Almech.] Madrid: Nacional, 1954. 1: 129-43.

Teillet, Suzanne. *Des Goths à la nation gothique. Les origines de l'idée de nation en Occident du Ve au VIIe siècle.* Paris: Les Belles Lettres, 1984.

"Ten Primitives in the James E. Roberts Collections of Paintings." *Bulletin of the Art Association of Indianapolis Indiana: The John Herron Art Institute* 11.5-6 (May-June 1924): 35-44.

Thiset, Anders. *Danske adelige Sigiller fra det XV, XVI og XVII Aarhundrede.* Copenhagen: C.A. Reitzel, 1905.

—, and Ludvig Peter Wittrup. *Nyt Dansk Adelslexikon.* N.p.: n.p., 1904.

Thompson, Edward A. "The Conversion of the Spanish Suevi to Catholicism." *Visigothic Spain: New Approaches.* Ed. Edward James. Oxford: Clarendon, 1980. 77-92.

—. "The End of Roman Spain." *Nottingham Medieval Studies* 20 (1976): 3-28; 21 (1977): 3-31; 22 (1978): 3-22; 23 (1979): 1-21.

—. *Romans and Barbarians. The Decline of the Western Empire.* Wisconsin: U of Wisconsin P, 1982.

Thorpe, Lewis. *Gregory of Tours. The History of the Franks.* London: Penguin, 1974.

Tito Achen, Sven. *Danske Adelsvåbener. En heraldisk nogle.* Copenhagen: Politiken, 1973.

—. "Muslingeskallen I heraldikken." *Konkylien og Mennesket.* Copenhagen: Industrimuseum, 1983-4. N.pag.

Torres Rodríguez, Casimiro. *La Galicia romana*. La Coruña: Fundación Barrie de la Maza, 1982.
—. *El reino de los Suevos*. La Coruña: Fundación Barrie de la Maza, 1977.
Torres Villarroel, Diego de. "La romería a Santiago: Pronóstico para el año de 1738." *Extracto de los Pronósticos de el Gran Piscator de Salamanca desde el año de 1725 hasta el de 1753*. Salamanca: Pedro Ortiz Gómez, n.d. 213-26.
—. "Peregrinación al Glorioso Apóstol Sant-Iago de Galicia (1737)." *Juguetes de Thalia. Entretenimientos de el Numen, varias poesías lyricas, y cómicas que a diferentes assumptos escribió ——*. Salamanca: Antonio Joseph Vilargordo y Alcaraz, 1752. 58-77.
Tour Guide Spain. Paris: Michelin, 1989.
Tranoy, Alain. *La Galice Romaine. Recherches sur le nord-ouest de la péninsule ibérique dans l'antiquité*. Paris: Diffusion de Boccard, 1981.
—. *Hydace. Chronique*. 2 vols. Sources chrétiennes 218-9. Paris: Editions du Cerf, 1974.
Turgeon, Art. "Crowds fete holiday with Federal Hill food, fun." *Providence Journal-Bulletin* 9 Oct. 1995: C1, C3.
Valiña Sampedro, Elías. *El Camino de Santiago. Guía del Peregrino*. León: Everest, 1985.
Van Dam, Raymond. *Gregory of Tours. Glory of the Confessors*. Liverpool: Liverpool UP, 1988.
—. "Images of Saint Martin in Late Roman and Early Merovingian Gaul." *Viator* 19 (1988): 1-27.
—. *Leadership and Community in Late Antique Gaul*. Berkeley: U of California P, 1985.
—. *Saints and Their Miracles in Late Antique Gaul*. Princeton: Princeton UP, 1993.
Van Herwaarden, Jan. "El culto medieval de Santiago en los Países Bajos." *Santiago: La Europa del peregrinaje*. Ed. Paolo Caucci von Saucken. Barcelona: Lunwerg, 1993. 357-71.
—. "The Origins of the Cult of St. James of Compostela." *Journal of Medieval History* 6 (1980): 1-35.
Vàrvaro, Alberto. "L'Espagne et la géographie épique romane." *Actes du XIe Congrès de la Société Rencesvals (Barcelona, Aug. 1988). Memorias de la Real Academia de Buenas Letras de Barcelona* 22 (1990): 295-330.
Vázquez de Parga, Luis. "Le pèlerinage après le moyen âge." *Bulletin de l'Institut français en Espagne* 46 (Dec. 1950): 222-4.
—, José María Lacarra, and Juan Uría Riu. *Las peregrinaciones a Santiago de Compostela*. 3 vols. Madrid: C.S.I.C., 1949. Rpt. Pamplona: Iberdrola, 1992.
Venantius Fortunatus. "Ad Martinum episcopum Galliciensiem." *Carminum Libri, Monumenta Germaniae Historica. Auctorum Antiquissimorum* 4. Ed. F. Leo. Berlin: n.p., 1881.

Vielliard, Jeanne. *Le Guide du pèlerin de Saint-Jacques de Compostelle.* Mâcon: Protat Frères, 1938.

Vieillard-Troiekouroff, May. *Les monuments religieux de la Gaule d'après les oeuvres de Grégoire de Tours.* Paris: Honoré Champion, 1976.

"Virgin Mary has home page in Cyberspace." *Providence Journal-Bulletin* 17 Sept. 1995: A7.

Vives. José, ed. *Oracional visigótico.* Monumenta Hispaniae Sacra. Serie litúrgica 1. Barcelona: C.S.I.C., 1946.

—. "Santoral Visigodo en Calendarios e Inscripciones." *Analecta sacra tarraconensia* 14 (1941): 31-58.

—, and Angel Fábrega. "Calendarios hispánicos anteriores al siglo XII." *Hispania sacra* 2 (1949): 119-46; 339-80.

Wagner, Peter. *Die Gesänge der Jakobusliturgie zu Santiago de Compostela aus dem sog. Codex Calixtinus.* Collectanea Friburgensia 29 [NF 20]. Freiburg: Kommissionsverlag, 1931.

Walker, Franklin. *Irreverent Pilgrims: Melville, Browne, and Mark Twain in the Holy Land.* Seattle: U of Washington P, 1974.

Ward, Benedicta. *Miracles and the Medieval Mind: Theory, Record and Event 1000-1215.* Philadelphia: U of Pennsylvania P, 1982.

Werf, Hendrik van der. "The Composition 'Alleluya Vocavit Jesus' in the Book Named 'Jacobus'." *De Music Hispana et Aliis: Miscelánea en honor al Prof. Dr. José López-Caló, S. J.* Eds. Emilio Casares, and Carlos Villanueva. Compostela: U de Santiago de Compostela, 1990. 1: 197-207.

—. *The Oldest Extant Part Music and the Origin of Western Polyphony.* Rochester NY: [By the author], 1993.

Werlauff, Erik Christian. *Danebrog og Danebrogsordenen.* Copenhagen: Wegener, 1872.

Wey, William. "An English Pilgrim to Compostela." Trans. James Hogarth. *Medieval World.* 5 (Mar./Apr. 1992): 15-19.

—. *The Itineraries of William Wey.* Ed. George Williams. Roxburghe Publications 76. London: Nichols for the Roxburghe Club, 1867.

Whitehill, Walter Muir, et al. See *Liber Sancti Jacobi.*

Williams, John, and Alison Stones, eds. *The* Codex Calixtinus *and the Shrine of St. James.* U of Pittsburgh, 3-5 Nov. 1988. Jakobus-Studien 3. Tübingen: Gunter Narr, 1992.

Winchester, Simon. "The long, sweet road to Santiago de Compostela." *Smithsonian* 24.11 (Feb. 1994): 65-75.

Winstead, Karen A. "The Transformation of the Miracle Story in the *Libri Historiarum* of Gregory of Tours." *Medium Aevum* 59.1 (1990): 1-15.

Wolf, Kenneth B. *Conquerors and Chroniclers of Early Medieval Spain.* Liverpool: Liverpool UP, 1990.

Wood, Ian N. "Gregory of Tours and Clovis." *Revue belge de philologie et d'histoire* 63 (1985): 249-72.

Wright, Craig. *Music and Ceremony at Notre Dame of Paris: 500-1500*. Cambridge: Cambridge UP, 1989.

Index